SOMERSET CRICKETERS 1946 – 1970

Also Available:
SOMERSET CRICKETERS 1882-1914
SOMERSET CRICKETERS 1919-1939

"Prepare to be surprised and enchanted at every turn of the page"
Vic Marks (Somerset & England Cricketer,
Writer and TMS Commentator)

"Without exception these are excellent profiles ...
immensely well written"
Martin Chandler (*Cricket Web*)

"Pieces together a compelling story"
Somerset County Gazette

"Enjoyable and brilliantly researched"
Anthony Gibson (BBC Cricket Commentator)

"There are gems to be found on every page"
Roger Heavens (*The Cricket Statistician*)

SOMERSET CRICKETERS 1946 – 1970

STEPHEN HILL & BARRY PHILLIPS

HALSGROVE

First published in Great Britain in 2018

British Library Cataloguing-in-Publication Data
A CIP record for this title is available from the British Library

ISBN 978 0 85704 325 2

HALSGROVE
Halsgrove House,
Ryelands Industrial Estate,
Bagley Road, Wellington, Somerset TA21 9PZ
Tel: 01823 653777   Fax: 01823 216796
email: sales@halsgrove.com

Part of the Halsgrove group of companies
Information on all Halsgrove titles is available at: www.halsgrove.com

Printed and bound by Parksons Graphics, India

Contents

Bill Alley – a larger-than-life Australian who arrived at the County Ground at the age of thirty-eight in 1957 and proceeded to light up Somerset cricket for a decade with his age-defying exploits. The Somerset supporters loved him and he in turn would make Taunton his home for the remainder of his life. SOMERSET CRICKET MUSEUM

Foreword & Acknowledgements

This is the third in a series outlining the life of each Somerset player in chronological order of debut appearance. Where two or more players share a debut, they are listed in the order shown on the relevant scorecard. Our trek through the annals of Somerset cricket continues with a biographical summary of the 113 men who made their first appearance from 1946 until 1970. Over the course of those twenty-five seasons, the county belatedly threw off the shackles of amateurism. The committee finally began to put in place the elements that would in time bring success (although the trophy cabinet would remain graced only with the presence of a surfeit of wooden spoons until the late 1970s).

We include in our opening chapter a brief transcript of an exchange at the annual meeting where the imperious attitude of the committee in general and the President in particular comes as a shock to modern eyes and ears. If the tenor of exchanges between the powers that be and players and supporters has changed, then so – in relation to its predecessors – has the nature of this volume. For the first time we encounter the living as well as the dead. Barry and I were able to meet venerable former players now in their nineties and still as sharp as ever, and others whose memories are fading but were able to share some precious recollections with us. Also included in the mix are some of our boyhood heroes, who patiently signed their autographs for us half a century or more ago as we stood in the old pavilion, and whose exploits we tried, without any notable success, to emulate. We acknowledge our debt of gratitude to everyone who has helped us in our endeavours, in particular our wives, Kate and Wendy, for their support, and the Somerset Cricket Museum for allowing us unfettered access to their archives. We are grateful, as well, to everyone at Halsgrove. This has been another gruelling but fulfilling undertaking, involving many helping hands. Listed below are the people we should like to thank. If we have forgotten anyone, we hope that we will be forgiven. Our thanks go to:

Jo Altmann, John Archer, Nick Baker, Michelle Baldwin, Mike Barnwell, Dave Beach, Len Beel, Steve Bindman, Geoff Bisson, Magnus Bowles, Dickie Brooks, John Brown, Bill Buck, Patrick Bucklan, Charlie Carter, John Castle, Stephen Chalke, Greg Chappell, Cheryl & Tony Clarkson, Geoff Clayton, Fiona Colbert, Claire Collingwood, Rowland Conibere, Miles Coope, Joan Courtenay, Jill Cowles, David & Janet Cox, Clive & Joan Davey, John Davies, Ann Deshon, Frances & Tom Dickinson, David Doughty, Ann Earls-Davis, Daryl Edmonds, Peter Eele, Paul Ekins, Carol England, Philip Fussell, Fay Galley, Mandy Gorey, Wendy Greetham, Michael Groves, David Gurr, Sue Hall, Mick & Wendy Hanna, John Harris, Ben Hill, John Hill, Phil Hill,

Greta Hills, Stuart Hirst, Teresa Hodges, Trevor Holmes, David Hughes, Richard Isbell, Rev. Gordon Jeanes, Steve Jennings, Caroline Jones, David Kemp, Roy Kerslake, Tehzeeb Khan, David Lambden, Stuart Lambert, Will Langdale, Mike Latham, Stephen Lawrence, John Lee, Neil Leitch, Vince Lindo, Rev. Malcolm Lorimer, Joanna Mackleston, Tracey McMahon, John Martin, Judith & Neil Mitchell, Mark Nicholas, Mike Nicholson, Simon Northcote Green, Vicky Oldham, Sue Ouvry, Tony Pearson, John Peters, Lewis Pickles, John Roberts, Pat Robinson, Peter Robinson, Adrian Roote, Brian Rose, Fred Rumsey, Dennis & Diana Silk, David Smith, Jonathan Smith, Roger Smith, Bala Srihdar, Allan Stuttard, Margaret Sully, Tony Sutton, Derek Taylor, Trevor Tollerfield, Sam Tonks, Graham Tripp, Roy Virgin, Margaret Walker, Ed Walter, Martin White, Alan Whitehead, Terry Willetts, Ann Williams, Mark Williams, Colin Wilks, Mark Willoughby, Ray Windsor, David Wood, Peter Wynne-Thomas.

STEPHEN HILL

Harold Stephenson (left) and Maurice Tremlett (centre), with a young autograph hunter in hot pursuit. SOMERSET CRICKET MUSEUM

1946

"1946 will always be known as Gimblett's Year."

Somerset Year Book

Championship Position: 4 of 17

County sides were given a boost when the Chancellor of the Exchequer offered sports clubs a concession on Entertainment Tax, intended to help them reinvest in facilities and reduce admission prices where possible for a public starved of uplifting spectacles. The County Ground at Taunton had emerged relatively unscathed from the Second World War, during which it had been utilised by the National Fire Service and the Ministry of Food, with *Wisden* noting that the pitch 'seemed in good condition'. There were grumblings, however, about the fact that around the ground the unsightly debris from temporary buildings remained uncleared for many years. The loss of head groundsman, Harry Fernie, was a blow. He had been forced to retire through ill health after twenty-four years in the role and his protégé, Cec Buttle, was appointed his successor. The catering proved more problematical with rationed food, tea and alcoholic drinks all 'in very short supply'.

Somerset ended up on the losing side in their first four matches but they recovered admirably. MCC took a dim view of proceedings when John Barnwell, standing in as captain in the absence of Bunty Longrigg, manufactured a result at Pontypridd with his Glamorgan counterpart, Johnny Clay. In a rain-affected game, Glamorgan were fed 'declaration bowling' by Frank Lee and Trevor Jones in order to match Somerset's first innings total of 51 for 1. The expectation was that there would be a tight result, although Somerset collapsed in their second innings, with seven of the eleven failing to trouble the scorers and Glamorgan won at a canter. Barnwell and Clay were subsequently reprimanded but the spectators had gone away happy enough. As the *Bath Chronicle* noted, 'MCC condemned this "cricket by arrangement" but public opinion swayed towards the sporting actions of the two captains'.

Somerset were blessed by the reunion of a number of favourites who had adorned the pre-war years and – combining their accumulated wisdom – surprised observers by

John Daniell — at the heart of the club since his debut as a player in 1898, he remained the most influential figure in Somerset cricket in the years immediately after the Second World War. SOMERSET CRICKET MUSEUM

reaching the dizzy heights of fourth position. Harold Gimblett had added solidity in defence to his attacking flair, a grumbling appendix foreshortening a season where he fell agonisingly short of 2,000 runs. Teacher Micky Walford had arrived in the summer holidays to share the burden. Frank Lee had operated with his usual understated efficiency at the crease. In a season that belonged primarily to batsmen, Arthur Wellard had recalled past glories with the ball — slower than in his prime but still a fine enough exponent of the art of bowling to take 119 wickets. Veteran wicket-keeper Wally Luckes had played his part, too, with seventy-six victims, a third of them stumped.

In truth, though, this was more a swansong than a bright dawn chorus. For many of the old faithfuls, their aching bodies were creaking, not unlike Somerset cricket as a whole. Meanwhile, leading lights such as the club President, Richard Palairet, or John Daniell, the man who would replace him the following year, clung on to the long-gone past. Here were two men who had made their debuts for the county in the nineteenth century and longed for the return of a Golden Age. The sparkling Championship campaign led them to feel vindicated in clinging to their belief in amateurism. They held fool's gold in their hands.

Their high-handed dismissal of the efforts of the newly-formed Supporters Club is indicative of their narrow-mindedness. The *Somerset County Herald* provides us with a transcript of the exchange between Richard Palairet and E. C. Reynolds that took place at the annual meeting early in the 1947 calendar year (and is described in the piece as 'the liveliest in its history'). Reynolds was speaking on behalf of the Supporters Club, who had a membership of 600 and wished simply to be officially acknowledged by the committee. Palairet had earlier confirmed the committee's refusal to do so. Reynolds had asked if a reason could be given.

RP: No, sir

ER: Does that mean to imply that the whole matter is definitely closed?

RP: Yes, very definitely closed

ER: Then I can only assume that the Somerset County Cricket Club does not wish to have any support

RP: I do hope you will not assume anything of the sort

It would be some years before the club officials ceased to cling firmly to their belief in the virtues of amateurism and began to think about the novel idea of trying to lay their hands on trophies.

Among the new faces to appear in 1946, the professional Johnny Lawrence would prove an excellent addition, Micky Walford would light up the scene during the school vacations and George Woodhouse would later serve as captain.

Somerset CCC in 1946. The team is made up primarily of players who had first appeared prior to the Second World War. The only newcomers are Johnny Lawrence and George Langdale.
Back row: *H. Gimblett, F. S. Lee, A. W. Wellard, R. F. Trump (Scorer), W. H. R. Andrews, H. F. T. Buse, J. Lawrence.* Front row: *W. T. Luckes, A. T. M. Jones, N. S. Mitchell-Innes, E. F. Longrigg, C. J. P. Barnwell, G. R. Langdale.* SOMERSET CRICKET MUSEUM

352
John Lawrence
11 May 1946 v. Essex, Taunton

Johnny Lawrence was born on 29 March 1911 in Carlton in the Rothwell district of Leeds, an area famed for its tender sticks of rhubarb and tough cricketers. Somerset's first debutant after the Second World War could very easily have been Billy rather than Johnny. With his birth not yet registered by the time of the 1911 census in early April, he is listed as William. His mother, Annie (née Hayton), was a Yorkshire girl. Johnny's father, Samuel, hailed from Staffordshire and worked as a foreman shunter, overseeing the uncoupling and redirecting of goods wagons. This was dangerous work, as the wagons were still moving along a gentle gradient when they were separated. Samuel did indeed suffer serious injury and by the time of the Second World War was wheel-chair-bound and living with his son, having lost the use of his legs in an accident.

It is claimed that Johnny had decided by the age of three that he wished to become a professional cricketer and that he trained his dog to retrieve the ball as he practiced incessantly. A leg-spin bowler and a competent batsman – good enough to be regarded as an all-rounder – he established a name for himself in the Bradford League, playing for Windhill (near Shipley) until 1937 while he undertook an apprenticeship as a master joiner before going on to make coffins. He then spent a year as Liverpool Northern's professional in 1938. He returned to Windhill for the 1939 season, but was offered the chance to join Somerset, initially playing for the Second XI.

Immediately prior to the 1938 season he had been married at the Methodist Church in Rothwell to Mary Clarkson, the daughter of a colliery underground onsetter (responsible for loading up the lifts before their ascent from below ground). Both committed Methodists, Johnny and Mary would have six children together. Rothwell would be their home but during the summers Johnny would

Johnny Lawrence – his indoor cricket school in Rothwell provided Somerset with a continuous flow of Yorkshire-born talent. SOMERSET CRICKET MUSEUM

Johnny Lawrence – an important contributor to team spirit during a period when results were not always encouraging. SOMERSET CRICKET MUSEUM

decamp to Taunton or Bridgwater, living in a caravan, sometimes joined by the family, while he played for Somerset. In August 1939 he had joined Cannington, near Bridgwater, while Somerset took a good look at him. His time with Cannington was deemed a success and included a return of 10 for 10 in a match against Wembdon in August 1939. Astonishingly, Wembdon, who were bowled out for 26 runs, still managed to win by 6 runs. We can safely assume that the match was played on a stinker of a wicket.

His Methodist beliefs remained an important part of his life and influenced a number of decisions, such as his insistence of being a conscientious objector for the duration of the Second World War, when he continued to use his skills as a master joiner, based at home in Yorkshire and acting as a member of the ARP Demolition Squad. He also found time to appear in cricket matches in the North of England, often encountering the irrepressible Somerset player Bill Andrews, who was extolling Johnny's virtues in the local papers ahead of the 1946 season.

Johnny made an immediate impact with Somerset, not just with his batting and bowling but also with his brilliant and sometimes showy close-fielding, characterised by acrobatic leaps, a trademark roll each time he caught someone and even, on occasions, somersaults. Johnny was possessed of an ebullient personality and his enthusiasm

Johnny Lawrence – an ebullient leg-spinner who developed into a useful all-rounder. SOMERSET CRICKET MUSEUM

for life and for the game of cricket was an important contributor to team spirit. Writing in *Growing Up With Cricket*, Alan Gibson states that Johnny 'was a jolly, kindly man, and perhaps the biggest contribution he made to Somerset cricket was his laughter and comradeship in the dressing room, at a time when things were generally going wrong'.

Another service to his adoptive county was a steady stream of Yorkshiremen whom he introduced to the County Ground. This began with his close friend Miles Coope and continued when Johnny set up an indoor cricket school in Rothwell and, over the years, alerted the county to any budding talent. Sadly, the very best of his charges – including, for example, Geoffrey Boycott – were usually claimed by Yorkshire, Graham Atkinson being arguably the one exception.

As for his contributions on the field of play, Johnny is described as a stubborn batsman and an 'extraordinarily slow bowler'. Mick Hanna, an occasional Somerset keeper, who played with Johnny in a number of friendly fixtures, asserts that his slow delivery was what led to his only ever being a very good rather than a great leg-break bowler. Mick also recalls the problems he and others among the ranks had in understanding Johnny's strong Yorkshire accent in the early days. In 281 matches over ten seasons from 1946 to 1955, Johnny took 791 wickets at 24.88 apiece. In a steadily improving batting career, he averaged 20.43, including three centuries and forty-six half-centuries.

As a result of his beliefs, he refused ever to play on a Sunday, even though this was likely to have a substantial impact on his finances during his benefit season of 1954 – the Sunday exhibition matches and friendlies usually drawing large crowds. As it happened, his principled stand would evince a positive response from many like-minded members of the public who supplemented his benefit fund with donations.

Johnny parted company with Somerset at the end of the 1955 season and thereafter played league cricket in his native Yorkshire for a number of years and with great success. After selling his cricket school at Rothwell in 1976 to his daughter and son-in-law, he went on to open a further indoor cricket school – named Lordswood – in the grounds of the new family home in Toulston, near Tadcaster. The enterprise was later taken on by his son, Stephen.

Long after his departure from the County Ground, Johnny evoked fond memories among his teammates and supporters. Fellow Somerset cricketer Eric Hill wrote of him that 'I have … to my everlasting pleasure, seen this diminutive … optimist confound the best in the land with his high tossed spinners.'

Johnny died at home in Toulston at the age of seventy-seven on 10 December 1988 as a result of a heart attack. His son, Miles, also played for Somerset.

353
George Richmond Langdale
22 May 1946 v. Warwickshire, Birmingham

Hot on the heels of Johnny Lawrence, another Yorkshireman made his debut for Somerset. George Langdale's link with the county was through marriage. In November 1944, by then a captain in the R.E.M.E (the Royal Electrical and Mechanical Engineers, responsible for the maintenance of equipment), he was married in Hazelbury Plucknett to Violet Rosalie Patricia Haskins, daughter of the vicar in the village. The couple had met while he was stationed in Somerset. Prior to joining the war effort in 1941, he had enjoyed a more placid existence as a school teacher.

Born on 11 March 1916 in Thornaby-on-Tees, where his maternal grandparents ran a baker's shop, George was the son of Helena (née Richmond) and Horace Wilson Lang-

G. R. Langdale – shown taking the field with Derbyshire Second XI while still a student (top) and as a member of the Somerset team (bottom). COURTESY OF WILL LANGDALE & VICKY OLDHAM

dale. Helena very probably continued to assist her parents in the bakery and confectionery shop after her marriage in 1912 and at least until the time of George's birth, while Horace worked as a blast furnace manager for the North Lincolnshire Iron Co. and enjoyed success as an opening batsman in club cricket in the Scunthorpe area. With his father's work taking the family to various locations, George was educated in Jarrow, Middlesex High School and finally Clay Cross Secondary School, before being offered a place at University College, Nottingham, to complete a BSc in Mathematics. He proved an outstanding student cricketer and was invited to captain the UAU, who called on players from all the universities apart from Oxford and Cambridge. He is described in the *Sheffield Daily Telegraph* as 'a stylish and punishing left-hand bat and a useful right-arm change bowler' and his feats with both bat and ball bear this out. In 1936, playing for UAU on a London tour he secured hat tricks on successive days against first Dominion Students and then Cricket Club Conference. He was drafted into the Derbyshire team in 1936, the year in which they secured the County Championship. He was aged twenty at the time. Then in 1937, he hit 212 not out in 120 minutes for Nottingham University against a Nottingham Forest team. His appointment as captain of the UAU XI followed in 1938. After graduating, George was offered employment as a Maths teacher at the City of Norwich School and while there he played for Norfolk.

His sojourn in Norfolk lasted only two years as a result of the Second World War and at the end of hostilities he would maintain his ties with the Army, teaching for a number of years at Sandhurst. During the summer vacations, he and his wife, Violet, decamped to Somerset and George was welcomed into the fold at the County Ground. When Somerset approached Yorkshire's captain, Brian Sellars, enquiring about the suitability of a player about whom they knew very little, Sellars apparently responded by informing the county that 'he'll do for you'. It was perhaps intended as a droll observation about cricket in Somerset but has subsequently been interpreted as a disparaging aside. Either way, Brian Sellars would be required to eat his words when George was galvanised into scoring 146 against Yorkshire on his home debut for Somerset.

Over the course of four seasons, in which he appeared twenty times, he averaged 19.87 with the bat. In addition to his century, he completed three half-centuries. He took 20 wickets for Somerset at 37.80 apiece. His last appearance was in 1949 and by the 1951 season he had become disenchanted with the Somerset hierarchy. The last straw was the Weston Festival, when – demonstrating that the officers of the club were perhaps guilty of favouring those whom they knew, rather than the most skilled practitioners – Somerset chose J. P. Sainsbury (grandson of a former Somerset captain, Ted Sainsbury) over George, despite the fact that it was clear the former was struggling to make any runs at first-

George Langdale OBE.
COURTESY OF WILL LANGDALE & VICKY OLDHAM

class level. He therefore threw in his lot with Berkshire, captaining the side on a number of occasions and becoming a winner of a Minor Counties Championship medal to add to his County Championship honour. Among his outstanding performances for Berkshire was a return of 10 for 25 against Dorset at Reading in August 1953. According to writer David Foot he was by then bowling 'unplayable off-breaks' rather than the medium-paced deliveries of his younger days.

He left Sandhurst to take up a post as a senior lecturer at Welbeck College for the Ministry of Defence. He often used cricketing examples to render difficult concepts understandable and became a regular contributor of learned articles in the *The Mathematical Gazette*, his papers including such mouthwatering subjects as *The Slide Rule*, *A Simple Course on Astronautics* and *Wisden Cricketers' Almanack and the Teaching of Statistics*.

He had been divorced and then married for a second time in 1961. George and Marian (née Wainscoat) – who hailed from Worksop but was based in Scarborough at the time of their wedding – would have three children together. He was awarded the OBE in 1981 for his services to Education. His son, Will, remembers his father joking that when he looked at the names of the Army Board who had made the recommendation for the award, he noticed that he had taught every one of them in the past.

George's passion for the game of cricket remained undimmed throughout his life. After his playing days were over he built up an impressive library of books about the game, including a valuable *Wisden* collection.

He died in Mansfield at the age of eighty-six on 24 April 2002 and was survived by his wife, Marian, and their children.

354
William Cecil Caesar
1 June 1946 v. Leicestershire, Melton Mowbray

Bill Caesar – a footballer noted for his 'robust methods'.

Bill Caesar's birth certificate gives his date and place of birth as 18 November 1899 in Battersea, although throughout his life he always celebrated his birthday on 25 November, suggesting a clerical error by the registrar. He was the eldest of five children of William Stephen John Caesar, a plumber, and his wife, Hannah Maria (née Robinson), referred to in some documents as 'Annie'. Bill's well-spoken daughter, Jo, jokes that the registrars no doubt struggled to understand the cockney accents of her forebears.

Bill joined the Savings Bank directly from school at the age of fourteen. Taken on as a 'boy clerk', he would work in the Civil Service throughout his adult life, his career only interrupted by his involvement in the Second World War. Having falsified his age in order to sign up with the Royal Fusiliers, he was wounded in action in France and transported to a military hospital in Ludlow, fortunate not to have had his leg amputated as a result of complications. It no doubt helped his recovery that he was a fit young man and a confirmed teetotaller who resolutely refused ever to enter a pub. Bill would later relate that he and a fellow wounded soldier celebrated the armistice by sharing a glass of orange squash together in a café in Ludlow.

A talented all-round sportsman, he was awarded the Warren Fisher Cup in 1925 (donated by the first Head of the Civil Service and subsequently presented annually to the outstanding sportsman across all departments). The announcement in the in-house periodical describes his 'exceptional pace and accuracy as a bowler' and refers to his exploits in the Civil Service Championship Final of 1924. Playing for the Savings Bank, Bill had claimed 9 wickets for 10 runs and scored an unbeaten half-century against the Southampton Civil Servants. He had already won wide renown as an amateur footballer, famed in particular for his free kicks, which were struck with tremendous power. In 1924 he had played at right-half for an amateur England side against South Africa. There followed a tour of Australia as part of a representative F.A. squad, among whom he was the only amateur. The participants were invited to take part in the F.A. Charity Shield match the following October.

Bill enjoyed a long career with Dulwich Hamlet in the 1920s, but also played as an amateur for a number of other teams. Former teammate, Edgar Kail, for a while an automatic choice for England, stated that 'a game in which Bill Caesar takes part can never be dull: the most colourful player in the amateur game, whatever he does, the crowd pick him out from the start'. One of the more unfortunate examples of a spell in the limelight occurred in 1931 when, with Hayes FC struggling with injuries, Bill was drafted into the side as an emergency replacement (for Alf Butcher) in the FA Amateur Cup Final. Sadly, he gave away a late penalty as a result of a hand ball and Hayes therefore lost. A press report in the *Chelmsford Chronicle* of 1937 notes that having returned from suspension for some overzealous play and now appearing as an inside-left for Chelmsford, his 'robust methods raised the ire of a section of the crowd'. He is however described in another source as 'a big, husky right half whose burliness belied the subtle art of footwork and deft passing in his repertoire'. The roll call of

clubs for whom he played also included Leyton FC, Kingstonian, Harwich, Barking, Walsall, Fulham (for whom he made just one first team appearance) and Brentford (whose Second XI he captained, though he made his league debut for them in October 1929).

He was married in 1929 to Gladys Hilda Baillie, the daughter of an electrical engineer. They would have two daughters. Bill later began a new career within the Civil Services as a member of the Admiralty staff, who were relocated to Bath as a result of the Second World War, taking up occupancy in a mixture of private schools and hotels, and he continued to play both football and cricket in the city. A report in the *Sunday Mirror* of 1945 notes that 'Bill Caesar, [the] old England and Dulwich Hamlet amateur, took seven for 29 for Bath against West of England'. Bill's debut appearance for Somerset at the age of forty-six came fully twenty-four years after his one and only previous

Bill Caesar leading out the Bath CC team. COURTESY OF BARRY PHILLIPS

first-class appearance – for Surrey against Scotland. Drafted into the Somerset side in 1946, he played in three matches, averaging 4.66 with the bat and taking 10 wickets at a respectable 21.40 apiece, by this time in his life bowling at medium pace.

Having remained in Bath after his retirement from the Civil Service, Bill returned to London in 1980. He died in Richmond on 5 April 1988 at the age of eighty-eight.

355
Richard Charles Peters
1 June 1946 v. Leicestershire, Melton Mowbray

R. C. Peters – a successful fast bowler for Somerset Police and Taunton CC.

Dick Peters was born in Chew Magna on 12 September 1911. His father, John Henry Peters was a general haulier who was also employed as the parish clerk and was married to Edith May (née Clements) who hailed from nearby Blagdon.

Dick opted for a career in the police force and there are clues as to his career path in the club sides he represented at cricket. In the mid-1930s he was a leading member of a strong Frome team described as having a 'deadly attack'. In 1936 he was appearing for Claverham and then, in the years immediately prior to the war, he was based at the police station in Upper High Street, Taunton.

Dick was married in 1941 to Iris Kathleen Jarman, a Taunton girl whose father was an insurance agent. They would have a son and daughter together.

He was making a name for himself as a fast bowler, appearing regularly for Taunton CC and for Somerset Police, the second of these formed in 1943 and becoming serial winners of the Baker Cup – the twenty-over competition for club sides in the Taunton area. His appearances in three successive finals between 1943 and 1945 would have made him familiar with the County Ground and he was known to a number of Somerset players whom he had played with or against. Indeed, he had been a regular member of R. J. O. Meyer's XI, who kept the West Country cricket fans (and the participants) entertained during the war years.

By the time of his appearance for Somerset in 1946, he had become a member of the CID unit based at Yeovil. In the absence of Somerset stalwarts Arthur Wellard and Horace Hazell, both of whom were injured, Dick was offered a chance to make his debut as an amateur alongside fellow newcomer Bill Caesar. In the event he bowled only six overs, taking 0 wickets for 18 runs and made a total of five runs, being dismissed once. This was his only first-class appearance, although he retained his association with the club, playing for Somerset Club & Ground – these matches acting as a proving ground for fringe players – and continuing to enjoy success playing for Somerset Police and Taunton CC. A report of the Baker Cup Final of 1950 reveals him playing as captain for the latter and leading his side to victory with bowling figures of 3 for 14.

As for his work, as befits one of the sleepier corners of the country, newspaper articles suggest that much of his investigative effort entailed probing matters such as fraud rather than any notorious crimes. In one instance, he was praised for his work in bringing to justice Ernest Merry, who had attempted to defraud the renowned company of Fox Brothers in Wellington. Lloyd H. Fox had requested that his thanks for the work carried out by Detective Sergeant Peters should be brought to the notice of the chief constable. It was noted that 'never has a commendation been more deserved'.

Having retired from the police force, Dick Peters died at the age of seventy-eight in Weston-super-Mare on 26 October 1989.

Dick Peters takes the field.
COURTESY OF JOHN PETERS

356
Frederick Castle
8 June 1946 v. Gloucestershire, Taunton

Fred Castle was born on 8 April 1909 in Elham, Kent, the son of Albert Castle, a tailor, and his wife, Alice Sarah (née Jenner). Fred grew up playing alongside Les Ames, another cricketer from the village, but one who enjoyed rather more fame as a one of the greatest wicket-keeper batsmen. The pair remained good friends, although whereas Les Ames went on to Folkestone for his secondary education, Fred was educated at Canterbury Grammar School. Here he captained the school cricket and football teams and appeared for the Kent Schools XI, being praised in one report for his 'quick wrist work'. In addition we are informed that he 'keeps the ball "on the carpet"'. After leaving school, he attended Goldsmith's Teacher Training College, University of London. His first teaching appointment, in 1929, was at St Peter's School in Folkestone and after two years there he moved to St Leonard's School in Hythe. In 1934 he was married to Doris Winifred Sanders, the daughter of a merchant navy captain. They would have one child, a son. Fred's first headmastership was at Knockholt Church of England School near Orpington. He had already established a reputation as a useful club cricketer, captaining the Hythe XI and also playing hockey for Kent and football for Crystal Palace, although records of any first team appearances are elusive. He was also beginning to demonstrate that he was not averse to the limelight, being lauded for his recitations of poetry, particularly works of the patriotic variety by the likes of Rupert Brooke and Laurence Binyon.

In 1941, he was made headmaster of Oldfield Boys' School in Bath. It was hoped that at the age of thirty-one, he would bring some youthful vigour to proceedings, with the previous incumbent having been there for thirty-eight years. Fred immediately threw himself into the local community, as indeed did his wife, Doris, who was a noted and enthusiastic participant in amateur dramatics. A report in the *Bath Chronicle* notes that 'in the short time [Fred] has been playing for the local side, he has done some spectacular scoring'. He was winning acclaim not just for his cricketing and teaching ability but also for his skills as a magician. A member of the Association of the Inner Magic Circle (Silver Star), his performances as an amateur entertainer were in the news on a frequent basis, one newspaper noting that at the Chilcompton Christmas Party 'for over an hour [he] held the children spellbound and mystified the elders with his wizardry'. Elsewhere, immersing himself in the Bath community as a singer in the local pantomime, he was 'in fine form as Ali Baba'.

His young pupils must surely have hero-worshipped him. The same cannot be claimed for the local Labour Councillors. In 1946, five Labour members of the Bath Education Committee argued that there should be a vote to reverse the decision to allow Fred leave of absence during term-time to play for Somerset during the Bath Festival. As the *Somerset County Herald* reported, others argued that 'his appearance would bring prestige to the school and the Education Committee'. Councillor Tom Jones stated that his objection was not to Fred's appearance in the team but to the fact that the ratepayers were being asked to continue paying a salary while Fred enjoyed his jolly. Councillor Huntley nailed his colours to the mast by asserting that 'nine out of ten firms would be tremendously pleased to see one of their employees chosen and would pay his salary gladly'. The Tory view prevailed, but even then the matter refused to die down.

Fred Castle – a man whose many talents included an impressive array of conjuring tricks. SOMERSET CRICKET MUSEUM

This was apparently not the first case of disgruntlement stirred up by Fred Castle. A report in the *Bath Chronicle* notes that 'Mr Castle is a man of exceptional versatility and talent. As well as being an able headmaster, he shines at cricket, hockey and at conjuring. Objections had earlier been raised by a group of professional conjurers that Castle's amateur activities were undermining their livelihood but that attitude only strengthened the public's interest in Mr Castle's displays of magic.' The writer concludes by making comparisons with the debate over Fred's release for the Bath Festival, suggesting that 'there are no Pecksniffs on the cricket field. It is a pity there are some on the Education Committee'.

There were no objections when Fred left in July 1946 for Denmark, having been selected to play for the England team on a hockey tour, after some outstanding performances for Bath, Somerset and the West of England. Mercifully, the matches had been scheduled for the school holidays. In the event, the England Hockey XI managed two narrow wins out of two, although this was regarded as no great triumph against a country with only 700 participants at that time.

Fred Castle on his wedding day.
COURTESY OF SUE OUVRY & JOHN CASTLE

Mick Hanna kept wicket to and was captained by Fred over a number of seasons at Bath and he observes that his captain was an extraordinarily bright man, not necessarily the most technically gifted of off-spin bowlers but 'able to out-think many batsmen'. He also confirms that Fred was 'fiercely competitive and berated anyone who dropped a catch off his bowling'. Fred's Bath side were apparently only ever allowed one round of drinks after any away game on the basis that he always had some evening performance as a singer or magician to get to.

He would play twenty-three times for Somerset, averaging 20.78 with the bat and taking only one wicket for 43 runs, also stepping in to captain the side in 1949 in the absence of George Woodhouse. His efforts away from the sporting arena continued unabated. He encouraged his pupils to take to the stage, producing plays and forming a school brass band and choir. One report notes that 'Mr Castle has acted commendably in introducing his scholars to the majesty of Shakespeare's jewelled English'. Setting a fine example, he joined the Bath Operatic and Drama Society (perhaps persuaded to do so by his wife, Doris), a reviewer stating that 'he uses his pleasing baritone voice well and plays with a spirited abandon and a sense of joie de vivre'.

There was perhaps much sadness and an eerie calm after Fred left Bath. In 1956, he moved to Bournemouth to take up his final teaching appointment as headmaster of Portchester School. He retired in 1968 and enjoyed a long and happy period thereafter in the Bournemouth area, even when he and his wife, Doris, had to enter sheltered accommodation in a local nursing home. Fred cared for Doris in the final years as her health and sight deteriorated. When his wife died in 1996, he moved to Cornwall to be closer to his son. He died at the age of eighty-eight on the 17 May 1997 in Portscatho.

357
George Edward Sealy Woodhouse
13 July 1946 v. Middlesex, Taunton

Although he was generally known within the family and in business as Edward, he was equally comfortable being referred to as George in cricketing circles. George Woodhouse was born on 15 February 1924 in Blandford Forum and brought up in nearby Iwerne Minster. His father was Colonel Harold Sealy Woodhouse of the Dorsetshire Regiment and his mother was Ruth (née Strange). George's father would die 'on war service' at the age of forty-nine in 1943, having served in both the First and Second World Wars. Two of George's uncles also died as war heroes: one in 1917 and another at Dunkirk in 1940.

George was a member of a dynasty who owned the brewery firm of Hall & Woodhouse, founded in 1777 and based in Blandford Forum from the latter part of the nineteenth century, having earlier been operating in the nearby villages of Dewlish and Ansty. George Edward Illingworth Woodhouse had married Hannah Dodge, a niece of Robert Hall, in 1847 and Robert appears to have taken a shine to his nephew-in-law, in time handing the running of the business to him. From this point, other members of the Hall family ceased to have any involvement and generations of Woodhouses (including George, as a fourth generation Chairman) would run the company. They continued to expand with a combination of good management, successful innovation, continuous investment and shrewd acquisition. New ideas had included one of the earliest registrations of a trademark – the company's badger motif – in 1875 and the first instance of beer being sold in cans in the UK in 1936. By the 1930s the company had swallowed up a number of local competitors and owned 135 pubs and a flagship hotel – the Crown Hotel in Blandford. The number of pubs has now risen to 220.

George was educated at Marlborough College and proved a successful schoolboy sportsman, captaining the school first team both at cricket and rugby. In 1942 he was invited to become vice-captain of the Lord's Public Schools XI at the headquarters of cricket, having already appeared there for Marlborough versus Rugby School. He then spent a year at Trinity College, Cambridge, before joining the Coldstream Guards.

Following the cessation of the Second World War, he was able to play sport on a regular basis and for a while captained the Dorset rugby XV, also appearing for the combined Dorset and Wiltshire team. From September 1950, he played for Bath RFC as a full-back. One report from October 1950 relates an incident where, in a match between Gloucestershire and Dorset & Wilts, Gloucestershire inadvertently drove a

G. E. S. Woodhouse — Somerset's youthful captain who went on to become chairman of his family's brewing business in Dorset. SOMERSET CRICKET MUSEUM

maul into an upright, which collapsed and in the ensuing melee, the crossbar fell onto a prone George Woodhouse, injuring his thigh. In an age when substitutes were anathema and to leave the field of play was a rarity, George was obliged to hobble through the remainder of the game.

He played cricket for Somerset on fifty-eight occasions between 1946 and 1953, averaging 20.68 with the bat, including one century and seven half-centuries. Although he was a useful medium-pace bowler at club level, he only ever bowled four overs in the first-class arena, taking one wicket for 8 runs. In 1948, he was asked to share the captaincy with 'Mandy' Mitchell-Innes and Jake Seamer. George in fact became, at twenty-four, the youngest captain at that point in the club's history. Recognising his limitations as a cricketing tactician, he turned regularly to the seasoned pros for help before making decisions. The following season, he took on the sole responsibility for captaining the club, but could only do so for one year as he was needed thereafter in the family business. Blind to the irony and resistant to the idea of a professional captain, the club then advertised for applicants for the joint role of amateur captain and paid secretary at a salary of £750 per annum. Stuart Rogers would in fact step into the breach but as an amateur captain with no secretarial duties.

George was married in 1953 to Moyra Debonnaire Haggard, the daughter of a schoolmaster, Victor Ernest Debonnaire Haggard, who must be one of the few people blessed with a stirring noun and three evocative adjectives for a name. George and

George Woodhouse leads the Somerset side out against Australia at Taunton in 1948. Shown left to right are: H. L. Hazell, W. T. Luckes, H. F. T. Buse, H. Gimblett, M. M. Walford, M. F. Tremlett, J. Redman, G. E. S. Woodhouse, H. E. Watts, M. Coope, A. W. Wellard.
SOMERSET CRICKET MUSEUM

Moyra would have four children. He would play cricket for Dorset from 1954 until 1964, as and when his work and family commitments allowed. He continued to be involved in the successful running of Hall & Woodhouse and was generous in helping out Somerset cricketers who were in need of winter employment or jobs after their retirement from the game. Long-term servant of the club Bertie Buse, for example, was invited to run a pub after his return from a stint coaching in South Africa.

In 1962, George was appointed Chairman of the company and remained so until his death. He also became High Sherriff of Dorset in 1977 and later Deputy Lieutenant. He died of a heart attack at his home in Fontmell Magna at the age of sixty-three on 19 January 1988. The running of Hall & Woodhouse passed to his sons, David and Anthony.

358
Michael Moore Walford
31 July 1946 v. India, Taunton

Micky Walford was an amateur sportsman of genuine class who, had he been a full-time participant in the game, would probably have graced the England cricket team. He was born on 27 November 1915 in Norton-on-Tees in County Durham, the son of Adolphus Augustus Beddell Walford, a London-born chartered accountant, married to Helena Christian Wynn (née Moore), who hailed from the Isle of Man and was the daughter of a sailcloth manufacturer. Micky was a shy, earnest character, although the description perhaps fitted his three siblings, too. None of the two boys and two girls was ever married.

Sent to Rugby School, he proved a sporting star and was selected in 1934 to play both for the Lord's Schools at cricket and for England Schoolboys at rugby. He had played in 108 consecutive matches for his school over four seasons at cricket, hockey and rugby. It is believed to be by some considerable distance a record for the school. He then went on to Trinity College, Oxford, and became a triple blue at the three sports. Whether through luck or supreme fitness, he had avoided injury at all levels of sport until 1938 when, shortly after having been offered a teaching post at Sherborne School in Dorset, he was demonstrating to a fifteen-year-old pupil in the Third XV how to tackle and succeeding in breaking his collar bone. To add to his woes, having already played for Durham and in England rugby trials, he had just been given Sherborne's blessing to play for Harlequins each Saturday.

As well as being injury-free and a brilliant sportsman during his student years,

Micky Walford – 'Somerset's brilliant schoolmaster batsman'. SOMERSET CRICKET MUSEUM

Micky Walford – a shy, earnest character.

Micky was also a bright young man, selected by Oxford University to represent them in an inaugural Transatlantic Spelling Bee against Harvard, broadcast on the radio by the BBC. The teams lined up but one newspaper reporter notes that whilst the undergraduates must have suffered lapses as a result of knowing that millions were listening in, some of the words 'flew backwards and forwards across the Atlantic before the host could find someone to spell them correctly'. The reporter expresses surprise that words such as 'trachea' and 'truncheon' should have foxed the undergraduates, though their inability to spell 'daguerreotype' is perhaps more understandable. Two nations, as the truism goes, separated by a common language, though united, it seems, by the inability of their elite to spell.

Having been offered a post as a schoolmaster at Sherborne, Micky's career as a teacher was interrupted by the Second World War, when he served with the Royal Corps of Signals, having signed up in 1940. On returning to Sherborne he approached Somerset about the possibility of playing for them in the summer, having previously turned down an approach from Warwickshire, who were aware that no first-class county had a claim on his services. His impact was immediate. On his first-class debut, he scored 141 not out against an Indian attack already softened up by a brilliant century from Harold Gimblett. This would in fact herald a productive partnership between the two men. Gimblett was able to share the burden of holding together a weak batting side with another intense and quiet player of undoubted class. Furthermore, here was a man who could draw out the competitive instincts of an established pro who never liked to be upstaged at the crease. Whilst never great friends, they respected one another hugely. There was perhaps some resentment on Harold's part that he was required to struggle through the early season when the pitches favoured the bowlers and his opening partner then turned up in July and August to reap the benefits of batting on hard and true surfaces. But Micky is quoted as saying of Harold Gimblett that 'I was a great admirer of Harold .... At times I considered he was as talented as Wally Hammond'.

In 1946, Micky Walford was sixth in the national batting averages and the following season his success continued, with a series of masterful displays including a highest score of 264 against Hampshire. The *Daily Mail* referred to him as 'Somerset's brilliant

Harold Gimblett (left) and Micky Walford (right) at Weston-super-Mare in 1950:
a fine pair of opening batsmen, they spurred one another on to greater heights.
SOMERSET CRICKET MUSEUM

schoolmaster batsman'. Elsewhere, he is referred to as 'Wonderful Walford' with his batting – particularly his perfectly-timed and well-placed cover-drives – described as 'delightful'. In fifty-two matches for the county between 1946 and 1953 he averaged 40.90. An occasional spin bowler (bowling left-arm orthodox in contrast to his right-handed batting) he took one wicket for 71 runs. He had also continued to enjoy success as a hockey player, making seventeen appearances for England and captaining the Great Britain team who won silver at the 1948 Olympics.

Somerset allowed him to slip through their fingers when they asked him to relinquish his special registration (as a non-resident) so that it could be accorded to Peter Wight, who was available on a full-time basis. As Peter Roebuck put it in his history of the club, 'too easily a splendid player was lost'. Micky went on to play Minor Counties cricket for Dorset from 1954 until 1962. This prickly, quiet and direct man spent his whole working life at Sherborne. He was Head of Economics for sixteen years, a housemaster – a caring teacher whose shyness some misinterpreted, much to his chagrin, as 'stand-offish behaviour' – and a dedicated coach who spent countless hours grounding pupils in the essentials of cricket and rugby. He died in Sherborne on 16 January 2002 at the age of eighty-six.

1947

"I am proud of my old school tie and what old
school ties have done for Somerset Cricket"

John Daniell (President of Somerset CCC and Former Captain)

Championship Position: 11= of 17

As the *Somerset County Herald* observed, 'from the prominence of fourth place, Somerset sank to the oblivion of sharing eleventh position'. Richard Palairet had stood down as President, to be replaced by former captain, John Daniell. The committee continued to be criticised by the Supporters Club in particular for being 'inefficient and unbusinesslike' with 'too much of the old school tie' about them. John Daniell remained implacably of the view that professionalism was a necessary evil that must be borne begrudgingly.

R. J. O. Meyer – the founder and headmaster of Millfield School who agreed to captain the team, despite suffering from debilitating back problems. COURTESY OF BARRY PHILLIPS

If those who ran the club proved resolutely consistent, then the same could hardly be said of the team's performances which ranged from the double triumph over eventual champions Middlesex to woeful totals of 25 against Gloucestershire and 28 versus Derbyshire (where they lost within a day). The captain for the season was Millfield School's maverick headmaster, Jack Meyer, whose decision-making was as wayward and unpredictable as the team's results. It seems strangely appropriate that a man beset with back problems should have been leading an ageing side embracing senescence. As for individuals, Maurice Tremlett's astonishing match-winning debut, a melding of natural talent and youthful fearlessness, had the national sports reporters hailing him – prematurely and mistak-

The Somerset team who played at Chesterfield in 1947. Bill Andrews was twelfth man and would later complain that he spent much of the season as the county's bag carrier.
Back row: M. Coope, H. Gimblett, W. H. R. Andrews, M. F. Tremlett, H. L. Hazell, H. F. T. Buse, J. Lawrence. Front row: F. S. Lee, W. T. Luckes, R. J. O. Meyer, G. L. Courtenay, A. W. Wellard. SOMERSET CRICKET MUSEUM

enly – as a future linchpin of English cricket. In addition, as reported in the local press, 'Walford, in one glorious month, became outstanding' with a string of fine performances including a highest score of 264. He ended the season with an average of 67.28. Harold Gimblett, too, enjoyed some success. Obliged to carry the weight of responsibility on his shoulders through the early part of the season and on some sticky wickets, he mustered a creditable 1,539 runs. Arthur Wellard was the leading wicket-taker, though no bowler achieved the landmark of 100 wickets.

At the end of the season, Frank Lee (whose Testimonial Year this had been) left to pursue a distinguished career as an umpire (a trail that a surprising number of Somerset players would follow). Among the debutants, only Maurice Tremlett would have any notable impact as a player, although opening batsman Eric Hill later became a familiar figure at the County Ground as captain of the Second XI and for many years as a local journalist.

359
Eric Hill
10 May 1947 v. Middlesex, Lord's

[signature]

A successful and stylish batsman of great promise at schoolboy level, Eric Hill was never able to make the grade as a professional cricketer. Other events in his life would demonstrate that it was never courage that stood in the way of his becoming a successful first-class opening batsman. Nor was it a wont of application.

Eric was born in Taunton on 9 July 1923. His father, Charles Reginald Lyndon Hill, known as Chas, ran a sweet shop on East Reach, Taunton, and was married to Evelyn May (née Shattock). A fervent Somerset fan, Chas would run a flag up the flagpole at his shop whenever Somerset recorded a victory. He sent Eric to Taunton School and, determined that his son should have every opportunity to make it as a cricketer, Chas funded coaching sessions for the boy at the County Ground, where he came under the wing of Arthur Wellard. It was perhaps less helpful to Eric's development that A. E. 'Talbot' Lewis, a useful Somerset all-rounder prior to the First World War, took to Eric as his billiards companion.

Eric's hopes of graduating from the Taunton School team into the county side were put on hold as a result of the Second World War. He volunteered for the RAF in 1941 and was chosen to serve as an observer in a Photographic Reconnaissance Unit, joining 554 Squadron at Benson in Oxfordshire. In the days long before the advent of satellite technology, his task was to undertake long-range sorties, obtaining aerial photographs, often while under the threat of attack. In the vast majority of cases, these were two-man flights and Eric's regular companion as pilot was Frank Dodd, later an air vice-marshal. In 1944, by now a flight sergeant, Eric played his part in a perilous flight to track the German Battleship *Tirpitz* (named after the German admiral famed for having established his country's navy) which was hounding the Allied convoys to Russia off North Norway. The two men were aware that locating the ship would be problematical as it was at the extreme of the range of their de Havilland Mosquito aircraft and other similar sorties had ended in disaster. After refuelling at Shetland, they eventually located their quarry, but when the Germans opened fire, the pair had to turn sharply, at which point, the Perspex casing of the cockpit blew off, along with their navigational and communication equipment. Obliged to cruise above the clouds to conserve fuel, they continued for a further four hours, with the fuel gauge by then hovering at or about zero. A break in the clouds revealed that, miraculously, they were within reach of Wick Airport where an exhausted Frank Dodd completed a perfect landing.

Awarded the DFM for his actions, Eric was commissioned shortly thereafter and would later be awarded the DFC 'for gallantry and devotion to duty on air operations'. He had by then also taken part with Frank Dodd in a 10.5 hour flight of over 10,000 miles to revisit the *Tirpitz*, now stricken and half-submerged. It was the longest Photographic Reconnaissance sortie of the war.

Having returned to civilian life, Eric played his first game for Somerset as an amateur in a stirring victory over Middlesex at Lord's. Set 176 for victory, Somerset were reeling at 101 for 5 when Eric and Wally Luckes dug in, setting the stage for fellow-debutant, Maurice Tremlett, to win the match 'with a number of lusty blows'.

He was offered a professional contract the following season. This in itself is of note. Times had changed. The war had been a great leveller.

Eric Hill – a local boy who went on to become a familiar figure at the County Ground as a reporter.

It was no longer regarded as a source of shame for a former public schoolboy to be paid to play the game he loved. Although Eric was blessed with good reach and helped by some fine coaching, he was never able to make his mark for the county he had supported for as long as he could recall. Some said he was unlucky to be dismissed by spectacular catches on a regular basis but, often bogged down, he would resort to the occasional risky shot. The bare facts are that in seventy-two first-class matches between 1947 and 1951 he averaged 15.92, compiling six half-centuries along the way. To add to his woes, Eric was already beginning to suffer from back pains that would dog him for the rest of his life.

He turned instead to journalism. Employed by the *Somerset County Gazette*, he continued to follow the fortunes of his beloved Somerset. He and others supporters watched, aghast, as Somerset propped up the County Championship in successive campaigns. Chas Hill was rarely running his flag up the flagpole at the family sweet-shop in those dark days. The acidic tang of his lemon bonbons was more in evidence than the sweet taste of victory ever was. Eric may have failed to turn around the county's fortunes with a bat in his hand, but he put his journalist's pen to good use, colluding with fellow scribes Ron Roberts and Bob Moore to lobby for change in 1953. The committee dug their heels in and civil war erupted, things being brought to a head when it was agreed that a no confidence motion would be debated in the near-deserted town hall at Weston-super-Mare in the late afternoon – a time and place where the rank and file, most of whom had no means of transport, would be horribly outnumbered. As a sop, the three musketeers were given roles on the committee and Eric was handed the captaincy of the newly-formed Second XI, a task he undertook with aplomb.

The fortunes of the club slowly turned around and Eric Hill's journalistic career progressed seamlessly. He became a reporter for *The Daily Telegraph* and, was given a helping hand by fellow journalist Ron Roberts, who generously gave Eric's writing career a boost in 1954 when he left Taunton to travel, handing all his contacts on to his protégé. As a freelancer, Eric's services were called on by the likes of *Wisden* and he also acted as a correspondent for England's overseas Tests, assisting Ron Roberts. Eric took up residence during the season at the old press box at the County Ground. His colleague and former school friend Alan Gibson later wrote an affectionate tribute, claiming that although Eric ruled the roost in the cramped facilities after the departure of Ron Roberts, his bark was worse than his bite. An iron gauntlet, he reckoned, masking a velvet glove.

Eric was married in 1959 to Dorothy Bonella. The couple lived for many years in Sampford Brett. They had no children and in 2006, no longer able to drive, they moved to nearby Williton, with its greater selection of services. Eric died on 27 July 2010 in Williton Hospital at the age eighty-seven, having devoted much of his life to the county cricket club he adored, including half a century as a journalist and freelance reporter. In the end he was struggling with back and hip problems and had made the decision to hand his broken body to medical science.

Eric Hill – his successful sorties during the Second World War were more noteworthy than his performances as an opening batsman for Somerset.
SOMERSET CRICKET MUSEUM

360
Maurice Fletcher Tremlett
10 May 1947 v. Middlesex, Lord's

Maurice Tremlett holds a unique place in Somerset's history as their first professional captain. Once he had found his feet, he would lead the county to their best season since the days of Herbie Hewett in 1892. Between Hewett's departure in 1893 and the appointment of Tremlett in 1956, the county had been led by a variety of men – from the charge-of-the-light-brigade types unversed in strategy such as Sam Woods or John Daniell to the dour and uncommunicative Jack White. Former players speak of Maurice's ability to bring the very best out of a disparate bunch of players, generating great team spirit. Bill Alley regarded him as the finest skipper he had ever encountered and stated that, lacking a main strike bowler and therefore having to manufacture creative declarations for much of his tenure, his captain learned to judge a challenging declaration to perfection. In truth, Maurice was an instinctive cricketer who was always eager to take a risk and ring the changes. Sometimes he got it horribly wrong but he grew into the role. His cause was not helped by the fact that throughout his tenure he never gained the full support of the committee, many of whom found him too lacking in deference for their taste.

Maurice's other contribution to the Somerset folklore was his outstanding debut at Lord's when he took a total of 8 wickets for 67 runs and steered Somerset home to victory with a fearless knock of 19 not out. The twenty-three-year-old was applauded off the pitch by the Middlesex side.

Born on 5 July 1923 in Stockport, he was the son of Eustace Cecil Tremlett, known as Cecil, and Maude Hilda (née Carter). Cecil worked for many years as an engineer for the Postal Service, moving to Taunton shortly after his son's birth. Maurice was educated at Priory School, leaving at a young age to become a brewery clerk at Rowbarton, working for Arnold & Hancock. The firm had been formed from a merger between S. W. Arnold at Rowbarton and the Hancock Brewery in Wiveliscombe. As a teenager, Maurice had already begun to make a name for himself playing for Stoke St Mary CC and Taunton CC. During the Second World War he served first with the Army Northern Command and in the latter part of the conflict as a trooper in the Royal Armoured Corps. He was approached by Gubby Allen at the end of the war and invited to play for Middlesex but turned down the opportunity, preferring to remain loyal to the county he lived in and had supported as a boy.

Maurice was a very useful fast-medium bowler and a forceful batsman with his powerful lofted drive a particularly effective shot. Although he bowled off a short run he was devastating, placing the ball invariably on a good length and moving it both ways. The

Maurice Tremlett – Somerset's first professional captain. SOMERSET CRICKET MUSEUM

problems began when Gubby Allen, still watching the young man's progress and determined to draw him into the Test arena, insisted that Maurice should adopt a longer run-up and add a yard of pace. Maurice was fast-tracked into the England side and played three Tests in 1948 but took only 4 wickets at 56.50 apiece and averaged 6.66. His potency as a bowler had evaporated. Gubby Allen's ministrations had been a disaster from which Maurice never recovered, though it is said that he remained a fine exponent in the nets. He focussed instead on his batting and topped 1,000 runs on ten separate occasions. The 1951 season, when he scored more than 2,000 runs, proved his most prolific, the achievement acting as a spur to Harold Gimblett to exceed the total the following season.

Maurice Tremlett watched by A. V. Bedser (left) and A. J. McIntyre (right) of Surrey.
SOMERSET CRICKET MUSEUM

Maurice had been married in Taunton in 1948 to Melina (née Cousins). The Hampshire cricketer Tim Tremlett was their son and Chris Tremlett of Hampshire and England their grandson.

Appointed captain of Somerset in 1956, Maurice's greatest achievement was surely to take a rag-tag team who had propped up the Championship table for four seasons – a 'happy band of jokers' as Bill Alley self-deprecatingly called them – and drag them to third place in 1958. The spur for this outstanding achievement had arguably been Maurice's sacking at the end of the 1957 season for one drunken escapade too many at the Grand Hotel in Swansea. Reinstated after the intervention of Dennis Silk – a man able to bridge the divide between the more boisterous of the players and the starchier element among the committee – Maurice had become a man on a mission.

He played 353 games for Somerset, averaging 25.93 with the bat, including fifteen centuries and took 326 wickets at 29.04 apiece. He also appeared for Hawke's Bay and Central Districts in New Zealand. After standing down from the Somerset captaincy at the end of the 1959 season – when his eyesight and his zest for the game both showed a marked deterioration – he left the scene in 1960 and, in a reprise of his earlier career with the Rowbarton brewery, was employed by Guinness.

He died in Southampton on 31 July 1984 at the age of sixty-one after a long and painful battle with cerebral cancer. This was perhaps linked to a sickening blow he had received in 1953 when he took the full force of shot from Tony Woollett of Kent which left a marked indent on his forehead. At the time, Maurice had been rushed to hospital. The trauma had affected his vision thereafter but had not dented the courage and enterprise he had already demonstrated as a captain and a player.

361
Miles Coope
24 May 1947 v. Gloucestershire, Taunton.

M Coope

Miles Coope was born in Gildersome, near Leeds, on 28 November 1916. His father, Fred, was a music teacher, already in his forties when he was married to Edith (née Crowther), a schoolteacher. Brought up with two sisters, Miles combined the sensitivity of a talented pianist and organist with skill as a hard-hitting batsman and bowler. On leaving school he undertook a seven-year apprenticeship as a piano restorer in a shop in Leeds, later recounting that he was obliged to work without pay for the first twelve months and that thereafter his weekly salary began at 2s 6d, with a further 2s 6d per week added each year. He was offered the opportunity to take on the business at the end of his training but declined, on the basis that he wished to have the flexibility to try his luck as a professional cricketer. Although he would carve a career in league cricket and the first-class game, this was a supplement to his work as a French Polisher and piano tuner, rather than an end in itself. In many ways, this freed him to express himself as a batsman. An exquisite timer of the ball, he could dominate bowlers in club cricket and took delight in hitting the ball out of a ground. His bats were made for him by Clough & Ward, who had a workshop attached to a pub in Drighlington, a short distance from his home village of Gildersome. They were commissioned with surplus weight in the lower part of the bat in order to assist him in his efforts.

A diffident, gentle-natured man, Miles became a close friend of Yorkshire-born Somerset cricketer Johnny Lawrence and – like Johnny – he was a conscientious objector, working with the Forestry Commission for the duration of the Second World War. His posting to Laverton would prove fortuitous. A member of a team assigned the task of felling a forest, he lodged with a farming couple whose daughter would become his wife. He was married in 1944 to Olwyn Sarah (née Watson), with whom he would have three children, all born in Yorkshire, the couple residing for a while in Drighlington. He was by then establishing his reputation as an opening batsman with Leeds CC at Headingley when the *Yorkshire Post* reported ahead of the 1947 season that the 'right-handed batsman from Drighlington has been granted special registration by MCC to play as a professional for Somerset'.

As had been the case with Johnny Lawrence, Miles had played on a number of occasions for Yorkshire Second XI and recognised that he would not progress further in a strong Yorkshire side. He was never able, though, to replicate the success of his friend

Miles Coope — 'one of the most delicate late cuts ever paraded in the West'.
SOMERSET CRICKET MUSEUM

at Somerset, although cricket historian David Foot notes that 'he had one of the most delicate of late cuts ever paraded in the West'. Over three seasons until his release at the end of 1949 he appeared seventy times, amassing 2,718 runs at 20.90, including two centuries. He also took 8 wickets at 59.87 apiece, bowling leg-breaks at something approaching medium pace.

From 1950 he returned to playing league cricket in Yorkshire, initially as a professional for Salts CC in the Bradford League. At the time of writing he retains the Bradford League record for the fastest half-century, completed in eleven consecutive balls. His son, Miles Jnr, recalls that fishing nets would be deployed to retrieve balls from the nearby canal and they were much in evidence that day.

Miles never showed any desire to stray far from his birthplace. After having lived in Drighlington in the early years of his marriage, he returned to Gilderstone. From a young age he had been the organist at the Baptist chapel in the village of his birth and he enjoyed his genteel life as a French polisher and piano tuner, working from his home, where he also stored a number of Steinway grand pianos, hired out for performances. He was in demand for a number of local events and among his clients was Dame Fanny Waterman, the internationally renowned pianist, piano teacher, and for much of her life doyen of the Leeds International Pianoforte Competition.

Miles's death was sudden and unexpected. He had come home on a Monday in great pain but determined that his ailment was insufficient to merit a visit to the local GP. Faced with a stubborn refusal to seek help, his son, Miles Jnr, quietly explained the problem to a Leeds-based doctor whose piano Miles Snr tuned. The doctor duly called in, claiming he was 'just passing' and, on seeing Miles's condition, promptly had him rushed to hospital. By the Friday, Miles had died in St James's Hospital in Leeds. The cause of death was given as kidney failure and acute pancreatitis. The date was 5 July 1974 and Miles was fifty-seven at the time.

Miles Coope, Bill Andrews and Johnny Lawrence enjoying net practice. Bill would recommend both players to Somerset.
COURTESY OF
STEPHEN LAWRENCE

362
Geofry William List Courtenay
4 June 1947 v. Sussex, Taunton

Geof Courtenay was the younger brother of fellow Somerset cricketer Peter, who had played for the county in 1934. Born in Castle Cary on 16 December 1921, Geof was one of four sons of Percy Donald Athon Courtenay and Ethel Florence (née Donne). Percy was an England hockey international who had spent time in the military before taking over his own father's watch-making and jewellery business in Weymouth. He later became a 'gentleman farmer' before finally retiring to Burnham-on-Sea where Ethel died of cancer in 1938, while only fifty-one years old. Geof was sixteen at the time.

Geof Courtenay – left Somerset to teach in Edinburgh.
SOMERSET CRICKET MUSEUM

Educated at Sherborne School, he proved an excellent all-round sportsman, in the rugby and hockey first teams for two years and the cricket team for three years. He and fellow Somerset cricketer Peter Deshon were the outstanding performers, opening the batting together for the cricket First XI for two of those years. Geof was also a fine tennis player, a report in the local paper of his exploits at Burnham-on-Sea hinting at his competitive nature by describing his as a 'tremendous fighter'. On leaving school at the age of eighteen, he was accepted into the Officer Cadet College in Bangalore, from whence he was commissioned as a second lieutenant and served in Burma until 1946, receiving the Burma Star.

After returning to civilian life, he lived briefly in Burnham-on-Sea, staying with his father and his brother, Peter. In June 1947 he played in four first-class matches for Somerset, averaging 9.42 with the bat. After scoring a creditable 34 in his maiden innings, he struggled to make further runs. Unclear about what career he wished to pursue, he struck up a conversation while playing cricket in Minehead that year and was offered a job as a schoolmaster at Cargilfield, Edinburgh's most venerable independent preparatory school, established in 1873. From such chance meetings the course of our lives can be determined. Geof would remain at Cargilfield teaching Maths and Games for nearly twenty-seven years.

He continued to play cricket and hockey at Grange, the latter for Edinburgh Northern (subsequently renamed Grange Hockey Club). Having immersed himself in the local sporting scene, Geof was selected in 1950 to play inside-left for Scotland at hockey in the match against Ireland. Not everyone was pleased. The reporter in *The Scotsman* felt moved to write: 'I deplore the fact that such a large number of 'Anglos' are to take part', though Geof no doubt gave heart and soul for his adoptive country.

Between 1952 and 1957 he joined his brothers in Dorset each year during school holidays and while there would play cricket for Dorset. In 1953, he was selected to play for the combined Minor Counties XI against the touring Australians in a match deemed first-class. Writing in May 1953, the *Somerset County Gazette* reports that he 'was approached with a view to leading the Gloucestershire side this year. Courtenay, a schoolmaster, apparently felt that, much as he would have liked to take it on, his scholastic career must come first and so reluctantly turned it down.' He was, however, able to make himself available to play in three first-class games for Scotland between 1955 and 1957.

Geof's life took a new turn when he met a cousin of two of his pupils. He and Joan Rennie Simson were married in 1958 and would have two daughters together. Joan's father held the rank of colonel and had served in the Royal Army Medical Corps and been taken prisoner by the Japanese in Hong Kong, though he lived to tell the tale.

Joan was nine years Geof's junior and – in her mid-eighties at the time of writing

G. W. L. Courtenay: st Taylor b Card 43 (Scotland v. MCC at Lord's in 1956).
COURTESY OF JOAN COURTENAY

– relates that her husband lived for sport, but after the birth of the two girls restricted his games of hockey and cricket to Sundays. He remained in her words 'a man's man', having been raised with three brothers and boarded at a boys' public school before spending time in the army and becoming immersed in team games.

The untimely death of his brother and fellow Somerset cricketer, Peter, while Joan was expecting their second daughter had come as a blow and Geof, too, would die too young, succumbing to cancer in Edinburgh on 17 October 1980 at the age of fifty-eight. He had spent his whole working life at Cargilfield School and had become part of the fabric of the institution.

The blessings of a life spent enjoying sport but the curse of an untimely death had been visited on both of Somerset cricket's Courtenay brothers.

363
Anthony Vickery
14 June 1947 v. South Africa, Taunton

Tony Vickery was born on 26 August 1925 in Taunton, the only son of Fred Vickery, a fishmonger with a shop on Taunton's South Street. His mother was Annie (née Hayward) and the family lived a comfortable life in Mansfield Road in the town. Educated at Eastcombe Prep School he then went on to Huish's Grammar School where as well as performing well academically, he proved an outstanding young cricketer. In September 1943, the local newspapers were reporting with great excitement about the eighteen-year-old who had scored over 1,300 runs in school and club cricket at an average of 44.00 and taken 118 wickets at under 5.00 runs apiece. He left that year for Bristol University where he was drafted into the University First XI in his first year and would later captain the side. He was not only taking wickets and scoring centuries with alacrity but is also described as 'brilliant in the field'.

He would graduate from Bristol with a BSc in 1945 before going on to study for an MSc (awarded in 1948). The *Somerset County Herald* of 1945 would note that Tony was 'just twenty and since the age of fourteen has made 1,000 runs every season. He is one of Somerset's most promising recruits'. The newspaper goes on to report that 'he bats in a very attractive way and, like Harold Gimblett, excels in the hook stroke', adding that 'in one game at the Exeter County Ground, when Vickery had made 57, he hooked a ball and his partner was run out attempting a seventh run. No overthrow was included.' One is left to marvel at the ability of the fielding side to conjure such a calamity.

Another side capable of the calamitous was of course his county side. Perhaps they

Tony Vickery – a prolific schoolboy batsman whose brief first-class career failed to match Somerset's heady expectations. SOMERSET CRICKET MUSEUM

hoped that here was another Harold Gimblett, another fairy tale of a local prodigy arriving in a blaze of glory. With their hopes raised to fever pitch, they would be sorely disappointed, for Tony Vickery never made the inroads his admirers had hoped for. In six first-class appearances he would average only 8.09 with the bat, a far cry from his performances prior to his introduction. The reasons behind his failure are spelt out in the *Somerset County Herald* when a reporter asks in 1948: 'Can Vickery, a natural ball player if ever there was one, master that nervous indecision early in an innings and blossom into a fruitful run-getter?'

Tony Vickery, who enjoyed many years of club cricket in Cheshire. COURTESY OF OXTON CC

The question would remain unanswered because he left in the latter part of 1948 to take up a position working in the laboratories of Lever Brothers in Port Sunlight. Here he continued to score freely in club cricket, appearing initially for a Neston side captained by Lancashire and England's Ken Cranston. Later he would become a stalwart of Oxton CC in the Cheshire league. In 1949 Somerset granted permission for Cheshire to register him and he appeared for them in Minor Counties cricket until 1959.

He had returned to Taunton in 1948 and guested for the town not at cricket but for Taunton Town FC, having previously played as inside-left for the town's Avimo side during his student days. The local report upbraids the home supporters for barracking one of their own after he sustained an injury and struggled on manfully. Raucous interventions from supporters were clearly not confined to Somerset's County Ground.

Tony Vickery would spend the whole of his working life with the Unilever organisation. In 1955 he was married to fellow researcher Beryl Betton. That same year, he was promoted from the Lever laboratories to Prices (Bromborough) Ltd. Sited adjacent to Port Sunlight, the business had been started in 1919 with the production of Price's candles but by the 1950s specialised in the production of fatty acids. Two years later he was made Joint Home Sales manager of Price's and in 1960 he became Sales Director. In 1967 he joined the board of Joseph Crosfield Ltd (a soap manufacturing part of the Unilever empire).

Tony was still turning out for Oxton CC until 1977, although by then in their Second XI, helping to bring on the youngsters. He lived with Beryl until her death in 2001 in Whitegate, a village near Northwich in Cheshire. Tony remained there until he died at the age of eighty-seven on 27 May 2013. The couple had had no children. Tony Vickery may never have met his native county's high expectations after his extraordinary exploits as a schoolboy cricketer but, looking at his life as whole, he had enjoyed a metaphorical good innings.

364
Frederick Leslie Angell
21 June 1947 v. Leicestershire, Bath

[signature: Angell]

Les Angell was born on 29 June 1922 in Norton St Philip. His father, Frederick Charles, a painter and decorator, was married to Elsie (née Ratcliffe). Educated at the City of Bath School, Les soon demonstrated his talent, winning the school cup in his final year as best all-round cricketer. By 1937, at the age of fifteen, he had joined the Lansdown club in Bath, albeit in the Third XI in his first season. He had established himself as an opening batsman when the Second World War intervened and he served with the RAF in the Middle East and Italy.

He was offered a professional contract by Somerset who were at the time seeking an opening partner for Harold Gimblett as a result of Frank Lee's departure to become a first-class umpire. Like Frank, Leslie was a sound and technically correct batsman, happy to be in Harold's shadow, shoring things up and enjoying the pyrotechnics as Harold chanced his arm against opposing bowlers. *Wisden* would later record that 'small, neat and stylish, Angell was the ideal foil for the explosive hitting of Harold Gimblett'. Whereas Frank Lee had accumulated a significant number of runs, Les was never quite able to replicate that success. Between 1947 and 1956 (when his contract was not renewed), he averaged 19.15 with the bat in 132 appearances. Included in this were one century and sixteen half-centuries. His average is perhaps unflattering, given that he was often required to stand aside when amateur batsmen – specifically Hugh Watts, Gerry Tordoff and Micky Walford – were available during the summer months, when the pitches had hardened. Only an occasional bowler in the first-class game, he conceded 31 runs without taking any wickets. He was also regarded as a fine slip fielder, taking fifty-four catches for the county.

Historians of the club consistently describe him as being a technically correct but wary batsman at county level, more commanding in the environment of club cricket. We are offered an account of his methods by H. J. Channon, writing in the *Somerset County Herald*. He states that:

> *Angell bats placidly, quietly and soundly, watching the ball till the last fraction of a second ... His batting is characterised by a quiet, concentrating and polished orthodoxy that is prepared to play every ball on its merits.*

He was a popular team member, described by one colleague as 'a very quiet man, extremely shy'. The *Somerset County Gazette* would report that 'nobody in the county team has been more popular'. He was known to many as 'Seraph', as a result of his surname, although the moniker could just have readily sprung from his serene demeanour. There was amusement whenever Arthur Wellard, having failed to grasp the allusion, referred to Les as 'Sherriff'. No one appears to have corrected Arthur.

When not employed by Somerset as a pro, Les worked as an engineering draughtsman in Bath and was an integral part of the local cricketing scene, compiling over 20,000 runs including thirty centuries for Lansdown, to which were added numerous wickets. Donald Bradfield praised the 'disciplined batting of Leslie Angell' in *The Lansdown Story*, the definitive history of Somerset's oldest club side. He writes that 'for many years Angell was the sheet anchor of Lansdown, and he scored a thousand runs almost every season in the years 1959 to 1970'. He adds that 'for sheer consistency of scoring over a long period of years Angell is without a serious [Lansdown] rival'. He captained the side for eleven seasons and became President of Lansdown CC between 1983 and 1986, describing the ground as his 'other home'.

Preoccupied with work and cricket in his early years, Les had been married in 1965 at the age of forty-two to Jennifer Mary Flint. Jenny, as she was known, was a receptionist, aged twenty-six and the daughter of a magistrate clerk's assistant. The couple would have a son and daughter.

Les continued to go quietly about the business of his sporting, working and family life in Bath until his death in the city on 9 October 2014 at the age of ninety-two. He is survived by his wife, Jenny, and their children.

Les Angell (top) also shown (bottom, left) with Gerry Tordoff. SOMERSET CRICKET MUSEUM

365
David Peter Tower Deshon
9 July 1947 v. Nottinghamshire, Wells

Born on 19 June 1923 in Marylebone, Peter Deshon was the son of Frederick George Tower Deshon, who hailed from the Bath area and became a career soldier, reaching the rank of colonel. Peter was fourteen when his father died, having retired to Tor House in Wiveliscombe. Frederick had been married in 1921 in his mid-forties to Audrey Victoria Bryant Branson, the daughter of a coffee merchant.

Peter was educated at Sherborne, where he was coached in the latter part of his schooling by Somerset's Micky Walford. He opened the batting along with fellow Somerset cricketer Geof Courtenay and enjoyed success with some free-spirited batting. The *Old Shiburnian* of 1940 reveals that 'Deshon was in very good form, but was occasionally inclined to play carelessly. He now has a great variety of strokes and he played with great confidence'. In August 1941, he appeared for South Public Schools against the North at Lord's and compiled 109 not out before lunch with the score at 179 for 1. His partner for most of the morning was a young Trevor Bailey, later of Essex and England. Peter was also a member of his school rugby team for three years, captaining the side in his final year. *Illustrated Sporting & Dramatic News* reports in 1940 that 'D. P. T. Deshon has excelled both as a full-back and place-kicker'.

With his late father and his paternal grandfather having enjoyed distinguished military careers, there was a strong likelihood that Peter would join the Army on leaving school. In October 1942, he was offered a commission as a second lieutenant in his father's old regiment, the Royal Artillery. He continued to play cricket when his Army commitments allowed, appearing for Somerset Colts, Somerset Stragglers Juniors and for Wiveliscombe CC, where he kept wicket and had much success with the bat.

Peter saw service in Europe during the Second World War. He landed on D-day from a troop ship with bombs dropping all around and spent the next year fighting his way through France and Germany. He was involved in the liberation of Bergen-Belsen concentration camp, which left a lasting impression, as it did for most of the soldiers who witnessed the effects of the atrocities inflicted on the Jews. He was promoted to the rank of lieutenant immediately after the war.

He was invited to play in a trial match for Somerset at the beginning of 1947 and played four first-class games for Somerset between 1947 and 1953, never fulfilling his early promise, averaging 11.71. His availability for the county was severely limited and indeed for much of this period he was in Tripoli. He also played cricket for the Army on a number of occasions. He remained with the Royal Artillery at the Staff College where, fast-tracked for higher office, he had risen to the rank of major in 1957. The following year he retired with that rank, though the Army tried their best to keep him. His retirement, at the age of thirty-five, was prompted by a chance conversation with a fellow cricketer who invited him to become part of a packaging business that was starting up in Alton, Hampshire.

In 1959, he was married to Anne Cecilia Capel, whom he had met at Staff College. Anne was the daughter of retired Air Vice-Marshal Arthur John Capel who owned the manor and its estates in the small village of Chipstable, approximately four miles west of Wiveliscombe. Already familiar with the Capel family, Peter had once dated Anne's elder sister. Anne's great-grandfather, Arthur, had bought the manor in 1839 and it has passed down the family, coming into Anne's possession in 1979. Meanwhile Peter and Anne had moved to Alton to be close to his new employment and the couple settled in Hartley Mauditt House near Alton where they would have three daughters. Peter was fully immersed in the new business venture but still found time to play cricket well into late middle age for such teams as Hampshire Hogs and Free Foresters. He continued to manage his business until retiring in 1988.

He died of a heart attack at the age of sixty-eight at Heathrow Airport on 18 January 1992 when about to fly up to Scotland for his grandson's christening. Anne remained at Hartley Mauditt House until moving to nearby Alresford in 2001.

D. P. T. Deshon of the Royal Artillery – he played four first-class matches for Somerset. COURTESY OF ANN DESHON

1948

"It cannot be claimed that the sharing of the captaincy among several amateurs was successful."

Somerset County Herald

Championship Position: 12 of 17

Unable to secure the services of any amateur on a full-time basis and unprepared to countenance the notion of a professional as captain of the side, Somerset appointed three captains: 'Mandy' Mitchell-Innes, Jake Seamer and George Woodhouse. They were nevertheless obliged to turn to others to fulfil the skipper's duties. Little wonder, then, that the *Somerset Year Book* acknowledged that 'this year's form might perhaps be suitably described as undistinguished'. Somerset's President, John Daniell, wrote of 'a lack of really class batsmen, the most elementary ideas of calling or running between the wickets, a lack of quick or even medium-quick bowler and a lifeless fielding side'. Harold Gimblett alone was singled out for praise. *Wisden* also observed that 'far too much responsibility fell upon Gimblett', whose 1,798 runs included four centuries, the only ones notched up by the team. Writing in the *Somerset County Herald*, H. J. Channon bemoaned the fact that 'in the past, Somerset county cricket was thrice blessed when 'Varsity cricketers after coming down could play regularly the whole season, but the nation's slogan today is "Work! Work! Work!" and the situation must be accepted'. Times had changed but the club's officials remained impervious to calls for new attitudes. A polite request on the part of Arthur Wellard that they

1948 Eastbourne
The scoreboard at Eastbourne in August 1948, recording Harold Gimblett's record-breaking triple century against Sussex.
SOMERSET CRICKET MUSEUM

might consider a ground collection as a bonus for his teammate, Harold Gimblett, in recognition of his wonderful triple-century at Eastbourne was met with a brusque rebuttal on the part of Somerset's Secretary, Brigadier Lancaster, who informed Arthur that making runs was what Gimblett was paid to do.

Horace Hazell achieved a 100-wicket haul. Now approaching forty, the ageing process was not an issue for a left-arm spinner who – even in his prime – was memorably described by John Arlott as the only man slow enough to keep wicket to his own bowling. Barely any quicker but also enjoying a successful season was Johnny Lawrence who saved his best performances for matches against the county of his birth. His 6 for 29 against Yorkshire at Harrogate was followed by a 6 for 35 at Taunton, including a hat trick. Maurice Tremlett fell just short of the double with 958 runs and 83 wickets. Among the debutants, Stuart Rogers would later step in to captain Somerset as indeed would Harold Stephenson, drafted in from the North-East as the replacement for wicket-keeper Wally Luckes.

Somerset take the field against Hampshire at Bath in 1948. Shown left to right are: W. T. Luckes, H. E. Watts (capt), H. F. T. Buse, M. F. Tremlett, F. L. Angell, H. W. Stephenson (in a rare appearance as a fielder), M. Coope (partially hidden), A. W. Wellard, H. Gimblett, H. L. Hazell, J. Lawrence. COURTESY OF BARRY PHILLIPS

366
Stuart Scott Rogers
5 May 1948 v. Glamorgan, Newport

S.S. Rogers [signature]

Stuart Rogers was welcomed into the Somerset fold after coming to Somerset's attention as a Cambridge undergraduate. Born in Muswell Hill, London, on 18 March 1923, he was the son of Reginald Samuel Rogers and Marjorie (née Prince). Reginald worked his way up from the position of junior clerk in the stock exchange, becoming a financial advisor and company director. Educated at Highgate School, Stuart was made captain of the First XI and toured Canada in 1939 with a British Public Schools team. He went up to Pembroke College, Cambridge, and gained blues both at cricket and football, the former after having established his credentials with an unbeaten century in the Freshmen's trial. During the vacations he played for Hornsey CC in North London, on one occasion scoring 144 runs in under an hour. He also made appearances for Middlesex Club & Ground. Nor had he forsaken football. A skilful forward, he played for the prestigious Corinthians team.

After leaving Cambridge he served in Burma (now Myanmar) during the Second World War in the 6th Ghurkhas and the Chindits, under the command of Orde Wingate. On returning to civilian life he would follow in the footsteps of his father and become a stockbroker, in time becoming a partner in the firm Keith, Bayley and Rigg.

Although he could on his day take on a bowling attack with great style, his shot selection was often overly ambitious. Such limitations might have given Middlesex cause to hesitate about selecting him but not so Somerset. He appeared in 1948 and 1949 while George Woodhouse captained the side. At this point, prior to the 1950 season, Somerset advertised for a captain and secretary on a salary of £750 per annum, in order to allow them to pay lip-service to the notion of an amateur skipper. Any secretarial duties were by no means onerous and in truth the running of the club would fall into the lap of Air Vice-Marshal Taylor. In the event, Stuart Rogers was persuaded to take on the role of captain while also continuing his work at the Stock Exchange. Some of his team members could not resist the temptation to refer to S. S. Rogers as 'The Good Ship' and his tactical naivety would mean that he often frustrated the seasoned pros, sometimes to the point of near-mutiny. Somerset cricketer David Kitson would note that 'Rogers used to captain by the clock and you could set your time to his changes. Ellis Robinson [who had enjoyed long bowling spells while at Yorkshire] was not best pleased.' To be fair to Stuart, he knew his limitations and often sought

Stuart Rogers – demonstrated a 'never say die spirit as befits an ex-Chindit captain'.

Stuart Rogers (above) giving a passable impersonation of a Mr Whippy ice cream.

SOMERSET CRICKET MUSEUM

advice from the affable Horace Hazell, who was always more likely to lead the community singing rather than any mutiny. Given their shared fondness for a tipple, the pair would often ruminate over the day's play in a nearby pub. Through it all, Stuart refused to be bowed by circumstance and his 'never say die spirit as befits an ex-Chindit captain' is praised in the *Somerset County Herald*. H. J. Channon would write that 'Stuart Rogers has an engaging natural charm of manner' and that he 'chases a cricket ball as if he has held the world's record for the hundred yards'. Whilst the Somerset committee might have been wiser to have turned in 1950 to a knowledgeable pro, Stuart Rogers should be praised for giving the role his all.

He played for his adoptive county from 1948 until 1953 and over the course of 118 matches averaged 19.08, scoring three centuries and eighteen half-centuries. A very occasional bowler, his two wickets came at 63.00 apiece. One of those matches – the fixture with Surrey at The Oval in 1950 – also featured his younger brother, Michael Scott Rogers. Michael had been a regular attendee at the nets at the County Ground and had stepped into the breach as twelfth man when Eric Hill's knuckle was broken. His enthusiastic contribution in the field included one catch.

Stuart was married in Taunton in 1951 to Margaret Helen Findlay, who hailed from Scotland, where her father had farmed in the North East of the country, subsequently opting for warmer climes and becoming a planter in Trinidad before finally retiring to Taunton. Stuart settled in the town for a while, appearing for Taunton Town FC in the winter of 1952.

At the end of the 1953 season, he left to focus on his work as a stock broker and was perhaps relieved to have shed the burden of captaining the county side. He continued to live for a while in Taunton, where his three children were all born, but by the mid-1960s had made Chesham his home and tried his hand at farming, perhaps leaning on the advice of his wife and her family. He died on 6 November 1969 at the age of only forty-six at the General Hospital in Amersham, Buckinghamshire. The cause of death was cirrhosis of the liver and, given the absence of any inquest, it is safe to assume that Stuart's reputation as an imbiber must have been well established.

Stuart Rogers – setting off for a single (top) and leading Somerset out at Glastonbury
(bottom), followed by Gerry Tordoff (partially hidden), Harold Gimblett, Horace Hazell and
Maurice Tremlett. BOTH SOMERSET CRICKET MUSEUM

367
Harold William Stephenson
5 May 1948 v. Glamorgan, Newport

[signature]

Registered at the time of his birth as William Harold Stephenson, Harold was born on 18 July 1920 in Haverton Hill, Billingham, County Durham. His father was William Henry Stephenson, a fitter and turner at an engineering works, involved in construction, married to Mary Isabel (née Hall), for a while a cloakroom attendant at a local skating rink. Harold had already established his reputation as a fine wicket-keeper and forceful right-handed opening batsman for the Durham Minor Counties side when he was recommended to the Somerset Committee as a reserve and replacement-in-waiting for the ageing Wally Luckes. A contemporaneous report states that the man who recommended Harold in 1947 was his retiring Durham captain, D. C. H. Townsend. Others have later attributed the introduction to Stockton-born Micky Walford who might perhaps have acted as an intermediary. At the time, Harold was a metal worker and in order to encourage the move he was not only offered a two-year professional contract under special registration rules but was also offered a chance to continue his trade as a metal worker at the Avimo factory in Taunton. He was also sought-after as a footballer. Having played in wartime for Darlington FC at inside-left, he was in discussions with Yeovil Town before in the end joining Bath City and subsequently settling down as a gritty half-back for Taunton Town.

By the time of his relocation, Harold was already married to Constance (née Horton), with whom he would have four children. Their wedding had taken place in 1944. He proved a fine acquisition for Somerset. Known to teammates as 'Steve', after Harold Gimblett had observed that two Harolds in the dressing room would be one too many – 'You'll be called Steve', Gimblett had concluded. The moniker had stuck. A dapper man – but for his oversized pads – and garrulous, he was a chirpy presence who stood up for his fellow pros and brooked no nonsense from the amateurs who ran Somerset. Despite this, the sheer weight of the argument in his favour meant that he would almost inevitably be appointed captain of the side in 1960. Colin McCool had also been mentioned as a candidate but makes it clear in his memoirs that he would never have accepted the poison chalice, had he been offered it. In the event, blessed with a fine opening bowling attack of Ken Palmer and Fred Rumsey, Harold would lead the team to a vertiginous third place in the County Championship in 1963.

Season after season he would perform outstandingly behind the stumps, regarded by most on the county circuit as a brilliant operator. His efficient keeping was evident from the outset. During the 1949 season, he did not concede a single bye as Surrey ran up 501 for 3 at The Oval. By 1950, he was widely tipped to go to Australia as deputy to Godfrey Evans. As *Cricket Monthly* would explain, he had 'one foot on the gangplank of the Australia boat' when on the eve of the selection meeting he made

Harold Stephenson – a wicketkeeper who demonstrated lightning reflexes and deft handiwork.
SOMERSET CRICKET MUSEUM

two costly errors, spilling chances offered by the Yorkshire batsmen Vic Wilson and Willie Watson. Sadly for Harold, their captain was Norman Yardley, a member of the selection committee, who opted for Arthur McIntyre of Surrey. Harold had blown his chance. Although he would later be selected in a number of representative games and take part in tours, he was never awarded a Test cap.

Many have written or spoken of his superb technique as a wicket-keeper. In the *Somerset County Herald*, H. J. Channon writes that 'there is nothing spectacular about his keeping, and nothing vociferous about his appealing ... Everything is done smoothly, quietly, neatly, and most efficiently.' In addition, he is described as 'a gay adventurer with the bat' with his running between the wickets said to be 'intelligent and enterprising'. He was however dogged at various times by back problems, a broken finger and also a torn leg muscle, the last of these in a match against Glamorgan in 1958 when the versatile Chris Greetham was required to stand in as keeper. In April 1959 the club announced that his contract would not be renewed until he had proved his fitness. By the following month, the issue had been put to bed.

Over the length of an outstanding career that stretched from 1948 until 1964 (including the last five seasons as captain), he would play 427 first-class games for Somerset, averaging 20.02 with the bat and accounting for over a thousand victims, 694 of them caught and 312 stumped.

His relationship with authority was often prickly. While his part in the Common-

Harold Stephenson attempts a stumping and George Lambert appeals at first slip.
SOMERSET CRICKET MUSEUM

wealth tour to India and Ceylon of 1950-51was uncontroversial, he found himself in the centre of a diplomatic row when, during the MCC tour of Pakistan in 1955, he, Brian Close, Donald Carr and Roy Swetman kidnapped the Pakistani umpire Idrees Baig and poured water over him as a prank, supposedly as a result of some unfavourable decisions. Harold also had a major falling out with Somerset President Bunty Longrigg during the Bath Festival of 1964. Asked by Longrigg to choose which pros should be dropped to make way for one or two amateurs, he responded that if the President wanted to make changes, he should perhaps skipper the team himself. Bunty Longrigg snubbed Harold at the club's annual dinner, mentioning not a single word about the retiring captain's outstanding career. There was further friction when his retirement was announced in the press before Harold himself had agreed. A subsequent report noted that 'his decision to retire at the end of 1964, announced in the press, cannot yet be confirmed. Much will depend on his form and fitness.' Subsequent events would suggest that Bunty Longrigg won the day. Between 1965 and 1968 Harold turned out for Dorset while still living in Taunton,

There was never any doubt about his popularity among the players or their admiration for him. Describing his memories of 'Steve', John Harris fondly recalls not just the lightning reflexes and deft handiwork but also the fact that 'he was always coughing because he smoked like a chimney'.

Having initially arrived with plans to work for Avimo during the winters, Harold took on other employment. During his captaincy he worked in the winter months in the offices of the South Western Electricity Board (SWEB) and after retiring from the game became a brewery rep. He remained in Taunton until his death in the town on 16 January 2008 at the age of eighty-seven.

368
Peter Arthur Onslow Graham
5 May 1948 v. Glamorgan, Newport

Born on 27 December 1920 in Kurseong, a hill station in the Darjeeling district of West Bengal, Darjeeling, Peter was the son of Herbert Walter Onslow Graham, known as Walter, a member of a family of tea planters who for five generations had owned a tea company named Imporient. Peter's mother, Phyllis Ann, hailed from Ludlow.

Sent to board at Tonbridge School, Peter was an affable boy, more interested in sport than he was in his studies. He represented the school at cricket, rugby, fives and

P. A. O. Graham – 'he is nearly as fast as Arthur Wellard was in his prime'.
SOMERSET CRICKET MUSEUM

boxing. At cricket he proved a late developer. He bowled very fast and very wildly until, in his final year at the school, there was a late flowering that saw him put in some impressive match-winning performances for his house and school teams. When it came to batting, he was regarded as a died-in-the-wool tail-ender.

After resitting his School Certificates, he left Tonbridge in December 1938, having failed to progress to the Sixth Form. Earlier that summer he had appeared for Somerset Colts during the school holidays whilst residing with his parents, who had retired to Burnham-on-Sea. It would appear that neither Peter nor his father had any further involvement with the family firm.

Enlisting with the Indian Army as a second lieutenant and leaving for India in December 1940, Peter served with King George's Own Ghurkha Rifles and was awarded a Military Cross for his bravery in 1945. By the time he left the Army in 1946, he had risen to the rank of temporary major.

The following year he was offered a job in Abadan with the Anglo-Iranian Oil Company but this was clearly not a success, given that he left after just one year and returned to live with his parents in Burnham-on-Sea. He then spent some time being coached at the Alf Gover Cricket School and began to make a name for himself at the Burnham-on-Sea cricket club. He was given an airing by Somerset, initially in a friendly against Glamorgan at Newport, where, according to the *Somerset County Herald*, 'Graham certainly impressed when he bowled in the first innings …. with three very good wickets all clean bowled.' The newspaper later adds that 'he is nearly as fast as Arthur Wellard was in his prime. When bowling at the County Ground in practice this week he kept a length and moved the ball quite a lot.' The coaching had not been in vain. If there were any last-minute concerns about his elevation to the first-class game, these would have evaporated when he returned figures of 7 for 28 for Burnham CC against Clark, Son & Morland CC, with all seven victims clean bowled. There can be no doubting his ability to bowl at the stumps at pace. In the event he played six times for Somerset, all bar one of the games in 1948 and the other, in 1953, when he returned home to Burnham-on-Sea. He took seven wickets in total at 45.14 and eked out an average of 9.11 with the bat, demonstrating that his batting had improved slightly under the tutelage of Alf Gover.

After his initial brief stint in the Somerset fold, he left for Shropshire to learn about farming from an uncle on his mother's side of the family, though not every lesson was applicable as he planned to farm tobacco in Rhodesia. He would be based there for thirty years until the late 1970s, by then in his fifties. He had returned to the UK ahead of his marriage in Norwich in 1954 to Enid Janet Alford, an occupational therapist and daughter of a doctor, with whom he had at least one daughter and son (with precise records difficult to locate). He left his farm at a time when the writing was on the wall

Peter Graham – left England to run a tobacco-growing farm in Rhodesia, later Zimbabwe. SOMERSET CRICKET MUSEUM

for the white farmers as Rhodesia – shortly to be renamed Zimbabwe – tore itself apart in a brutal civil war. Peter retired to the island of Jersey, having purchased a property overlooking the Royal Jersey Golf Course in the parish of Grouville and would remain there until his death on 2 March 2000 at the age of seventy-nine.

369
Joseph Edwin Bucklan
5 May 1948 v. Glamorgan, Newport

J E Bucklan

His birth was registered with the surname Buckland but for most of his life he referred to himself on all official documents such as marriage and death certificates as Bucklan. Indeed, his original surname came as a surprise to his wife and family when they unearthed his birth certificate at the time of his death. To add to the confusion, he was known throughout his adult life – among friends, family, teammates and work colleagues – as Paddy, the name adopted here.

Born on 24 September 1916 in Lingfield, Paddy was the sixth of nine children of Allan Leonard Buckland, a bricklayer, and his wife, May (née Davey). May had previously been married to a Charles John Allen but had been left a widow in 1907, with two infants to bring up. The longsuffering May's first child had arrived in 1904 and the eleventh and last in 1925. Their home on Baldwins Hill, Lingfield, must have been a crowded place and money would have been in short supply as evidenced by Allan's Poor Law application for financial support in 1912. May died in 1937, at the age of fifty-one.

The loss of his mother was in all probability the spur that led Joe to shake off his past and seek a new life as a twenty-year-old. Immediately after her death he left home and joined the merchant navy. This was almost certainly the time that he became no longer Joseph Buckland but Paddy Bucklan (or in formal circumstances Joseph Bucklan). He never again returned to his family home.

Paddy would later state that he served briefly during the Second World War in the tank regiment and was redeployed owing to a burst eardrum. Press reports note that he became a private in the Royal Electrical and Mechanical Engineers (REME) and was stationed in Bridgwater. Although the work was inevitably shrouded in secrecy, it is assumed that he was involved in the construction of Bailey Bridges at the converted British Cellophane Ltd factory. Whilst based there he met Eileen Gladys Fry, a typist and secretary whose parents – Alfred and Lily Fry – owned and ran the Fleur de Lis Hotel in St Mary Street. Confusingly, she was known as Jane. The twenty-eight-year-old Paddy and twenty-four-year-old Jane were married on 16 June 1945. They would have three children together.

Paddy played cricket for Bridgwater CC as early as 1945. He was a left-arm, fast-medium swing bowler, slightly built, but if the mood took him he could generate genuine hostility, as the local newspaper reports would sometimes attest. Clive Davey – also a Somerset player and for many years a club teammate – referred to Paddy as a 'fiery' bowler and highly competitive, although as a man he was gentle-natured and never known to raise his voice or to swear. He was the mainstay of the Bridgwater CC bowling attack immediately after the war and throughout the 1950s. Invariably named as P. Bucklan in the club records, he was regularly among the wickets and Somerset finally took notice when veteran wicket-keeper Wally Luckes recommended him to the county, having played with him on a number of occasions. It was announced in 1948 that 'Bucklan will play as a temporary professional' meaning that he would be paid a match fee only if asked to represent the county. Paddy duly appeared in the non-Championship season opener, a three-day friendly against Glamorgan at Newport, and acquitted himself well with a total of 3 wickets for 55 runs and 17 undefeated runs with the bat. Just how temporary a pro he would be was made apparent when he was not selected again. Paddy would at least be able to claim that he was never dismissed in first-class cricket and had come away with a bowling average of 18.33 that most would be eminently satisfied with.

Returning to club cricket, he continued his outstanding success. He would make an appearance as an amateur in the Somerset Second XI in 1950 after the vice-captain of Bridgwater CC had voiced his frustrations at the March 1950 AGM, over the way his teammate's claims had been ignored by Somerset. It was noted that 'they have a devastating bowler in P. Bucklan but ... he never made an appearance for the county last year when he took 90 wickets.'

Paddy would remain rooted in his adoptive county, residing in Bridgwater. He and Jane had spent the first eleven years of their marriage living in the Fleur de Lis, helping Jane's parents with the running of the public house. Paddy initially worked during the day as a joiner for the Bridgwater builders, Harris Bros and Collard Ltd. His mother-in-law was a member of the Collard family and among the firm's projects was the house built for Jane's parents. Paddy's next employment involved a return to British Cellophane Ltd. This was a tiring time with a

Paddy Bucklan – a 'devastating bowler' for Bridgwater CC.

growing family, regular commutes to the Midlands to the head office of parent company Courtaulds and evening work in the pub. Little wonder that Jane expressed her frustration that Paddy was continuing to play cricket. Their son, Patrick, relates the tale of the time when his father announced that he was off to play cricket where-

J. E. (Paddy) Bucklan takes the field in his only appearance as a member of the Somerset XI:
a friendly fixture against Glamorgan in May 1948. Left to right: *J. E. Bucklan,*
M. Coope (partially hidden), H. F. T. Buse, E. Hill, P. A. O. Graham, N. S. Mitchell-
Innes, S. S. Rogers, H. Gimblett, H. W. Stephenson. COURTESY OF BARRY PHILLIPS

upon Jane threw Paddy's kit into the stream that ran at the bottom of their garden.
Having retrieved the soaking kit, Paddy promptly left for his match.

Cricket notwithstanding, the couple worked well as a team, taking on a new challenge of running another pub – The Queen on Bridgwater's High Street – until 1972.
Paddy was still rising to the challenge of two jobs, having become a skilled pattern
maker, crafting tools for the manufacture of moulded packaging, first for Borden UK
and subsequently for TMB Patterns Ltd in the town. He continued in this line of work
until retiring at sixty-five but was then recalled and asked to spend the next five years
training up a successor. At seventy, this hard-working man – determined never again
to witness the penury he had endured as a child – finally relaxed and enjoyed his final
days with Jane on Chepstow Road in Bridgwater.

Paddy was a sixty-a-day cigarette smoker throughout his adult life. Given this, it
perhaps comes as no surprise that this once-pacey bowler should have succumbed to
lung cancer. He died in Bridgwater on 18 February 1989 at the age of seventy-two.
His was, in the words of his wife, 'a quiet funeral, as he would have wanted'. His death
was officially registered as 'Joseph Edwin Bucklan'.

370
Michael Antony Sutton
23 June 1948 v. Oxford University, Bath

The Cricketer of January 1993 announced the sad news of the death of Tony Sutton, with a brief summary of his career as a cricketer. The news came as a surprise to many, not least to Tony. In early 2017, at the age of ninety-five, he was able to look back with some amusement at an incident that elicited much embarrassment and apologising on the part of the magazine's editor, Richard Hutton. As Tony pointed out in his letter to *The Cricketer* regarding his obituary, he had already got his revenge in early by twice claiming the wicket of the editor's father, Len Hutton, during his first-class career. All was well that ended well. Tony was sent a case of champagne which he invited friends and family to help him consume at his Obituary Party. Guests were encouraged to attend dressed either in mourning clothes or cricket gear and, as photographs attest, Tony was full of life and decked in his I Zingari blazer and cricket whites.

He was born on 29 March 1921 in Weymouth. His father, William Moxhay Sutton, married to Barbara Marie (née Corballis), was a career soldier who rose to the rank of brigadier in the Royal Tank Regiment and was at one time ADC to King George V. Barbara's mother hailed from Taunton, where the family's home was Creechbarrow (christened Creech Castle by subsequent owners) and her father was an Irish landowner.

Together William and Barbara would have three children, including Tony's twin sister, Sybil Mary (who was later married to Winston Churchill's private secretary, Donald Hay).

Tony attended Ampleforth, a leading Roman Catholic boarding school based in North Yorkshire, and starred both in the rugby and cricket teams, in the latter as an off-spin bowler. In 1940 he was invited to represent the North of England Public Schools. Also academically gifted, he had won an exhibition to study History at Oxford but joined the war effort instead. While a cadet in the Royal Armoured Corps he gained a fine reputation not so much for his abilities as a soldier – which are not in doubt – but for his skills as a conjurer. One report includes an image of Cadet Tony Sutton pulling a duck out a tin helmet as his take on the traditional rabbit out of a hat. Somerset could have done with a few more metaphorical

Tony Sutton walking out to bat at Lord's. COURTESY OF TONY SUTTON

rabbits out of hats in that era, though there tended to be ducks aplenty. When it came to the business end of the war, Tony was involved in the Normandy landings as a lieutenant with the Westminster Dragoons, equipped with flail tanks, although he modestly points out that he regarded as the real heroes those (such as his elder brother in the same Regiment) who landed on the first day to provide mine-free lanes off the beach. Tony was later awarded the Military Cross for his bravery in jumping from his tank to rescue an injured crewman from another tank whilst under heavy fire during fierce fighting in Southern Holland. He would be granted the Legion d'Honneur by the French Government in 2016 as a surviving veteran who had contributed to the liberation of France.

He left the Army at the end of hostilities to go up to Worcester College, Oxford, not on the basis of his original exhibition but as a Kitchener Scholar for able students with a father in the military. While at Oxford, he was awarded blues both at cricket and rugby. He also played as a second-row forward for Richmond.

On leaving Oxford University, he was articled to Stone, King and Wardle, a firm of Bath solicitors. Here he continued to immerse himself in the local sporting scene, playing rugby for Bath and Somerset and joining Lansdown CC. The *Somerset County Herald* announced with great excitement in May 1948 that the 'off-spinner and Oxford blue M. A. Sutton … has been having nets in Taunton'. Having played in eighteen first-class matches for Oxford, taking 46 wickets at 25.52, he only ever played once for Somerset, that being against his alma mater. He took one wicket for the county at a cost of 44 runs and averaged 13.00 with the bat.

His brief sojourn in Bath was ended when he qualified as a solicitor and moved to Teignmouth to join the firm of Tozers, of which he became in time a partner. He played cricket for the South Devon club in Newton Abbot and in 1954 for Devon, continuing to enjoy club and wandering cricket for sides such as Somerset Stragglers, Devon Dumplings, I Zingari and Free Foresters until he was nearly sixty. He also retained an interest in rugby and was President of Teignmouth RFC for several years. He was married in 1958 to Bridget Gillian Mary Fawcett, known as Gillian, with whom he would have five children. He describes himself as a country solicitor who had a particular interest and specialism in helping Roman Catholic institutions such as his Diocese and monasteries and convents. In later years he turned increasingly for recreation to tennis and golf and remained firmly rooted in Teignmouth after his retirement.

This former member of the Magic Circle performed no great miracles for Somerset in 1948 but did go on to stage an impressive resurrection in 1993, following the publication of his obituary. At the time of writing he is Somerset's oldest surviving former player and sharper than many a man half his age. It is to be hoped that he will conjure another few years and become the first Somerset player to reach the age of a hundred. Perhaps another complimentary case of champagne from *The Cricketer* would be a fitting way to herald that event.

Tony Sutton shakes hands with King George VI ahead of the Varsity rugby match (above) and impresses distinguished onlookers with his sleight of hand (below).
COURTESY OF TONY SUTTON

371
James Redman
31 July 1948 v. Gloucestershire, Bristol

Jim Redman was born in Bath on 1 March 1926. His father, Samuel Francis Redman, was a railway clerk, married to Mabel (née Sykes). Jim was their only child. He attended the City of Bath School, playing in the school cricket and rugby sides alongside fellow Somerset cricketer Mick Hanna. Whereas Mick went on to play rugby for his county, Jim enjoyed more modest success at the game, appearing at fly-half for the Bath Second XV (Bath United RFC). He played his club cricket for Hampset, the side so named because it was set up by one founder member from Hampshire and another from Somerset. The club was formed in 1940 and became successful after the war when the ageing members of Bath CC appeared determined not to yield up their places to the next generation. The newly formed Hampset team, peopled in large part by former pupils of the City of Bath School (Old Sulians), gained a reputation as a fit and youthful side, particularly noted for their fielding prowess.

H. J. Channon wrote in the *Somerset County Herald* that Jim was a 'right-arm, medium pace bowler with chief reliance on a good length', adding that 'his steady bowling makes batsmen play him with care'. Channon concludes that 'his bowling needs that extra polish that makes him better than a good club cricketer ..... He is young, sturdily built and a keen trier and may yet confound the critics.' Sadly and not through wont of effort, Jim never rose beyond the level of a successful club cricketer, though he had his moments. In a very weak Somerset side who spent much of their time propping up the Championship, he and Bertie Buse acted as a foil to an attack that relied primarily on spin bowlers. Between 1948 and 1953, playing as a professional, he appeared in 65 matches and took a total of 117 wickets at 35.63 apiece. His best performance was at Frome in 1951, when, against Derbyshire in conditions where he was able to impart marked swing, he took 7 for 23. Over the course of his career, he also averaged 12.34 with the bat. Mick Hanna relates an incident in 1948 when his former schoolmate and good friend was facing Keith Miller immediately after a lunch interval and the great Australian all-rounder fired in a fearsome bouncer that momentarily 'terrified the life out of Jim', who quickly ducked, only to see the ball sail over his head and realise that Miller had unleashed an Indian rubber ball. Keith Miller was never one to settle for the predictable. Such aberrations appear to have been tolerated by umpires in those times. The incident compares with the rather less menacing doughnut bowled by Somerset's Raymond Robertson-Glasgow to Bev Lyon of Gloucestershire, after a tea interval.

Jim and Somerset parted company at the end of the 1953 season. Married in 1948 to Jean (née Hooke), with whom he would have a son, he went into business, owning a sports shop in Salisbury for many years and turning out for Salisbury CC and, on occasions, for Wiltshire. He continued to run the shop until his early death in Salisbury as a result of cancer on 24 September 1981 at the age of fifty-five.

He was survived by his wife, Jean and their son, Roger. While Somerset cricket had been at a low ebb, this honest, hard-working pro had given of his best for his county and for his family.

Jim Redman – 'his steady bowling makes batsmen play him with care'.
SOMERSET CRICKET MUSEUM

1949

"SIR – West Country lovers should be proud of the Somerset
team who invariably go all out to win, and if they cannot win
are content to lose. This is the true spirit of the game which
is so lacking in the majority of other first-class counties.
GEORGE ATWOOD, Commander RN (Retired)."

Letter to *Western Gazette*

Championship Position: 9 = of 17

Commander George Atwood's letter to his local newspaper might have expressed his satisfaction with another season of mediocrity but not everyone was in agreement. There was consensus, however, that the season was lit up by the three Somerset victories at the Weston Festival, the first triple success since 1936.

Harold Gimblett set a new record for the county of 2,063 runs in the season (surpassing Frank Lee's 2,019 runs achieved in 1938), ably assisted in the latter stages of the season by the schoolmasters Micky Walford of Sherborne and Hugh Watts of Downside. With eleven centuries clocked up, the batsmen had arguably stepped up to the plate. The *Bath Chronicle* reports that 'Harold Gimblett has settled down to more subdued methods, mainly because of the responsibilities … of opening the innings'. It also congratulates Stuart Rogers for having demonstrated so much 'pluck' when batting with one hand against Essex at Bath after suffering a fractured finger. The paper notes that not everyone was prepared to knuckle down, observing in relation to Miles Coope and Eric Hill that 'their sometimes unorthodox strokes in matches, just when they appeared set, have caused disappointment in the camp'. As for the bowlers, Horace Hazell and Johnny Lawrence both exceeded 100 wickets but the absence of a penetrative quick bowler remained a major problem.

In summarising the efforts of their captain, the club stated in the *Somerset Year Book* that 'Mr Woodhouse, in his first year in full control of the side of such unpredictable qualities, showed himself imperturbable, ready to face any crisis and entirely unselfish'. There was some disgruntlement over the lack of fitness with 'singles and twos turned down' (Rogers and Stephenson excepted) and 'fielding and returns to the wicket were still open to criticism'.

There were great hopes for debutant Roy Smith, a Taunton boy, but he was never quite able to become a force in the first-class game.

Horace Hazell is greeted by the manager of Taunton Town FC ahead of a benefit match involving the Somerset cricket team at Priory Fields on 30 August 1949. The cricketers included within their ranks a number of talented footballers, although Horace could not claim to be one of them. Fred Lee (hidden in the photograph behind Horace's considerable bulk) was in fact a regular in the Taunton Town side and Maurice Tremlett had just signed a contract to play as their centre-half for the ensuing season. Taunton Town beat the Horace Hazell Benefit XI by 2 goals to 1. According to the Somerset County Herald, *Johnny Lawrence, playing on the left-wing, 'caused many laughs'. Stuart Rogers 'beat Burt with an unstoppable shot ten minutes before the end' after Eric Hill had 'hit the woodwork several times'. The footballers then rose from their slumbers to claim victory with two late goals. The players shown here are –* Back row: *W. R. Genders, R. Smith, E. Hill, A. W. Wellard, M. F. Tremlett, H. W. Stephenson.* Front row: *H. Gimblett, F. G. Lee (hidden), S. S. Rogers, J. Lawrence.* Foreground: *H. L. Hazell.* COURTESY OF BARRY PHILLIPS

372
William Roy Genders
22 June 1949 v. Cambridge University, Bath

In his two first-class matches for Somerset, Roy Genders would score a total of twenty-nine runs, substantially fewer than the number of books this prolific writer would complete during his varied and interesting life. He was born on 21 January 1913 in Dore, Derbyshire, the son of William Henry Genders, at the time a commercial traveller, and Mary (née Peat), a primary school teacher in the village of Eckington at the time of her marriage in 1911. Roy's father would go on to develop a successful business as a timber merchant, doing sufficiently well for the family to employ a maid and a cook.

Educated at King's School in Ely, Roy won a place at St John's College, Cambridge University, in 1932 and although a subsequent report states with unintended humour that he 'studied mushroom growing for two years at Cambridge', he in fact studied Natural Sciences. It is certainly true that he knew a thing or two about mushrooms. He would later enjoy recognition as the 'BBC mushroom grower' and his book *Mushroom Growing for Profit*, published in 1946, would become the oracle for budding fungiculturalists. Roy had in fact already had many gardening books published, having first enjoyed success as a writer in the early 1930s. One reference notes that the 'venerable English gardener Roy Genders' wrote approximately fifty books, some of them published posthumously. As soon as he had completed his education, Roy had set about earning a living through the sale of plants – initially aubrietias and violas, which he grew at his parents' home in Sheffield, aided by the gardener he employed. In 1944 he would take ownership of Fanshawe Gate Hall (a sixteenth century manor house in Derbyshire with eighty acres of farmland) and write of his experiences in his book *I Bought a Farm*, published in 1947. He is quoted as having concluded that there was more money to be had in writing about farming than there was in farming itself and in 1951 he abandoned that particular struggle. Indeed, throughout his life, Roy would reveal either a willingness to move on with decisiveness or perhaps a low boredom threshold.

From an early age, he had demonstrated some skill as a sportsman. The *Sheffield Independent* of November 1933 reports his selection at inside-right for St Albans FC while studying at Cambridge and notes that he had been on the books as an amateur at Sheffield Wednesday FC. He would also go on to represent Sheffield United FC and we are informed that at that time he had 'the ideal build', standing 5 ft 11 in tall and weighing 11.5 stone. While at Cambridge he played for St John's College at cricket, but failed to gain a blue and left without completing his degree. Prior to the war, he enjoyed success in club cricket in the Yorkshire Leagues. He would later write about his experiences in his book *League Cricket*, describing it within the book's pages as 'cricket in the raw, not the spit and polish county stuff, but the real 'blood and guts' warlike cricket which delighted these tough Yorkshiremen, reared on the windswept moors, who wanted some action for their money'. His honest account of the win-at-all-costs mentality that pervaded league cricket won admirers and critics in equal measure.

During the war, he continued to enjoy regular games of cricket. In 1942 he played for Heckmondwike and averaged 89.00. Then in the 1943 season it is recorded that, having joined the RAF, he amassed over 1,000 runs. The *Derby Daily Telegraph*, anticipating that he would be knocking on the door for a place in the Derbyshire team at the end of the war, states that 'if he is not a purist in stroke play he has a hearty drive that pleases the crowd'.

Immediately after the war he was engaged by Smethwick as a pro, opening the batting and also bowling leg-breaks, and the 1946 season also saw his maiden first-class appearances for Derbyshire. It was a busy year for Roy, with the publication of the first of his three authoritative books on greyhound racing. The announcement of its publication describes him as an 'author, Derbyshire cricketer, farmer and wartime flier'.

He was married in 1940 to Mary Beryl Thompson and they lived subsequently in Liverpool and Sheffield (which acted as Roy's base while he restored the manor and grounds at Fanshawe Gate Hall). He would have three children with Mary between 1942 and the winter of 1948 but spent much of his time after the war in Derbyshire and Worcestershire. He played five first-class matches for the latter county in 1947 and 1948 including two away matches but, whilst in Worcestershire, he was playing away in an entirely different sense. He had a child with Kathleen Rushe in early 1947, and two more children were to follow during the couple's stay in Woolavington, in Somerset. After his divorce from Mary, he married Kathleen in Bridgwater in 1951. Mary also

Roy Genders – a remarkable man who wrote numerous books on a dazzling variety of subjects.

remarried that same year.

The pace of his life had not relented. In 1949 he had been offered the position of pro for Penzance CC and had been granted permission by the council to live in a caravan sited on the cricket ground for the duration of the summer, in light of the housing shortage. His much-anticipated arrival was delayed while he took an extended trip to India. It was then cancelled entirely as he opted to play for Somerset as an amateur, after Johnny Lawrence alerted the county to his availability. In the event, he would play in only two first-class games for Somerset, averaging 7.25 with the bat and bowling only four overs without taking a wicket.

If his zest for cricket had diminished, the same could not be said for his writing, which continued unabated with an astonishing number of publications, including a history of Worcestershire CCC as well as offerings on all aspects of gardening and a volume on collecting trade and cigarette cards. Roy was clearly an avid collector, because his extensive accumulation of trade cards was sold after his death by Bonhams, a separate and unrelated but equally impressive collection of English drawings and watercolours having been sold by Christies in 1971.

This remarkable man was still writing at the time of his death in Worthing at the age of seventy-two on 28 February 1985.

373
Roy Smith
22 June 1949 v. Cambridge University, Bath

A diminutive character with a big heart, we are given an insight into Roy Smith's approach to the game of cricket by H. J. Channon, writing in the *Somerset County Herald*. Channon observes that 'Roy is in the nets at every possible moment and no day is long enough for practice' and that he 'pesters bowlers as to faults in his batting and gets them to bowl ball after ball until he has mastered it'. We are also informed that 'Roy's cup of enthusiasm brims over. He is a sparkling fieldsman.'

Roy also showed great promise as a footballer. At sixteen, he had been turning out for Ilfracombe as a centre-half, attracting the attention of Liverpool FC. Roy would happily inform people that he had the distinction of scoring a goal for the club in a friendly fixture, although sadly it was an own goal, which, he noted, rather scuppered his chances of a regular place. The following year, he had joined the ground staff at Tottenham Hotspur after three trials as a right-half. He was remoulded into a left back but a career in the upper echelons never materialised and he later plied his trade for a variety of local clubs in Devon and Somerset.

He was born in Taunton on 14 February 1930 (and not 14 April as listed in some sources). His parents, Edith May Quick and Albert Le Breton Smith, met while Albert was stationed in Taunton with the Somerset Light Infantry. Albert lived a chaotic life, regularly moving from one job to the next and adopting a casual attitude towards authority which proved disruptive during Roy's childhood years. Despite this, Roy retained happy memories of his upbringing until his mother died in 1943 of cerebral thrombosis. The thirteen-year-old boy was devastated by the loss. Albert's hastily arranged and shortlived marriage to Rose May Webber, recently widowed, proved one of his more hare-brained attempts to do the right thing for his son and soon descended into acrimony.

Roy Smith – a diminutive character with a sunny disposition and a big heart. SOMERSET CRICKET MUSEUM

Albert eventually settled down with a good friend, whom Roy's daughter remembers as 'Grandma Elsie, a very kindly lady who adored dad [Roy]' and brought stability to Albert and Roy's lives.

Roy was a pupil at Huish's Grammar School at the time of his mother's death but his father sold the family home in April 1944 and shortly thereafter decamped with Roy to Woolacombe, in Devon. Here, Roy completed his education at the grammar school in Ilfracombe while Albert, determined to start afresh, applied successfully for a licence to offer donkey rides on Mortenhoe Beach. There was a comical twist to events when Albert was issued with an ultimatum by the local authority that his licence would be revoked unless he replaced one of the more feral among the donkeys that was causing mayhem. Indeed Roy harboured vivid memories of being dragged along by more than one of the donkeys as he tried to bring them under control. Albert had been a man prepared to try anything but he clearly lacked an eye for a tame donkey. When not struggling to control the recalcitrant beasts, Roy would play football and cricket and was soon making waves with North Devon CC. Seen as an all-rounder, his main skills were as a slow left-arm bowler with news of his ability spreading beyond the bounds of Devon. In his first full season in club cricket, the seventeen-year-old had taken 119 wickets at 7.80 apiece. Over the next two summers he enhanced his reputation with some fine performances for Somerset Colts with bat and ball. He was drawn into the Somerset fold and offered a job in the office at the County Ground, working for Assistant Secretary, Nigel Daniell. Such was his burgeoning reputation

*Roy Smith in the throes of scoring 77 not out against Australia at Taunton in 1953.
Yawar Saeed is at the non-striker's end. The bowler is Jack Hill and the wicket-keeper is
Don Tallon.* SOMERSET CRICKET MUSEUM

that Somerset's captain, George Woodhouse – speaking in an interview with John Arlott – referred to Roy as 'the new Jack White'. Alas, Somerset's hopes would in time be deflated, though not through any lack of application on Roy's part.

After the club's Honorary Secretary, Brigadier Lancaster, had had a word in the right places, Roy undertook his National Service at Norton Fitzwarren, near Taunton, in 1949 and while based there he took 8 wickets for 56 in a trial match for The Army. He was selected to play against Oxford University although, on a wicket more suited to the seam bowlers, he was not asked to bowl. Meanwhile, the promising youngster was coached by Jack White on the basis that although the best deliveries were deadly, his line and length were erratic. Sadly, although he learned to replicate the great master's action and metronomic efficiency, his ability to take wickets was diminished. Somerset offered him a professional contract from the start of the 1950 season and persisted with him for 96 matches until 1955, but he never managed to live up to his early promise. He only ever took 19 wickets at 57.00 apiece. He also averaged 17.10 as a batsman and completed one century and nine half-centuries. A highlight was his 77 not out against the touring Australians in 1953 although he enjoyed a fortunate escape when one delivery hit the stumps but failed to remove the bails.

He had been a popular member of the side, a happy and smiling presence. He had also proved a man of principal, a committed teetotaller unprepared to countenance the gambling that was part of the culture in the dressing room. Perhaps their shared outlook was the reason for a close bond that existed between Johnny Lawrence and Roy. When not employed as a professional footballer in local circles, Roy was invited on occasions to take part in coaching sessions at Johnny's cricket school in Rothwell and stayed with the Lawrence family. His relationship with Maurice Tremlett was less cordial and Roy would later cite the moment their relationship took a turn for the worse. He had refused as a young rookie (appearing as twelfth man) to make a trip to the bookmaker's to place bets on Maurice's behalf.

Roy was married in 1954 to Mary Rutt, a dental nurse in Taunton and the daughter of Cyril and Hilda Rutt, who both taught at Huish's Grammar School. Mary would later quip that her father's response on hearing the news was to remark: 'Of all the boys who went through Huish's, you had to choose Smith.' Roy in fact got on well with Cyril and just as his childhood, for all the occasional setbacks, had been filled with fun and laughter, so it was with Roy and Mary and their two daughters.

Roy had previously found work where he could during the winter months above and beyond his time as a football pro and part-time cricket coach. Despite his being a teetotaller, he had been an employee at the Taunton Cider Company and he had enjoyed a period working for Stansells the Builders. He had even completed a stint as a conjurer's assistant working alongside his father. Albert had decided to become an illusionist after parting with his donkeys, but he had fallen ill and died shortly after his final appearance at Ilminster in 1952. Having realised that his time as a professional cricketer was drawing to a close and encouraged, perhaps, by his in-laws, Roy trained at St Luke's College, Exeter, to become a teacher and joined the staff at Huish's. His father-in-law, known to his pupils as 'Ginger' Rutt, was a strict disciplinarian and an object of terror for many a schoolboy. His firm methods were a counterpoint to the caring, cheerful and self-deprecating manner of his son-in-law. As well as teaching Maths, Roy took on responsibility for coaching the school cricket and football teams.

He left Huish's in July 1978 (when the comprehensive system was introduced to Taunton and the school became a sixth form college) and he began teaching in September 1978 at Monkton Heathfield on the outskirts of Taunton. He was not happy there, opting to take early retirement. He and his wife enjoyed a contented spell thereafter in Taunton but when Mary died in 1993, Roy could not face the prospect of remaining in the family home. He moved to Teignmouth and later Dawlish, living for many years with a companion who had long been a family friend. Following her death in 2013, he moved to Weston-super-Mare, close to his daughter, Jill. At the time of writing, he remains in the care of his loved ones as the problems of old age begin to beset him.

His sunny disposition with laughter and a smile never far away, his infectious enthusiasm and his quiet diligence all made him a much-loved teammate, teacher and family man.

Mary and Roy Smith on their wedding day in 1954. With them are Johnny Lawrence and Graham Atkinson. COURTESY OF STEPHEN LAWRENCE

1950

"One day in the masters' common room, a colleague told me
that he had seen an advert he thought might interest me –
Captain/Secretary of Somerset County Cricket Club. I applied
but returned after an extraordinary interview before a
committee of 43 – or so I was told. I neither had the time
nor the inclination to count them, but there seemed no
way I could work with them."

Charles Palmer (England Cricketer)

Championship Position: 7 = of 17

Somerset registered an enlarged squad of thirty-three players, including twelve
professionals, though the number was trifling when compared to the size of the
committee. In an attempt to entice a well-heeled member of the cricketing fraternity
to captain the club, Somerset advertised for an amateur captain who would be paid to
act as Secretary in order to preserve his notional amateur status. Charles Palmer's
recounting of his experience of the interview process is related by David Foot and Ivan
Ponting in *Sixty Summers*. Whereas Palmer walked away, the ebullient and hopelessly
optimist ex-Chindit Stuart Rogers appeared undaunted by the challenge, accepting
the role of amateur captain but not of Secretary. If enthusiasm rather than technical
ability won trophies then S. S. Rogers would have been a serial winner and he certainly
brought positivity to proceedings. In addition he 'set an example in the field', though,
sadly, most of his team were unable or unwilling to follow his lead.

After a sticky start to the season, Somerset ran into some form. Not the least among
their contributors was the ebullient and popular Johnny Lawrence who fell an agonising 19 runs short of completing the double. With a toothless pace attack, the spin-
bowling triumvirate of Johnny Lawrence, Ellis Robinson and Horace Hazell bagged
the bulk of the wickets, though they proved too few in number to press for any
honours. Predictably, Harold Gimblett was the stand-out batsman with another 1,782

runs to his credit. Micky Walford also offered brief but valuable support in the school holidays. 1950 was the year in which Maurice Tremlett broke through as a batsman with three centuries, though sadly his potency as a bowler had waned.

Among the new arrivals, Ellis Robinson – a seasoned pro from Yorkshire and a fine player, now past his prime – would make useful contributions, though he could suck the life and soul from a dressing room as surely as his fellow Yorkshireman, Johnny Lawrence, could light it up. Debutant Gerry Tordoff is of note in that he would later be appointed captain.

The Somerset team in 1950.
Back row: *R. Smith, E. P. Robinson, M. F. Tremlett, R. F. Trump (Scorer), A. F. Irish, F. L. Angell, H. W. Stephenson, J. Lawrence.* Front row: *H. F. T. Buse, G. E. S. Woodhouse, S. S. Rogers, H. L. Hazell, H. Gimblett.* SOMERSET CRICKET MUSEUM

374
Arthur Frank Irish
3 May 1950 v. Glamorgan, Cardiff

A. F. Irish

Although he was born in Dudley on 23 November 1918, Frank Irish was very much a Sidmouth man, living in the East Devon town for the vast majority of his life. His father, Arthur William Irish, at the time a cabinet maker in Sidmouth, had been married in 1913 but his first wife Sarah (née Burgoyne) had died as a result of complications after giving birth to their son, Cyril Arthur, who survived and lived to old age. Arthur William was remarried in 1917 in Dudley to Helen (née Fryer) who later gave birth to Frank. After the war, the couple settled in Sidmouth and brought up the two half-brothers there.

Frank's father set about building up two retail businesses – a barber's shop and a tobacconist's – in Sidmouth's Fore Street. He also took advantage of the influx of tourists each summer. Postcards of Sidmouth street scenes from the inter-war years often bear the imprint of A. W. Irish. The businesses were successful enough to support the family and Frank would in time take over the running of the enterprise.

During the Second World War he served as a sergeant in the Royal Army Medical Corps and while posted overseas he was married in 1943 in Helmich, Egypt, to Florence Maud Ferreira, a nurse who hailed from Port Elizabeth in South Africa.

The couple returned to East Devon and for many years Frank was a mainstay of Sidmouth CC. Although he had appeared for Glamorgan Colts in 1939, it was in playing for Devon that he made his name. For four seasons after the war he was a dominant force in Devonshire cricket. At club level he established a new record for Sidmouth when accumulating over 1,500 runs for them in the 1948 season, a record that was subsequently broken by fellow Somerset cricketer John Harris. The following season, Frank would amass a combined 2,500 runs in all club and county cricket.

In 1948, Devon had applied to become a first-class county but were rebuffed. They still harboured hopes that their wish would be granted but these were dashed – causing acrimony in some quarters – when Frank was poached after having been offered a professional contract by Somerset in 1950.

H. J. Channon, writing in the *Somerset County Herald*, wrote an account of Frank's style of batsmanship, leaving us in no doubt that he was an accumulator of runs rather than an adventurous stroke-maker. Channon writes that 'like Dartmoor granite, there is a pronounced solidity to his defence, but unlike granite, his batting so far for Somerset has hardly sparkled'. He adds that Frank Irish 'stays at the wicket a long time for few runs'. Channon signs off by describing him as 'a likeable fellow'.

Frank Irish – a Sidmouth tobacconist and a dominant force in Devon cricket in the years immediately after the Second World War. SOMERSET CRICKET MUSEUM

He played sixteen first-class games for Somerset, averaging 25.16 with the bat, including four half-centuries. After a bright start his form fell away when 'muscle trouble affected his footwork'. He was also given an airing with the ball. Channon notes that 'Irish did little bowling for Devon but he has developed into a useful change bowler of medium pace with a pronounced swing'. In the event, he took only 3 wickets at 68.66 apiece. He was offered the chance to extend his contract but, as *Wisden* would note, 'he did not care for the professional game'.

Frank returned to playing for Sidmouth and Devon and is described as 'a forthright and combative captain of the town club'. He made his last appearance for his home county in 1953. He continued to manage the shops his father had established in Sidmouth until his retirement and had no children to pass the business on to. He was predeceased by his wife, Maud and, having suffered badly with arthritis in his later years, died in Sidmouth on 17 July 1997, at the age of seventy-eight.

375
Frederick Gordon Kenneth Day
3 May 1950 v. Glamorgan, Cardiff

Ken Day was born in Yatton on 25 June 1919, the son of William Henry Day and Frances Mary (née Edbrooke) who were married in nearby Bladgon in 1913. William, an engine driver with the Great Western Railway was a widower at the time of their wedding and Frances a farmer's daughter, ten years his junior.

Ken followed in the footsteps of his father and was employed by the Great Western Railway, although as a clerk. He was married in 1945 to Phyllis Mabel Thorne, whom he had met while working for the GWR, where she was employed as a typist. The couple would have one child: a daughter.

He established his reputation as an outstanding club wicket-keeper and a solid and dependable batsman (good enough and patient enough to chalk up thirty centuries in club cricket). He came to the fore initially with Claverham CC and then enjoyed many fruitful years with Knowle CC. A report in the *Western Daily Press* of 1949

Ken Day of Knowle CC.

observes that 'Knowle have in Ken Day a wicket-keeper who has few equals in his job in Bristol'. Indeed, many observers, including Somerset player, coach and sometime journalist, Bill Andrews, felt that, had he been so minded, Ken could have succeeded in the first-class game as a professional keeper. He would in fact only play on seven occasions, each time as a stand-in for Harold Stephenson. In his debut, he proved his worth not only as a keeper but with his role in a stubborn ninth-wicket partnership alongside Horace Hazell. He would then play in six successive matches in 1956 when he was able to negotiate leave of absence to take the place of the injured Stephenson. His batting average of 18.27 in his seven games, including one half-century, speaks of a man comfortable in the elevated company. His contributions with the bat may not have set pulses racing but they were valuable, and writer David Foot describes Ken as stylish and correct.

Ken Day – played seven first-class games as a stand-in for Harold Stephenson. SOMERSET CRICKET MUSEUM

Later he would be employed for many years at a local shipping firm before then going on to work as an insurance manager. After retiring, Ken lived in Whitchurch, Bristol. He suffered in later life from motor neurone disease and finally succumbed to bronchopneumiona, dying in Keynsham Hospital on 9 December 1991 at the age of seventy-two. He was survived by his wife, Phyllis and their daughter, Annette.

376
Ellis Pembroke Robinson
3 May 1950 v. Glamorgan, Cardiff

Ellis Robinson was blessed both with a fine cricketing pedigree and a pair of large hands and long spinner's fingers that meant he was destined not just to become a successful bowler but a superb slip fielder, too. Trevor Bailey would write that, despite having reasons to be cheerful, Ellis was 'somewhat temperamental .... with a woebegone face, stoop and the conviction that the gods were not on his side'.

He was born and bred in Denaby Main, a mining community where it paid to have a certain strength of character. A report, admittedly written in 1899, twelve years before Ellis's birth, describes it as a 'village where nearly all of the men and most of the women devote their high wages to betting, where religion is forgotten, home life is shattered, where immorality and intemperance are rife, where wives are sold like cattle, and children are neglected'. It appears that the Robinson family rose above the general malaise. Ellis was in fact born in the village on 10 August 1911. His father, Ernest, hailed from Bradford and was a building foreman and sometime joiner who combined resources with his brother Luther (who had played first-class cricket for Nottinghamshire) to run a building company. Ernest was forty-four when Ellis was born and Ellis's mother was Ernest's second wife, Caroline Ellen (née Preston), who had previously worked as a housemaid. When they had been married in 1908, Ernest already had a son and two daughters. The couple would have a further six children. Ellis's sister, Marjorie, born a year after Ellis, would be the sibling with whom he remained closest.

The family building company was sufficiently successful for Ernest and his family to move to nearby Conisbrough, although the Robinsons retained their allegiance to Denaby CC, a club that Ernest had been instrumental in setting up and one that succeeding generations of the family would dominate, being described in one report as 'one of the best known cricketing families in South Yorkshire'. The existence of a family business also meant that Ellis never needed to scratch around for employment outside the cricket season.

When he first came to the attention of Yorkshire, he was playing primarily as a wicket-keeper batsman but was informed that the prospects of progression as a keeper were slim as Yorkshire felt they had a surfeit of men capable of fulfilling the role. Ellis therefore turned to spin. Making his debut in 1934, he would contribute strongly to Yorkshire's success, including Championship titles in the three years immediately

Ellis Robinson – 'a woebegone face, stoop and the conviction that the gods were not on his side'.
SOMERSET CRICKET MUSEUM

prior to the Second World War and a further table-topping season in 1946. Bowling his off-spin at a lively pace, he and the left-arm spinner Hedley Verity proved a strong pairing for their native county. Both men would join the RAF for the duration of the war. With Verity severely wounded in Sicily before being taken prisoner of war and dying of his wounds in 1943, Ellis was left to bear the brunt of the attack in 1946 and did so with great aplomb, taking a total of 167 first-class wickets and appearing for Players v. Gentlemen. His form would subsequently fall away when judged by his own high standards and he was allowed the dignity of resigning at the end of the 1949 season and given a grant of £1,500 in lieu of a benefit. He had earned the nickname 'Steely' while at Yorkshire, the name referring not to his resolve (which certainly fitted that moniker) but because he hit the ball so lustily when on song with the bat that on a tour of the West Indies with Yorkshire in 1936, the locals allegedly marvelled that his bat must be made of steel and named him accordingly. He left Yorkshire having taken 735 wickets for the county at 20.60 apiece and held 256 catches, most of them at slip, many of them spectacular and among them a record six held in one innings.

Yorkshire raised no objections when Ellis expressed a wish to play for Somerset, given that his sister, Marjorie, lived in Taunton. Eric Hill would note, dryly, that as a Yorkshireman, Ellis was never likely to pass up the opportunity for free digs. He was not required by the MCC to qualify by residence. In later years, Ellis would state that his three seasons with Somerset were an unhappy time, owing to his frustration with the lack of discipline at the club, with batsmen unprepared to knuckle down. He was also withering in his analysis of the way certain amateurs were parachuted into the side on the basis of their connections, while pros were expected to stand aside. Some teammates have suggested that things were not quite as bleak for Ellis as he reckoned. In a letter to Barry Phillips, Eric Hill would write in later years:

> He was a funny {strange} bloke in some ways but quite honestly he never gave the impression that he hated his time at Somerset. We used to pull his leg a lot but we had lots of fun, notably in 1951 when, prompted by Johnny Lawrence and Roy Smith, most of us took to carrying water pistols. Harold Gimblett missed a match after cutting his hand when trying to repair his pistol with a sharp implement while Harold Stephenson worked up a nasty blister on his trigger finger! Ellis seemed to enjoy all that trivial rubbish.

Perhaps he was not always the dour Yorkshireman he was often portrayed as being. There is no doubting that he brought some of his wiles and grit to proceedings. Over the course of eighty-nine matches for Somerset, between 1950 and 1952, he took 256 wickets at 28.55, added a further 75 catches to his remarkable tally and averaged 8.17 runs with the very occasional Wellardian onslaught against opposing bowlers.

He left at the end of the 1952 season to ply his trade in Yorkshire League cricket, where he felt more at home. Chat show host Michael Parkinson would later reminisce about fielding at forward short leg to the bowling of Ellis at Barnsley and being told, witheringly that 'tha' stands abart as if thi' knickers were starched'. Ellis saw out his cricket-playing days having gone full circle and rejoined Denaby CC (now Denaby & Cadeby CC), whom he had first played for as a boy. He was made an Honorary Life Member of Yorkshire CCC in 1982. Never married, Ellis collapsed and died at the age of eighty-seven at his home in Conisbrough on 10 November 1998. Active to the last, he had been dressing at the time for a planned game of golf.

377
George Gerald Tordoff
19 July 1950 v. Warwickshire, Edgbaston

Gerry Tordoff was born in Whitwood, Yorkshire, on 6 December 1929. His father, Reginald Percy Tordoff, was a professional cricketer, married to Ann (née Melvin). Reginald played for Whitwood Colliery CC for a number of years. Immediately prior to Gerry's birth he had topped the batting averages and would continue to appear for

the side after the war. He then became the pro at Castleford CC in 1948, the year before his death, when Gerry was nineteen, so that he never lived to see his son play first-class cricket.

Gerry was a pupil at Normanton Grammar School and went on to take a degree in Chemistry at Manchester University. Here he was a teammate of Lancashire and Somerset bowler Tom Dickinson, with whom he also appeared for the combined UAU side. He was brought to the attention of Somerset by Johnny Lawrence.

Gerry batted left-handed with what is described as a 'free style', which is to say he was often rather too adventurous to build an innings. He also bowled right-arm medium with what is termed 'a slinging action' in one source. Having first appeared for Somerset while a student at Manchester, he would then go on to complete a further degree at St John's College, Cambridge, over the 1950-51 academic year and while there

Gerry Tordoff – 'his speedy deliveries come at the end of a longish, bounding run'. SOMERSET CRICKET MUSEUM

Gerry Tordoff – brave enough to take on the captaincy of Somerset, a thankless task described at the time as 'the toughest job in cricket'. SOMERSET CRICKET MUSEUM

would gain blues both at football (playing at left-half) and at cricket. He had initially been brought into the Somerset team under a special registration when Harold Gimblett was called away on Test duty in 1950 but would not become a regular until the 1952 season, after he had left Cambridge.

Having been offered a three year commission with the Royal Navy, based in Portsmouth and serving as an instructor lieutenant on *HMS Vernon*, he was seen as an asset to the Royal Navy and Combined Services teams. Writing in the *Portsmouth Evening News* in 1954, 'Nimrod' includes an enthusiastic piece in praise of Gerry, reporting that:

> *Lieut. G. G. Tordoff, who does everything at speed, is the type of attacking player needed to brighten up English cricket ... His bold forcing qualities as a bat have been displayed repeatedly ... He can be most devastating as a bowler, his speedy deliveries coming at the end of a longish, bounding run. He whips the ball down with all the ferocity which his lithe, energetic body can impart to it.*

Nimrod's overenthusiasm was shared by the Somerset committee, although their blind faith in the youthful naval officer was coloured by an additional splash of desperation. In their defence, he had topped the 1954 batting averages at Somerset, albeit with only eight innings to his credit. A more measured account of his ability cites 'a technique that was considered a little loose'.

Ben Brocklehurst resigned the captaincy at the end of the 1954 season with Somerset now becoming serial recipients of the wooden spoon. The committee were determined that another amateur captain should be appointed and Gerry was persuaded that he was the man to take on the role described in one newspaper as 'the toughest job in cricket'. The Royal Navy duly agreed to release their man.

In the event, Somerset's insistence that an amateur should lead the side would do nothing to reverse their fortunes. Peter Roebuck would later accuse them of being 'in hot pursuit of a principle in defiance of all evidence'. Although Gerry would average a useful 25.44 (including three centuries) in 54 matches for a woeful Somerset side and would add 26 wickets at a rather expensive 46.03 apiece, he unfairly took much of the blame for another poor season. It was hardly his fault that at the age of twenty-five and a relative novice, he was unable to lead from the front. *Wisden* notes that 'he found the batting order a jigsaw puzzle without the right men to fill the holes'. A later report in *The Times* informs us that 'a forthright individual, he was popular with the younger players'. He was also comfortable enough in his own skin and sufficiently aware of his limitations to call on the advice of fellow Yorkshireman Johnny Lawrence. After one season he would return to a more rewarding career in the Royal Naval. Gerry would later state that the choice was taken from him after a dismal Weston-super-Mare Festival in which all three games were lost and he registered a pair in the last of these. In his words, 'the committee advised me to return to the Royal Navy'. He was

Gerry Tordoff hits out against Essex at Chelmsford in 1953 (top) and leads Somerset on to the field against Surrey at Weston-super-Mare in 1955 (bottom). Pictured (left to right) are: M. Walker, J. Lawrence, J. W. J. McMahon, B. Lobb (partially hidden), H. W. Stephenson, M. F. Tremlett, G. L. Williams, P. B. Wight, G. G. Tordoff, F. L. Angell.

SOMERSET CRICKET MUSEUM

94

replaced at Somerset by the county's first professional captain, Maurice Tremlett.

Married in 1958 to Marjorie Hope Leake, known as Hope, Gerry would have a son and daughter. If he had been disappointed by his relative lack of success as Somerset captain, this was no doubt ameliorated by his promotion to instructor lieutenant commander in 1958. He continued to represent his employer at cricket for many years and would also appear for Berkshire. After rising to the rank of instructor commander in 1968, he retired from the Royal Navy in 1972. Thereafter he became the registrar of St Martin's College in Lancaster, a teacher training college which later became part of the University of Cumbria. According to *The Times*, Gerry applied at one point - possibly at the time of the departure of Dicky Robinson – to become Secretary of Somerset CCC, but never received a reply. The lack of any response was likely to have resulted from Dicky's inefficiency rather than a more sinister motive.

Gerry died at home in Poulton-le-Fylde on 16 January 2008, aged seventy-eight.

378
William John Conibere
19 July 1950 v. Warwickshire, Edgbaston

Jack Conibere was born in Wiveliscombe on 11 August 1923, the son of William Conibere, a brewery lorry driver, and his wife, Emily (née Lovell). The couple would have three sons – Jack, Donald and Roy – all of whom played cricket and rugby for Wiveliscombe, with Jack talented enough to represent the county at both sports.

He left the local school in Wiveliscombe at the age of fifteen and was employed by the Arnold and Hancock Brewery in the town. At the outbreak of the Second World War, he joined the Royal Navy as an eighteen-year-old and subsequently saw service in the Indian Ocean, while based in South Africa. In his leisure time he represented the Royal Navy both at rugby and tennis. He then returned to Arnold and Hancock as a clerk. The Hancock family were strong supporters of the local rugby team and had been stalwarts of Wiveliscombe RFC since the late nineteenth century, with two of their number – Froude and Frank Hancock – winning international caps while another two – William and Ralph – represented Somerset at cricket.

As for Jack, a strongly-built and adaptable rugby player, he played at various times as a second-row forward, flanker or centre three-quarter. He was also the club and later the county place kicker. News of his prowess spread and Wigan attempted to sign him as a rugby league professional. He turned them down, opting to remain a rugby union player, and was shortly thereafter awarded his first cap by Somerset RFC. His

Jack Conibere – a highly-regarded county rugby player and pacey left-arm bowler from Wiveliscombe. SOMERSET CRICKET MUSEUM

cricketing career was also progressing smoothly. By 1949 his name was cropping up in the local press on a regular basis as he tore through other club sides bowling left-arm fast-medium pace and setting about the opposition bowlers with some vigorous though often short-lived pyrotechnics with a bat in his hands. A report from 1949 relates a more unusual encounter – a charity match – in which Jack hit 'six fours with a pickaxe before being bowled by Mrs Humphries for 33'. No one could accuse Somerset of a run-of-the-mill approach to honing the skills of their hopefuls.

A more conventional performance for Somerset Second XI against Wiltshire at Chippenham led to Jack's being invited to replace the injured Jim Redman. He had taken 5 for 16 in twenty-two overs, thirteen of which

Jack Conibere – turned down the offer of a professional career in rugby league.
SOMERSET CRICKET MUSEUM

had been maidens, and had hit a lusty 31 runs. Given leave by his employer, he appeared for Somerset on an amateur basis and began well on his debut with a bowling analysis of 4 for 66 followed by 2 for 39 – a creditable contribution towards Somerset's ten-wicket victory. Sadly, he would only take one further wicket in his next three appearances, leaving him with first-class figures of 7 wickets at 31.42 apiece. His batting average over the four games was 3.20.

Jack was married in 1951 to Mabel Rowland Osborne. Mabel had been a member of the RAF nursing service and had later taken up a senior nursing post at the Royal United Hospital in Bath before moving to Wiveliscombe to live with her aunt and uncle who were licensees of the White Hart Hotel, an establishment favoured by Jack and fellow members of the local rugby and cricket teams. The couple would have two sons and two daughters.

Jack would continue to play on occasions for Somerset Second XI until he was transferred in 1952 to Arnold and Hancock's Barnstaple depot. In 1955, the Arnold & Hancock brewery business was purchased by Ushers and Jack was recalled to Wiveliscombe where he and his young family lived until 1959 when he was promoted to a senior clerical role at the Ushers headquarters in Trowbridge, Wiltshire. He subsequently joined the stocktaking and valuation team, travelling around Oxfordshire and the West Country. Although his days playing competitive club sport were now behind him, he still found time to coach the youngsters at Trowbridge CC, but by the mid-1960s he began to suffer serious health issues and was admitted to Frenchay Hospital near Bristol in order to have half a lung removed.

Jack was a strong man and a fighter and soon returned to work, although in 1967 he left Ushers and joined Butlin's in a role similar to the one he had been undertaking in the recent past, his work now taking him all over the country. Perhaps tiring of the constant travel and time spent away from his family, Jack set himself up as an independent stocktaker and valuer but when the business failed to take off as he had hoped, he returned to the fold as an employee for a succession of companies in Torquay, among them a retail butcher in the town. Finally, he worked as a control and supply clerk at a meat wholesaling company named Weddel's (who were part of the Vestey Group). Jack was then diagnosed as having lung cancer. A fighter to the last, he was working until a mere ten days before his death in Torquay at the age of fifty-nine on 19 August 1982.

His ashes were interred not in Torquay but in the graveyard of St Andrew's Church, a matter of mere yards from the home in Church Street, Wiveliscombe, where he had been born and raised. Jack had never lost his love for the small market town whose rugby and cricket teams he had graced with distinction, where he had been educated and been given his first job and where he had met his future wife, Mabel. Wiveliscombe was also the place to which he had for a while returned to bring up his young family.

Jack had lived to see the arrival of only the first of his six grandchildren, one of whom would be named William John in his memory. Mabel would live to the age of ninety-two.

379
Michael Richard Gratwicke Earls-Davis
19 August 1950 v. Worcestershire, Worcester

Michael Earls-Davis was born in Camden on 21 February 1921. Although his name was registered as 'Michael Richard Oliver', he had been given the name Gratwicke by the time of his christening. His father was Thomas Richard Earls-Davis, an Australian, and his mother was Helen Norah Gratwicke (née Heasman). Helen's father, Dr

William Gratwicke Heasman, had played first-class cricket for Sussex. Her mother, Helen (née Pawle) also contributed to Michael's cricketing pedigree, coming from an established cricketing dynasty more recently represented by Michael's cousin, John Hanbury Pawle of Cambridge University and Essex.

Michael was eight years old when his father died. His mother was remarried a year later. Educated at Sherborne School, he was briefly at Cambridge University before joining the war effort as a member of the Irish Guards from 1941 and for the duration of hostilities. Wounded in action, he returned to England and played some wartime cricket for Sussex. On returning to civilian life he completed his degree at

Michael Earls-Davis as captain of Somerset Second XI. SOMERSET CRICKET MUSEUM

Corpus Christi College, Cambridge. Although he played cricket for the Varsity team, he missed out on a blue when Cambridge opted to bolster their batting strength and selected Barron Cangley in his stead.

Thereafter Michael took up a teaching post at Downside School, where Somerset cricketer Hugh Watts also taught. The two of them had been teammates at Cambridge and it is entirely possible that Hugh played a part in his friend's appointment. Michael would supplement his £300 salary by working during the summer holidays as secretary to E. W. ('Jim') Swanton, the well-known cricket journalist and author.

He was asked to captain the Somerset Second XI during the summer vacations. A right-arm medium-pace seam bowler, he batted left-handed. Invited to play for Somerset in August 1950 in place of Arthur Wellard – at the time only available for midweek games – he would make only one first-class appearance for the county, averaging 4.00 and taking no wickets at a cost of 18 runs. That was the beginning and the end of his County Championship adventure.

He would leave Downside in 1954 to become a member of staff at his alma mater, Sherborne School, and would remain there for twenty-four years until his retirement in 1978. A housemaster from 1966 until 1975, he also commanded the school's Combined Cadet Force, where it is said that he cut a dashing figure in his Irish Guards uniform.

After retiring from teaching, he acted as the Honorary Secretary of the Old Shiburnian Society from 1980 until 1992. He had been married in 1958 at the age of thirty-seven to Ann Raymond, a graduate of St Andrews University who taught at Sherborne School for Girls. Prior to this, it might be said that Michael had been wedded to the school. It had been his anchor from the age of eleven and would remain an important part of his life right through to the time when, at the age of seventy, he handed over the running of the Old Shiburnian Society.

He continued to live in the town of Sherborne, retaining an active interest in the school, until his death on 5 April 2016, at the age of ninety-five.

Michael Earls-Davis – associated for most of his life with Sherborne School.
COURTESY OF ANN EARLS-DAVIS

1951

"Somerset were signing the wrong sort of men, rejects rather than gifted youngsters eager for opportunity or sage professionals prepared to help for a season or two."

Peter Roebuck in *From Sammy to Jimmy*

Championship Position: 14 of 17

Buckling under the weight of expectation, Harold Gimblett was unable to continue playing in July. He came back all the stronger in August and ultimately accumulated 1,453 runs, which was just as well, given that Micky Walford was not around to share the burden during the school holidays, having elected to join an MCC tour of Canada. Maurice Tremlett continued to excel with the bat, amassing more than 2,000 runs and delighting the Somerset faithful with his cleanly-struck straight drives. Among the bowlers, it was again the spinners who claimed most of the spoils, Ellis Robinson in particular using all his wiles to capture more than 100 wickets.

Harry Parks, formerly of Sussex, was brought into the fold as a coach in the hope that he would be able to help bring on local talent and it was agreed that the squad would be built up with five or six youngsters added to the ground staff. The *Somerset County Gazette* noted that 'evidence that the club is serious is provided by the fact that already one fifteen-year-old lad has been placed on the ground staff and duly registered. He is John Harris, a Taunton boy whose parents now live in London.' John would in fact prove only a moderately successful fast bowler but in a later incarnation a fine first-class umpire. A fundamental problem for the county remained the absence of a competitive league which owed much to geography and the absence of sizeable competing conurbations. It should be added that the county did not always aid their own cause. Among the triallists ahead of the 1951 season was Len Coldwell, a fast bowler from Devon, whom Somerset allowed to slip through their fingers before he went on to enjoy a successful career with Worcestershire and England.

The only debutant of note in 1951 was Pakistan-born Khan Mohammad, a hostile bowler of Test Match standard who – sadly – was only able to appear for one game whilst studying at Bristol University. How Somerset could have done with him on a full-time basis.

380
Michael Hanna
19 May 1951 v. Nottinghamshire, Yeovil

M. Hanna

In his nineties at the time of writing, Mick Hanna will tell you that he 'can only manage five mile walks' these days and his wife Wendy will chip in, gently chiding her partner for being 'a soft Southerner'. They met through a rambling club, of which Mick had been a founder member, soon after his arrival in the city of Lincoln, in the 1970s. To be able to share the story of Mick's life – tales of his encounters with some of the greats of cricket – while being plied with Wendy's tea and cakes is a rare delight. He has an enormous fund of anecdotes and regards himself as blessed for having played alongside and against some great players. He still recalls his Somerset debut with great clarity, walking out with the pros, unaware that, as an amateur, he was able to claim the privilege of taking to the field alongside his skipper, Stuart Rogers. He also remem-

Somerset take the field against Nottinghamshire with Mick Hanna as their wicket-keeper at Johnson Park, Yeovil, in May 1951. Pictured (left to right) are: F. L. Angell, J. Redman, M. Hanna, E. Hill, R. Smith (partially hidden), S. S. Rogers, H. Gimblett, M. F. Tremlett, H. F. T. Buse, E. P. Robinson. COURTESY OF MICK HANNA

bers welcoming England's Joe Hard-staff to the crease with a deferential 'Good morning, Mr Hardstaff' and stumping Hardstaff while he was still in single figures – although the umpire begged to differ. 'You should have walked there, Joe', Harold Gimblett informed Hardstaff, smiling, between each over as the Notts batsman went on to make a century. Mick relays his admiration for Harold Gimblett, who proved a good friend, supportive of the young players and far removed from his reputation for surliness. Mick also recalls the terror he felt when he came in to bat against Northamptonshire and overhead the discussion over whether the ball should be handed to Frank Tyson, whom he regards as the fastest bowler he has ever seen – 'fast,

Sir Jack Hobbs coaches a young Mick Hanna.
COURTESY OF MICK HANNA

erratic and terrifying'. To Mick's eternal relief they opted for George Tribe.

Born in Camberwell on 6 June 1926, Mick was the son of Walter Hanna and Ada Elsie (née Dean), known as Elsie. One of his early memories is of being coached by 'a man with kindly eyes'. Only in later life did he come across a photograph of himself with Sir Jack Hobbs, with a caption confirming that when he was eight years old he had won a competition – hosted by the *Evening Standard* – to be coached by Hobbs.

His father was relocated to Bath in 1939 along with other employees of the Admiralty, including Surrey and Somerset cricketer Bill Caesar. For a while, the family was split with Mick evacuated to Deal, in Kent, while a brother and sister were sent to Dorking and the eldest brother to Maidstone. Having been reunited in Bath, Mick's parents would remain there. Elsie would later be elected Mayor of Bath.

Educated at the City of Bath Grammar School, Mick became captain both of his school cricket XI and the rugby XV. He also won prizes as a swimmer. He joined the Royal Navy as an eighteen-year-old and would complete three years of service. After training at Skegness and at Rosyth he was commissioned as a midshipman on the cruiser *HMS Jamaica* before being promoted to sub-lieutenant on the fleet minesweeper *HMS Serene*. He spent time in the Far East, minesweeping in preparation for the arrival of an Australian force who were scheduled to share the occupation of Japan before the USA made the decision to take sole responsibility for the country's reconstruction. He

Mick Hanna – scrum-half of Bath RFC and Somerset.
COURTESY OF MICK HANNA

retains vivid memories of the horrors of Hiroshima, which he visited in February 1946 when victims of the atomic bomb were still collapsing and dying in the streets. Mick's three years of service led to a lifetime's interest in the Royal Navy. His study is crammed with books on naval history and memorabilia and he has committed some of his own extensive research to print, writing two slim volumes about ships an uncle had served in during the First World War.

Married for the first time in 1951 to Mary (née Sheppard), Mick would have a son and daughter. A slim and sprightly character, full of zest for life, he was made for the roles of scrum-half at rugby and wicket-keeper at cricket. He starred at both sports for Bath, appearing for the rugby XV on 145 occasions. The *Bath Chronicle* talks of 'his darting through the middle, combined with speed off the mark, purposeful running and a rare eye for an opening'. He would in fact win county honours at rugby and cricket.

Based on his club performances and his appearances in the Second XI and Club & Ground matches, he quickly established himself as understudy to Somerset's professional wicket-keeper, Harold Stephenson. Mick was only called upon twice, though.

He averaged 2.50 with the bat. Although recognised by Somerset as the reserve wicket-keeper, he chose to pursue a career in Social Services, working initially for the Wiltshire County Council, looking after the needs of the physically handicapped, the elderly and the homeless. When Somerset decided to employ two professional keepers, Mick opted to play Minor Counties cricket for Wiltshire for many seasons. He was described in the

Bath Chronicle as 'a cool, competent wicket keeper ... who must be considered one of the best outside [first-class] county cricket'. His work in social care subsequently took him to Worcestershire, Hampshire and Derbyshire before he finally settled in Lincoln. For more than twenty years, Mick acted as a volunteer guide showing visitors around Lincoln Castle. He also retained his fitness through the rambling club he had helped to form and through which he met his second wife, Wendy (née Tennant), to whom he was married in 2000. As well as continuing to walk, he swims half a kilometre each week. He shows no signs of slowing down, despite his wife Wendy's skills as a cake-maker, as adept as Mick once was at the craft of wicket-keeping.

381
Khan Mohammad
1 August 1951 v. South Africa, Taunton

Khan Mohammad was a player of genuine class whom Somerset would dearly have loved to have had in their ranks on more occasions than his solitary match. They did indeed offer him a contract but he declined. A three-year qualification by residency would have been required. Biding his time with friendly fixtures or club matches, held little appeal. He would instead return to Lahore and would later leave an indelible mark in Lancashire League cricket and as a pioneer of Pakistani cricket. He in fact has the twin distinctions of bowling the first delivery and subsequently taking the first ever wicket in his country's inaugural Test Match, against India in Delhi in 1952. A pace bowler of genuine Test class had landed in Somerset's lap but only fleetingly. And their supporters were left to rue what might have been.

Born in Lahore on 1 January 1928, he was the son of Jan Mohammad, a timber merchant. One of three brothers, Khan attended Central Model High School in the city. He made his first-class debut for Northern India in 1947, shortly before Partition. He then played for Punjab University while reading History and Economics at Islamia College. Selected for Pakistan's 1948-49 tour to Ceylon, he took 14 wickets in the two unofficial Tests.

The newly formed Pakistan Board of Control agreed to fund coaching for him at Alf Gover's cricket school in London while he took a further degree at Bristol University. During his time at Bristol he was invited to play for Somerset against the South Africans. He would return bowling figures of 3 for 74 and 2 for 30 and average 10.00 with the bat, but despite his efforts Somerset lost the game narrowly. Having declined a three-year contract with the county, he returned to Lahore and played his part in

Khan Mohammad enjoyed an outstanding cricketing career as a league pro and as a Test player for Pakistan. COURTESY OF JOHN LEE

establishing Pakistan as a Test-playing nation. Somerset's loss was Pakistani cricket's gain. His devastating bowling against a touring MCC side in 1951-52 indeed opened the door for his home country to be granted the status of a Test side. In 1952 he would make his appearance in his country's inaugural Test and although his Test career would be limited to thirteen matches because of his contract commitments in Lancashire League cricket and a recurrent groin injury, he put down a marker by racing to 50 wickets in only eleven Test matches, a record that would remain until eventually surpassed by Waqar Younis in 1990. His success continued unabated – often combining with Fazal Mahmood to devastating effect – until Pakistan's tour of the West Indies in 1957-8. Returning after injury for the Third Test, he stepped into the breach after opening bowler Mahmood Hussain broke down in the first over.

Khan returned figures of 0 for 259 while Garry Sobers, at his brilliant best, recorded what was at the time the highest Test innings of 365 not out. It proved Khan's penultimate Test Match appearance and despite that drubbing he had still claimed an excellent 54 wickets at only 23.92 apiece in a superb Test career.

Reliant on tearaway pace in his early years, he gradually sacrificed speed for accuracy and over time became a proficient off-spin bowler when required to fill the spinner's berth. His time as a pro in Lancashire League cricket had begun in 1953 with two years playing for Lowerhouse CC. While at the club he was released to take part in the Second Test at Trent Bridge, when Pakistan agreed in turn to release a member of their squad to stand in for him in the league fixture. At the end of the 1954 season he announced his intention to return to Lahore and, demonstrating that he had picked up the English vernacular, he announced that 'the Lowerhouse boys are a splendid bunch of fellows'. He also informed a reporter that he was looking forward to meeting up with his 103-year-old grandmother and planned to help in the running of a family cotton business (from which one hopes his grandmother had been allowed to retire with good grace).

Cricket soon gained precedence over business when he agreed to lead a tour of England by the Pakistan Eaglets in 1955, bringing his experience to bear and making a guest appearance for Burnley against Bacup, chipping in with 4 for 35. Bacup must have been hugely impressed by what they saw because they duly signed him for the 1957 season as their pro.

He was residing in London by the time of his marriage in 1965 at the Ealing Register Office to Hamida Noor Mohammad, a widow four years his junior. He was still describing himself at the time as a cotton farmer, but thereafter he ran a travel agency business whilst also taking up coaching positions including at the MCC indoor school at Lord's, a young Wasim Akram being one of his charges. He also orchestrated a number of tours by Pakistani representative sides while regularly leading cricketing coaching camps in Pakistan. He achieved all this while running his travel agency in Ealing until a year before he was diagnosed with the prostate cancer that claimed his life at the age of eighty-one on 4 July 2009, in London. Much respected in his adoptive country, he had been revered in his homeland for his skills both as a bowler and later as a mentor and an elder statesman of Pakistani cricket.

382
John Popham Sainsbury
11 August 1951 v. Glamorgan, Weston-super-Mare

John Sainsbury was born in Weston-super-Mare on 8 January 1927 and came with a noteworthy cricketing pedigree. His grandfather, Ted Sainsbury, had captained Somerset during their first brush with first-class status. When Somerset were unceremoniously dumped from the top table in 1885, Ted had been one of the few among the fifty-nine men who had appeared for the county at the time who could walk away with their heads held high.

John's parents were Edward Alfred Sainsbury and Sylvia May Alice Sneyd (née Richards) whose paternal grandfather had been an admiral. After a spell in the military, rising to the rank of captain, Edward Alfred would join the family grain merchanting and oil cake business, originally set up by Ted. An old boy of Clifton College, John's father was well-known in local cricketing circles, a member of Somerset CCC and a benefactor to the Weston Festival, a jamboree much loved by Somerset supporters and holidaymakers. Indeed, some of the pros, understandably unhappy at being usurped by the amateurs, would claim that John's selection owed everything to his station in life and nothing to his abilities. Whilst the first-class game would prove a step too far, he had shown promise as a schoolboy cricketer. Sent to Clifton College, it is said that his father had threatened (hopefully in jest) that if John failed to make it into the school First XI he would be removed to a less illustrious institution. In the event he would in time captain the trinity of rugby, cricket and athletics teams. He would also hold the school

John Popham Sainsbury, whose grandfather, Ted Sainsbury, had captained Somerset in the 1880s.
SOMERSET CRICKET MUSEUM

discus and javelin records for many years and had the honour of captaining the Lord's Schools XI in his final year at Clifton. His 'bright and energetic batting' is praised in one report.

Having joined the family business directly from school, he left for a while to undertake his National Service in the Royal Navy. With the Sainsbury grain and oat cake business being based in Bristol, there was plenty of opportunity for him to indulge his passion for sport. Rugby appears to have been his favoured pursuit and he starred as a speedy left-wing three-quarter for Weston-super-Mare RFC and on a number of occasions for the Somerset XV. Although he was invited to take part in trials for the England rugby team, he never gained international honours.

There was much murmuring in the ranks when John was parachuted into the Somerset side ahead of men whom some considered more deserving. George Langdale was affronted not to have been selected and announced that he saw no future with the county. Ellis Robinson, at times among the most cantankerous of men, referred to John Sainsbury as 'an amateur who couldn't lay bat on ball.' In his two matches on his home turf, John registered three ducks and was then dropped while shaping up for his second successive pair before rallying and scoring the 16 runs that left him with a first-class average of 4.00. Here was another example of a player who had shaped well at schoolboy and club level but had struggled in more elevated company.

John was married in 1955 to Bridget Grindrod whose grandfather had started a business in 1910 that became a major South African conglomerate in the banking, logistics and transport businesses with the company being run by successive generations of the family. The couple would move to Rhodesia (Zimbabwe) where John would farm the Odzani Junction Estate, growing tobacco, cotton and maize. They would have two children and would later divorce.

His daughter recalls that 'he loved reading and had a command of the English language which is seldom heard today. His knowledge of sporting history, especially cricket and rugby, was phenomenal.' For the last eighteen months of his life John suffered serious ill health. An aneurism in his aorta was followed by kidney failure. He died in Old Mutare, Zimbabwe, on 24 August 2004 at the age of seventy-seven and is remembered in the region with great fondness, spoken of as a perfect English gentleman with time and a kind word for everyone. The same cannot necessarily be said of those who had been riled by his selection for two matches back in August 1951.

1952

"Looking ahead to the immediate future of Somerset cricket is not exactly a cheering prospect."

Ron Roberts in *Sixty Years of Somerset Cricket*

Championship Position: 17 of 17

In his review of Ron Roberts's history of Somerset cricket, published in 1952, Eric Stanger of the *Yorkshire Post* notes that 'Somerset are truer to themselves and their traditions when they scorn safety to seek that rare but so sweet swashbuckling victory against all sound opposition.' Neither man could have known how joyless the next few seasons would become, nor that Somerset were about to prop up the Championship for the first time since the dark days of 1913. At times, only Harold Gimblett was able to offer succour to the longsuffering supporters by displaying that Somersetshire virtue of fearless attacking cricket, whatever the odds. He amassed 2,134 runs in his Benefit Year, including five centuries. He had requested the Gloucestershire fixture at Taunton as his benefit match but had been told that he would have to opt for a less lucrative one. The man who continued to carry the side came away with the princely

The crowd at Morlands Athletic Ground in Glastonbury. The spectators enjoyed their first taste of Championship cricket in July 1952 when Somerset played Northamptonshire. They were treated to centuries by Harold Gimblett and Stuart Rogers. SOMERSET CRICKET MUSEUM

profit of £8 from the game against Northamptonshire at Glastonbury. Little wonder that when interviewed in later years and asked if he would change anything about his career he replied that he would have played as an amateur because they were so much better paid than the pros.

There was rejoicing when the popular Johnny Lawrence completed his maiden first-class century, taking part in a ninth-wicket stand of 133 with another of his Yorkshire-born protégés, debutant Bill Dean, in the match against India.

Once again, the majority of wickets fell to the spin of Hazell, Robinson and Lawrence, though too few of them to win any more than two matches in a total of twenty-eight.

Off the field of play there was a positive development when the Supporters Club was re-formed, managing a football pools operation that would eventually benefit from 55,000 participants and provide valuable financial help for the club. As well as purchasing properties which housed players cheaply, the Supporters Club also paid the Second XI expenses, to allow the team to continue competing in the Minor Counties Championship and funded the construction of a stand. Without this injection of much-needed capital, cricket in the county of Somerset would have been in a parlous state.

Some fresh young faces were introduced but none of the debutants would make a lasting impression on the game, although Ben Brocklehurst would later go on to captain the side.

The Somerset team who played Surrey at The Oval in July 1952.
Back Row: *R. F. Trump (Scorer), E. P. Robinson, H. W. Stephenson, M. F. Tremlett, J. Redman, F. L. Angell, R. Smith, J. H. Harris (Twelfth Man).* Front Row: *J. Lawrence, H. Gimblett, S. S. Rogers, H. L. Hazell, H. F. T. Buse.* SOMERSET CRICKET MUSEUM

383
Benjamin Gilbert Brocklehurst
3 May 1952 v. Yorkshire, Taunton

Ben Brocklehurst was a man of contrasts. A traditionalist with a fondness for military discipline, he was also bursting with creativity and iconoclastic ideas. He was born on 18 February 1922 in Knapton Hall in the small village of Knapton in Norfolk. His father, Ernest, who was married to Kathleen (née Evers), had made a successful living as a rancher in British Columbia before taking up residence first in the Manor House at Oulton near Lowestoft and subsequently in Knapton Hall. One of five children, Ben was educated at Bradfield College, representing the school at a variety of sports including football and tennis, and captaining the cricket First XI. He was also an outstanding athlete, competing in a public schools tournament in 1938 and winning the discus and high jump and coming away with the Victor Ludorum as the outstanding all-round athlete at the meet.

He went straight from school to serve in the Second World War, initially with the 10th (Home Defence) Battalion of the Devonshires, his connection with Devon being that his mother had moved to Budleigh Salterton after Ernest's death in 1935, when Ben was embarking on his teenage years. After suffering superficial wounds in the Bristol Blitz, he was subsequently offered a commission with the Royal Berkshire Regiment but became bored with building defences in East Anglia and requested a transfer to the Indian Army. While stationed in Wana his duties included the role of whipper-in for the Wana Hunt and in addition he utilised his free time to hone his skills as a highly competent artist, painting the walls of the officers' mess with his murals. Forty years later the building would be occupied by Osama bin Laden and Ben would quip that he hoped that his artistic output was appreciated by the new resident.

Among Ben's more unusual experiences was to have been mauled by an irate bear, in a life-threatening attack. The exit from the Kashmiri stage following his pursuit by the bear led to a spell in Burma (Myanmar) where he took command of a reconnaissance unit and was subsequently given the rank of lieutenant colonel, in charge of a cast of thousands of Japanese prisoners of war.

His military service over, he was married for the first time in 1947 to Mary Aileen Wynn, with whom he would have two children. He took to a new life as a farmer in Berkshire for eight years and it was during this period that he would be invited, having previously spent time residing in the neighbouring county of Devon, to become Somerset's captain. He was already known in the 'right' circles – which included MCC, I

Ben Brocklehurst – Somerset captain, farmer and magazine proprietor.
SOMERSET CRICKET MUSEUM

Zingari and Free Foresters, bastions of privilege and amateurism all – and seemed undaunted that he was taking on what many would have regarded as a disheartening and lost cause. He had inherited a side that propped up the County Championship and under his leadership they would continue to do so. He would play sixty-four times for Somerset between 1952 and 1954, in the second and third of those seasons as captain. Described as a 'forceful' right-handed batsman, he averaged 15.61, completing six half-centuries but never achieving the cherished three figures.

His reign as captain was doomed on three counts. Firstly, he lacked a wide enough pool of talent. Secondly, his stern and decidedly military approach to discipline went down badly, especially given that he struggled to make an impact with his personal contributions. Thirdly, any trust was undermined when he played his part

Ben Brocklehurst – a disciplinarian who lost the support of his team when he played his part in silencing calls for reform.
SOMERSET CRICKET MUSEUM

in crushing the revolt where Ron Roberts, Eric Hill and Bob Moore led something approaching a mutiny, urging the club to greet the modern age in order to turn their fortunes around. The plotters had hoped that Ben would stand up for the players. Instead, he spoke up against the proposed changes, dubbing the plotters Faith, Hope and Charity. From that point he had won the hearts of the committee but lost the dressing room.

Ever one to embrace a new challenge and easily bored with the status quo, Ben would forsake farming for the world of publishing. After working for a while on *Country Life* magazine he joined the Mercury House publishing company, persuading them to purchase *The Cricketer*, at the time a loss-making magazine. He would in fact buy the magazine from them in 1972, leaving Mercury House in order to run *The Cricketer* with his second wife, Belinda (née Bristowe), whom he had married in 1962 and with whom he had two children to add to his existing brood. His son-in-law, the England all-rounder Richard Hutton was for a while editor of the magazine. Ben merged the publication with *Playfair Cricket Monthly* and then in 2003 he sold the enterprise to Paul Getty who orchestrated a further rationalisation when he amalgamated the magazine with *Wisden Cricket Monthly*.

Ben had used the reach and influence of his monthly to establish The Cricketer Cup, where former pupils of certain public schools locked horns and later he funded a national village knock-out competition and a national Lord's Taverner's Trophy for fourteen- and fifteen-year-old boys. Although his aim was to subsidise these via sponsorship, he was known to dip into his own pockets as and when the need arose. An attempt to persuade the MCC to stage a World Cup with a final played at Lord's fell on stony ground being deemed 'too commercial'. Clearly Ben Brocklehurst was a man ahead of his time. He also set up a travel company offering Cricketer Holidays. By way of relaxation, he continued to paint and developed his garden at Ashurst, near Tunbridge Wells, and liked to visit the Ionian Isles, sailing in his cabin cruiser.

A man of many talents, always in restless pursuit of his next fine idea, he once wrote to *The Daily Telegraph* suggesting that matches played on ice and under floodlights might increase interest in the game. Ben Brocklehurst died at the age of eighty-five in Tunbridge Wells on 12 June 2007. He had not left much of an entry into the annals of Somerset cricket, but had certainly made his mark on the game in many other ways.

Ben Brocklehurst and Australian captain Lindsay Hassett in discussion with groundsman, Cec Buttle, ahead of the start of play at Taunton in 1953. The pitch proved to Hassett's liking. He scored 148 in a rain-affected draw. SOMERSET CRICKET MUSEUM

384
David Lees Kitson
17 May 1952 v. Hampshire, Portsmouth

David Kitson was born in Batley, Yorkshire, on 13 September 1925. His father, Thomas, was married to Annie (née Lees). Thomas's declared job as a 'shoddy manufacturing timber machinist' perhaps merits a brief explanation. He worked a heavy frame, manufacturing shoddy, a product that had been associated with Batley since the early nineteenth century when Benjamin Law, a resident of the town, had developed a method to combine finely shredded recycled cloth with new wool to produce an affordable woven material. The word has of course been commandeered to imply second-rate products or workmanship but shoddy had been a boon for those who could ill afford to buy woollen clothing and it certainly provided bountiful employment opportunities for the locals involved in the collection of rags and the manufacture of the material.

David began playing cricket in the Yorkshire Leagues as a teenager but in 1943, at the age of eighteen, joined the Army, finally returning to civilian life after the close of the 1947 cricket season. He had played for Wakefield CC and later for Park Avenue Bradford CC before being invited for a trial with Somerset on the recommendation of coach Harry Parks, who had watched him in action at Johnny Lawrence's indoor nets. On the basis of his performances he was offered a three-year contract commencing in 1952, on a special registration, with Yorkshire having raised no objections. A right-handed batsman who had been schooled in his native county to build an innings and not to yield his wicket lightly, he was correct in his methods, though lacked sparkle. He was firmly of the view that a lighter bat was preferable to a heavy one and that timing was at the core of batting technique. Although given a decent run in the early part of his first season, David never managed to establish himself in the side and would make only thirty-two appearances for his adoptive county, averaging 15.54 and completing five half-centuries. By his own admission, he found the experience a disappointing one. Speaking in the 1990s to Barry Phillips, he observed that:

> *Playing for Somerset was frustrating. You would work hard for a fifty with wickets tumbling at the other end and then find yourself dropped for the next match {to make way for an amateur}. There was often no Second XI match, so we used to play for local clubs when teams rang to ask for a player.*

He played on a number of occasions for Sidmouth CC and later for Glastonbury CC but after the challenges of Yorkshire League cricket, the happy-go-lucky West Country village matches soon lost their appeal. David admitted that he had lost interest in life as a professional cricketer by the end of his first season at Somerset.

He was married in 1956 to Bernadette Mary (née Leavy) and in June 1958 the couple left the country to live in South Africa. They would remain there for thirteen

David Kitson, who found the experience of playing for Somerset a disappointment.
SOMERSET CRICKET MUSEUM

years with David working in the chemicals industry, living near Durban and describing his occupation as 'dyer' but later becoming a representative selling textiles. After being made redundant, he returned to the UK to live with Bernadette in Hook Norton. He sold cars for a number of years for the Hartwell group in Oxford until he opted to retire in 1984, as he approached his sixtieth birthday. The couple then relocated to the village of Horton, close to Ilminster, in Somerset. The driving force for the move was perhaps Bernadette, who had been raised in nearby Taunton. She and David were both accomplished bowls players and would enjoy their retirement playing the game.

They were still living at Horton when David died in Musgrove Park Hospital in Taunton at the age of seventy-six on 6 May 2002.

385
John Henry Harris
24 May 1952 v. Glamorgan, Swansea

John Harris was born on 13 February 1936. His father, Jack, was married to Doris (née Ferdinando), the daughter of Somerset's head groundsman, Harry Ferdinando, known as 'Fernie'. Fernie was an eccentric figure, famed as much for his capacity for alcohol consumption as for his undoubted skills as a preparer of wickets. Indeed, when John's parents separated when he was only three, he would move in with his maternal grandparents in Taunton, so that Fernie would have a big influence on his grandson, though fortunately as a cricketer rather than as a drinker.

At the age of twelve, John went to live with his mother in London and attended the Cooper's Lane Secondary Modern School where he was encouraged by his sports master and was soon starring for Blackheath Wanderers and Crofton Park cricket clubs. He was invited to play for the England Schoolboys team and went for a trial with Kent who told him to 'come back in three years' time'. Having informed his headmistress that he still hoped to carve out a career for himself in the game, he was informed that 'cricket won't get you through life'.

His grandfather, Fernie, still an influential figure, despite having retired, approached Somerset captain Stuart Rogers and John was offered a two-week trial as a bowler of right-arm off-spin and a left-handed batsman. He was coached in the nets by Arthur Wellard, who – perhaps aware that Somerset had a surfeit of spin bowlers but were in need of some pace in their attack – invited John to 'bowl a bit faster', thus sparking his reinvention as a fast-medium bowler. At the age of fifteen he was offered a place on the

John Harris — a fast-medium bowler taken on by Somerset at the age of fifteen.

ground staff as a pro, helping out in a number of ways. John recounts the tale of a day spent with Cec Buttle in which he was taught to lay turf. Having absorbed the lessons, he went home and relaid a section of surplus turf in his grandfather's garden and was still proud of his efforts when Fernie came staggering home supported by two walking sticks (which he always relied on by then) and in a state of advanced inebriation, having spent the day supping at Scarlett's – a male-only pub in Taunton – with his drinking buddy, Lord Portman. Fernie took one look at his grandson's efforts, chuntered about what he saw as poor workmanship, lowered himself onto the lawn and proceeded to relay it so that it would have done justice to a bowling green.

John's career with Somerset never quite blossomed in the way the county had hoped. At the age of only sixteen, he was informed, thirty minutes before the start of his debut, that he would be replacing the injured Jim Redman. He says that he felt no nerves, though only because two of the more ebullient members of the team – Johnny Lawrence and Roy Smith – spent every moment 'chattering away', perhaps as a diversionary tactic.

In 1954 he commenced his National Service in York and for a while he appeared in club cricket in Yorkshire. He observes that he was struck by the winning mentality of the players he encountered, far removed from Somerset's more easygoing approach to life. When he returned he struggled to make his mark, spending time in the Somerset Second XI. Between 1952 and 1959 he made only fifteen first-class appearances, averaging 11.00 with the bat and taking 19 wickets at 32.05 apiece.

He then accepted the role of groundsman and coach at Framlington College, having been approached by Norman Borrett, a man who had similarly struggled to make his mark in the first-class game (with Essex) but who had excelled as a hockey player. John would remain there for five years, appearing on a number of occasions for Suffolk. He then took up a position as head groundsman at St Edmund's School, Canterbury, also coaching at the same time at Kent College in the city. The pull of the West Country proved irresistible, though, and he returned to become club captain and head groundsman at Sidmouth, also appearing for Devon in 1975. In 1978 he took over the groundsman's duties at Exeter. He was by now establishing a reputation as an umpire in club and Minor Counties cricket and was invited to join the list of first-class umpires in 1983, officiating in a combined total of nearly six hundred first-class or List A matches until his retirement in the year 2000. Although selected as a reserve, he never officiated in a Test Match.

For a while, he acted as chairman of the Somerset Former Players' Association before handing the reins to David Gurr. John has been twice married, first in 1956 to Marilyn Piercy and then in 1984 to Morag Elsbeth Jane Wardrop, the daughter of a Sidmouth veterinary surgeon. As a young woman brought up in less enlightened times, Morag had been denied the opportunity to become a vet. When the Drum Kennels at Sidbury in Devon came up for sale, the couple decided to deploy their considerable energy and a love of dogs to purchase and manage the enterprise. Already in his eighties, John Harris and his business both continue to thrive and he retains the same enthusiasm and zest for life he demonstrated as a fifteen-year-old rookie who had been taken under his wing by Somerset and England's Arthur Wellard.

386
Malcolm Walker
28 May 1952 v. India, Taunton

The production line of young Yorkshiremen recommended to Somerset continued apace with the introduction of Malcolm Walker, born in Mexborough on 14 October 1933. His parents were Bevan Walker, a plumber and glazier, and Florrie (née Phillipson), the daughter of a canal boatman. Malcolm's father and uncles were keen club cricketers and his brother, Graham, was offered a trial with Somerset, although he never broke through into the first-class arena.

Malcolm was schooled in the game from a young age, first appearing for Yorkshire Colts in 1951 at seventeen, having already impressed for Wombwell Main CC and then Salts CC in the Bradford League. He was also twice selected as twelfth man by Yorkshire, on the first occasion against Somerset at Taunton in June 1951, when four of the first team regulars were unavailable. The following year, he joined the nursery staff at the County Ground. Not yet qualified by residence in 1952, he was able to make his debut first-class appearance against the Indian tourists but his other games were limited to the Second XI.

Regarded as a promising off-spin bowler, he was also expected to develop into a useful stroke-playing batsman. In the event, things did not work out quite as well as had been hoped. Malcolm and Somerset parted company for the 1957 season, while he was engaged as a pro at Doncaster CC, only for Somerset and him to agree that they would join forces again in 1958. Between 1952 and 1958 he would make twenty-nine first-class appearances and would average 11.71 with the bat, while taking 28 wickets at 34.85 apiece.

Eric Hill, who captained the Second XI, was firmly of the view that Malcolm could have been a greater asset to a good batting side if he had come in at number six and been allowed to express himself. Eric would cite Malcolm's first-class century in that position, scored against Essex before he had had to withdraw from the side for the following match, having been taken to hospital with a grumbling appendix. Recast as an opening batsman in 1956, he struggled to make his mark. Eric also publically expressed his dismay in September 1958 at the news that Somerset had dispensed with Malcolm's services, considering him 'harshly treated'. He highlights his awareness that Malcolm's dismissal was down to an issue over 'attitude', adding that 'I know full well that Walker is of an independent turn of mind … I fear that I detect here something in the way of 'maintaining discipline' in the staff simply by sacking [those] who seem less amenable to it than most. I deplore it and believe it is wrong. From my experience, there is eminently as much goodwill and desire to succeed … as in anyone else and that correctly handled it will come out.' Malcolm's daughter, Judith, confirms that her father was a quietly determined man, and certainly not one inclined to conform.

Perhaps his most lasting contribution to Somerset's fortunes had been to show a young medium-paced bowler named Brian Langford, the art of off-spin bowling while he spent a fortnight lodging with the Langford family in Bridgwater. The rest, as they say, is history.

After leaving Somerset, Malcolm returned for a while to Yorkshire where he played cricket for Stainborough CC in Barnsley while working in the family plumbing and build-

Malcolm Walker – an all-rounder 'of an independent turn of mind'. SOMERSET CRICKET MUSEUM

ing business. He had been married in 1953 to Margaret Rose Best and together they would become licensees of the Effingham Arms in Bradgate, Rotherham. Malcolm had developed a passion for water skiing and he and Margaret would decamp whenever they could to their static caravan in Tuxford, Nottinghamshire. Margaret would steer the motor boat on the River Trent near High Marnham while Malcolm honed his skills. Having retired from the often gruelling licensing trade after nine years, the free-spirited couple moved permanently to the caravan site in Tuxford and when not engaged in water skiing were often to be seen on their motorbikes. Malcolm also deployed his skills as a plumber and maintenance man, working on a part-time basis for Newark and Sherwood District Council, also spending some time overseeing young offenders who had been obliged to undertake community work.

If his premature departure from first-class cricket was regrettable then this paled alongside his tragic early death. On 2 September 1986 he was riding his motorcycle on the A 6075 near Tuxford when a nineteen-year-old van driver turning right onto the B 1164 cut across him. The fault lay entirely with the young driver, who was subsequently sentenced. Malcolm suffered multiple injuries and his death was instant. He was fifty-two years old. Margaret bore the loss of her soulmate with great fortitude and was never remarried. At the time of writing she resides in Lincolnshire.

387
William Frederick Dean
28 May 1952 v. India, Taunton

W. F. Dean

Bill Dean was born in Leeds on 3 January 1926, the son of Frederick Wharton Dean and his wife, Lily (née Smiles). Fred managed a Coal Dealer's business in the city and was a successful club cricketer, captaining Middleton CC in Leeds for many years. Bill began playing alongside Fred at the age of thirteen and his name appeared almost immediately in the local press when, after having been handed the ball by his father, he proceeded to dismiss the great Herbert Sutcliffe, who was playing for Pudsey Britannia CC. It had been a sensational start to his career in Yorkshire League cricket. Bill was in fact a natural athlete who won junior tournaments at table-tennis and later became a skilled pool player.

On leaving school, he began his training as a chartered accountant but was obliged – somewhat reluctantly, according to his family – to serve as a pilot with the RAF. He was married in 1946 to Betty Maria Walker, with whom he would have one daughter, Susan. Betty, whose father was a tailor in Leeds, was five years Bill's senior, although – no doubt conscious of the age difference – Bill added four years to his age on the marriage certificate. By now, he was combining his work as an accountant with employment as a cricketing pro, on the payroll of Crewe LMR. The club was named after the London Midland Railway and a hazard all players had to overcome was the intermittent enveloping of the pitch with steam and smoke billowing from passing trains that caused play to be held up for a while.

Bill and Betty had settled in the village of Middleham, near Leyburn in Wensleydale, where the air was rather fresher than at Crewe and where many of his accountancy clients ran farms in the surrounding hills and dales. On the field of play he was a pace bowler sufficiently quick to have removed the front teeth of an opponent with a vicious bouncer for which he was sent off after being overcome with laughter. Bill would later state that the laughter was more an hysterical fit of the giggles than anything malicious, but it did his reputation as an intimidating fast bowler no harm. Deemed an all-rounder, there was less excitement surrounding his batting. The *Driffield Times*

Bill Dean —took part in a record ninth-wicket stand with fellow Yorkshireman Johnny Lawrence.
COURTESY OF THE FAMILY OF BILL DEAN

Bill Dean – felt obliged to change his name by deed poll to William Barrett, following some questionable business dealing which landed him in hot water. COURTESY OF FAMILY OF BILL DEAN

reported in August 1949 that while playing for Leeds Corinthians, he had been barracked by the Driffield crowd for his slow scoring, demonstrating the same stubborn defence later evident when appearing for Somerset against India.

He had also impressed Johnny Lawrence at the cricket school in Rothwell and Johnny duly brought him down to the County Ground where he was deployed in the nets during April 1952. The *Somerset County Gazette* reports that 'he is a useful all-rounder with special promise as a fast bowler'. He played for the Second XI against Gloucestershire Seconds with no great success but followed this up in the next game with a five-wicket haul. On the basis of this performance he was drafted into the side for the game against India. Although he opened the bowling in both innings, he failed to take a wicket but only conceded 17 runs in his ten overs. His stubborn stand as part of a record ninth-wicket partnership of 133 was what stood out, with Bill contributing 21 runs, ensuring that Johnny Lawrence was able to make his maiden first-class century.

Although there were discussions as to whether or not Bill would be offered a permanent contract with one special registration place up for grabs, he was never given the opportunity to play again. Instead, he joined Stockport CC as a pro until being replaced after two seasons by Australian Test Match player Colin McCool, who would go on to play for Somerset. Bill then went to ply his trade with a number of other clubs such as Morecombe CC in Lancashire and later Ashington CC, Benwell Hill CC and Percy Main CC in the North-East.

He was continuing to operate as a joint partner in an accountancy firm, working from his home in Middleham and filing the accounts for a number of local farmers when in 1957 he eloped with a sixteen-year-old farmer's daughter from Wensleydale, named Audrey Muir. Audrey's father was furious but her mother less so. 'She rather liked Bill,' Audrey confirms. Although they were never married, Bill and Audrey had two daughters, Sara and Joanna. For a while they lived in a caravan in the garden attached to the bungalow where the longsuffering Betty and her daughter, Susan, resided. Although aware that they were no doubt regarded as a scandalous couple in the closely-knit community, Bill and Audrey learned to live with the stigma.

With his cricketing days behind him, Bill directed his energies towards business and alongside his accountancy firm he established betting shops in Yorkshire and Durham. He landed himself in difficulties, with some of his business dealings proving as tangled as his personal life. He therefore decided to break with his past and change his name by deed poll to William Frederick Barrett (or Bill Barrett) as he set about building a new life. He subsequently opened a jazz club in Ilkley. Already a capable clarinettist, Bill learned to play the soprano saxophone and performed regularly at his jazz club. His other passion – fishing – offered a contrast to the jazz club and for a while this serial entrepreneur ran a fly farm, selling bait to various outlets.

In later life, having sold off his businesses, he ran a tax consultancy, advising accountants on updates in tax laws via a quarterly mailing. He was still running this tax advisory business in his sixties when he began to suffer from a slow-growing cancer, initially of the oesophagus and sternum. He was later informed that the source of the problem was likely to have been a traumatic blow he received when hit by a cricket ball in his younger days. His daughter Joanna confirms that Bill remained proud to the very last of his part in what was at the time a record ninth-wicket stand for Somerset in his only first-class outing. He was residing in York when he died in the city on 18 September 1994 after a spell in St Leonard's Hospice. He was sixty-eight at the time of his death.

References in some sources to W. H. Dean or William Henry Dean are erroneous.

388
Colin Gerald Mitchell
7 June 1952 v. Sussex, Hove

Born in Brislington on 27 January 1929, Colin was the son of Harold Mitchell, a radio and electrical wholesaler, and Edna May (née Cooke).

A natural all-round sportsman, he would shine in local sporting circles, although primarily for his skills as a footballer. A left-winger who was also a prolific goalscorer, he would play for Bristol University and Clifton St Vincent's and also has the distinction of gaining more county football caps for Gloucestershire than any other man. He was also good enough to be approached both by Bristol City and Bristol Rovers and was offered professional terms by Nottingham Forest but in all three cases declined the invitation. It appears that Colin was happier playing with friends and colleagues.

Having graduated from Bristol University, he enjoyed a full season of first-class cricket with Somerset in 1953 on an amateur basis before he became a teacher and

Colin Mitchell – a local teacher who played amateur cricket and turned down the opportunity to become a professional footballer. SOMERSET CRICKET MUSEUM

would thenceforth only be available during the summer holidays. In the event, he played in a total of thirty matches between 1952 and 1954, taking 53 wickets at 38.39 and averaging 7.44 with the bat. His moment of glory had come in the game against Worcestershire at Frome when he secured his best bowling analysis of 6 for 62 in the first innings and made his highest score of 26 not out before claiming a further five wickets in the second innings. Sadly, despite his heroics, Somerset lost. A right-handed batsman and a seam bowler at what was regarded at club level as fast-medium, he was awarded his county cap on the basis of his performances in 1953. No one would have begrudged this likeable and modest young man his recognition but it inevitably caused murmuring when the pro Brian Langford was not accorded the same status. The malcontents grumbled that it was one rule for the amateurs and another for the pros, and a decision motivated by the fact that the award would have entitled Brian to a pay increase. The debate about amateurism was refusing to go away.

For a period, Colin captained the Second XI and it is reported that he was one of the multitude of amateurs sounded out about taking on the captaincy of the First XI. For a combination of reasons – his natural diffidence, his commitment to his teaching career and the fact that he was bright enough to know what would have lain in store – he turned down the offer.

He was married in 1957 to Thelma (née Sage) and the couple would have a daughter. Colin continued to teach and live in Brislington until his retirement in 1993 at the age of sixty-four. He also spent twenty years coaching schoolboys in the Avon Education Authority at both cricket and football.

He had remained firmly rooted in Brislington, resisting all blandishments to move elsewhere. He died there on 13 September 2007 at the age of seventy-eight.

389
John Baker
16 August 1952 v. Lancashire, Weston-super-Mare

John Baker was born on 18 May 1933 in Weston-super-Mare, the only child of a detective inspector, Harry Baker, and his wife Winifred (née Chapman). John would later describe his parents as 'wonderful and infinitely kind', noting that his father taught him to play cricket and his mother taught him to play the piano. His achievements as a cricketer are on record but he also became an accomplished musician who briefly considered a career as a concert pianist. At the age of eleven he won a scholarship to Taunton School, although his time there was not entirely joyous as a result of 'the

John Baker – a teacher for many years at Bryanston School, 'he was reliant primarily on a good line and length'.

dreadful food' and 'the general brutality' that made him 'glad to leave'. He would write that 'I think I went into teaching partly to try to make up to another generation for some of the rotten things done to me'. He was a student between 1952 and 1954 at Bristol University (following in the footsteps of his mother, who had been one of the earliest of Bristol's women graduates). He then went up to Jesus College, Oxford, where he played five times for the Varsity side, although never against Cambridge. He did, however, come away with a batting average of 36.83 and seven wickets at 28.42 apiece. John had earlier played in nine first-class matches for Somerset between 1952 and 1954 with less impressive statistics to his name. He averaged 10.50 with the bat and his one wicket came at a cost of 204 runs. A tall, right-arm medium pace bowler, he cites Somerset's coach Bill Andrews as a major influence who helped him to bridge the gap between schoolboy and first-class cricket. Mick Hanna, who kept wicket to John on a number of occasions, relates that 'he was reliant primarily on a good line and length and was very hard for batsmen to get away'.

After leaving Oxford, John served for three years with the RAF in their Education Department, based at RAF Melksham in Wiltshire. He was then offered a teaching post at Millfield School, where he remained from 1958 until 1964, later joking that he spent his time 'largely on the breeding and rearing of pigs when not playing county cricket [for Dorset]'. He apparently tired of travelling between Millfield and Dorset to play cricket and hence applied successfully for the role of English teacher at Bryanston School on the outskirts of Blandford Forum in Dorset. He would remain there until 1997. Hugely popular among staff and pupils alike, he was possessed of a ready wit and was a man of great compassion. During his time at Bryanston he served as a housemaster and as Head of

English, also acting as master in charge of cricket for many years and even teaching the trombone, an instrument he had taken up 'in a moment of quixotic idleness' and mastered quickly. His skills as a pianist and as a writer of staff Christmas shows were also a feature of life at Bryanston. With an insatiable thirst for learning, he completed a PhD in 1985 at Birmingham University on early French literature, so that he was accorded the title Dr Baker for the final twelve years of his teaching career. He also completed an exchange year teaching in Reno in the USA.

Married in 1959 to Mollie Cross, he would have three sons, one of whom would follow in his footsteps and play for Dorset. Between 1960 and 1975 he had remained a stalwart of Dorset cricket although he continued to make appearances for Somerset Stragglers and in one memorable game against Sou'Westers in 1963 took all 10 wickets in an innings in 19.5 overs. He would look back with great fondness at two decades in the game he loved. Ever a modest man, he regarded it as a huge privilege to have played first-class cricket while a student. An avid reader, he loved to quote from literature and among his favourites were the words from Shakespeare's *Love's Labour's Lost*: 'He is a marvellous good neighbour, faith, and a very good bowler ...'

John continued to reside in Blandford Forum after his retirement from teaching and died in the town on 29 April 2015 at the age of eighty-one.

Fitness training at Taunton. John Baker is crouched in the central group, grappling with Roy Smith and held by Harold Stephenson and Malcolm Walker. In the the right hand group is Colin Mitchell, grappling with Ben Brocklehurst, Johnny Lawrence and Graham Atkinson. Bryan Lobb (far left) is also visible. SOMERSET CRICKET MUSEUM

1953

"Somerset County Cricket Club, which was heavily criticised at a special meeting held last week, yesterday decided to set up an emergency committee of five to consider reorganisation in administration of the team sub-committees."

Somerset County Herald

Championship Position: 17 of 17

At last there was recognition that the county was in crisis but when a stifling bureaucracy is in crisis, more often than not it is likely to reorganise itself rather than reinvent itself or, better still, dissolve itself. The deck chairs were rearranged on the *Titanic*. A number of influential figures began to voice their concerns over the mismanagement of the club. Among them was Eric Hill, who fired regular broadsides via the *Somerset County Gazette*, bemoaning the failure to give emerging talent a chance and railing against the inclusion of amateurs on an ad hoc basis. Such sentiments were evidence of the first stirrings of a revolt.

Ben Brocklehurst had agreed to step in as captain. In an interview, he admitted that 'it is distressing for me to hear how low we have sunk in the estimation of the cricket world' but added that 'I am optimistic about the prospects. I don't see how you can expect to get anywhere with a pessimistic outlook.' To believe that things will get better simply by an unshakeable belief that they will get better is to be in complete denial.

One of the county's only two victories was recorded at a Bath Festival more suited to the pages of *Alice in Wonderland* than *Wisden*. The opening fixture, against Lancashire – which Bertie Buse had selected to his eternal regret as his benefit match – was over by teatime on the first day. In their first innings, not a single Somerset man had reached double figures. There was widespread panic that the festival would prove a financial disaster not just for Buse but for the club as a whole. Groundsman Cec Buttle was summoned and he and Johnny Lawrence worked tirelessly to create something vaguely resembling a cricket pitch. Their efforts involved the liberal use of bull's blood and grass clippings which seemed to do the trick, though no one was exactly sure why or how. The fixture with Kent provided Somerset with a rare victory and marked the

130

emergence of seventeen-year-old off-spinner Brian Langford, whose fourteen wickets were complemented by a magisterial 146 scored by Harold Gimblett. And then against Leicestershire, although the match was lost, two days' play had been eked out and Langford had clocked up another eleven wickets, so that Somerset – at least temporarily – had a man (or perhaps more accurately a boy) at the top of the national bowling averages.

The end-of-season statistics told a story. Harold Gimblett had amassed 1,836 runs at 40.80 but the next most successful batsman had been plucky Roy Smith with an average of 26.13. Johnny Lawrence had claimed most wickets – 70 of them – though they came at 31.77 apiece. The uplifting signs were the astonishing arrival of Brian Langford and the first appearance of Guiana-born Peter Wight, who, still in the throes of residential qualification, had scored a stylish century on debut against the Australian tourists.

Among the other debutants, the introduction of England rugby international John Currie for one match added a little lustre rather than any runs, and Yawar Saeed would bring an exotic flavour and a sense of cricketing adventure rather than noteworthy performances.

The Somerset team in 1953.
Back row: *J. Lawrence, R. Smith, M. Walker, M. F. Tremlett, T. Tout (Scorer), J. H. Harris, D. L. Kitson, H. W. Stephenson.* Front row: *C. G. Mitchell, T. A. Hall, B. G. Brocklehurst, H. Gimblett, H. F. T. Buse.* SOMERSET CRICKET MUSEUM

390
Thomas Auckland Hall
2 May 1953 v. Worcestershire, Worcester

Tom Hall

Tom Hall was born in Darlington on 19 August 1930, the son of Maurice Howard Hall and Lilian Frances (née Auckland). Tom was a teenager when the family moved to Horbury in Yorkshire after his father's appointment as the Assistant Works Manager at Charles Roberts Ltd, overseeing the manufacture of railway wagons. He would inherit both the paternal skills as an engineer and a tall and strong frame that leant itself to pace bowling. He also benefitted from the education that his parents were able to fund at

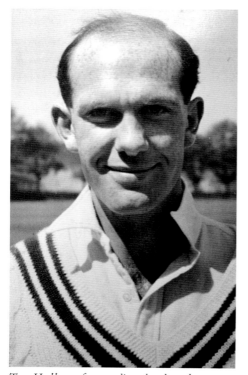

Tom Hall – a fast-medium bowler who broke the speed sailing record and later died when he fell from an express train.
SOMERSET CRICKET MUSEUM

Uppingham School. In his final year at the school – 1948 – he had captained the First XI.

Peter Roebuck describes Tom as 'popular and gregarious' and the interesting cocktail of exposure to the different worlds of a well-regarded public school and the less polished world of heavy engineering was perhaps what gave him his ability to rub along with players from all social strata. Having left Uppingham to train as an engineer, he began his working life, as reported by David Frith 'on the railways in Derby, shovelling coal into the locomotives as an engineering apprentice, and [on one occasion] surprising his friends by arriving at a hunt ball a few hours later resplendent in white tie and tails.'

He had previously been selected as an all-rounder for Derbyshire Second XI before his first-class cricketing adventure began in 1949 when he appeared for Derbyshire, the day after his nineteenth birthday. He would represent them as an amateur twenty-eight times but came down to Somerset in 1953 when there was a yawning gap for a pace bowler of substance. The fact that he was an amateur was deemed a considerable bonus. Tom certainly made some useful contributions as, in the words of David Foot, 'a wholehearted fast-medium bowler' who also demonstrated his worth on occasions, shoring up the tail with one half-century to his name for the county. He played twenty-three matches in total for Somerset, taking 63 wickets at 32.26 apiece and averaging 12.43 with the bat. He played for only two seasons, calling it a day after 1954.

Venturing gamely where others feared to tread, he courted and was then married in 1955 to Susanne Ray, the stepdaughter of Air Vice-Marshal Taylor, who ran Somerset at the time with curt military precision. The couple made a fresh start well beyond the purlieu of Susanne's stepfather when Tom set up a boat-building business at Rockland St Mary in Norfolk. He met Timothy Colman (of the mustard dynasty), later Sir Timothy, and the two of them worked together hatching their plan to beat the world speed sailing record with the boat christened *Crossbow*. They duly achieved their target at a competition staged off Portland, Dorset, with the record very much in mind. Tom was a member of the crew who achieved a new world-record speed of 26.3 knots which would twice be improved upon in 1980 as the team developed and raced *Crossbow II*.

His business did not perhaps benefit in the way he had hoped and it is reported that he was struggling financially when he fell from an express train near Arlesey in Bedfordshire on 21 April 1984. He was fifty-three at the time. The death was attributed indirectly to 'hypertension' and directly to 'multiple injuries' with a verdict, after two inquests, of 'accidental death'. Perhaps the exact circumstances can never be known. It was a sad and premature end to the life of a man, who, in the words of the late Peter Roebuck was 'remembered by friends as the nicest, staunchest, most honest of men' and whose death 'was widely mourned'.

391
John Derrick Stenton
27 May 1953 v. Surrey, Taunton

John Stenton (whose middle name is sometimes given incorrectly as Derek) was born in Sheffield on 26 October 1924, the son of Reginald Stenton and his wife, Dorothy (née Lingard). Reginald was a railway engineer and fireman at the time of John's birth (and later listed as a locomotive driver) and would have considered himself fortunate to be alive. He was a First World War hero who, as his son, John, would later write, 'was wounded four times and was very lucky to have survived the war'.

John Stenton – a teacher at Queen's College in Taunton at the time of his selection.
COURTESY OF JOHN LEE

John was educated at Woodhouse Grammar School where he demonstrated his prowess as an athlete and cricketer. During the Second World War he joined the Royal Navy and clearly impressed his superiors, given that he was appointed a young sub-lieutenant at the age of twenty in March 1945 serving on *HMS Tavy*, a frigate deployed in escorting convoys between New York and Liverpool. He was released from naval service a year later in March 1946 and was appointed a junior master in charge of Physical Education at Queen's College, Taunton. Small, lithe and neat, and an all-rounder, he bowled left-arm spin and is also described in reports as 'a forceful batsman' who opened on occasions for the Somerset Stragglers side. A report in the *Somerset County Herald* of 1949 notes that 'a young Yorkshire amateur J. D. Stenton, now resided at one of the Taunton schools, has received intensive coaching from George Hirst and Len Hutton. He is a bowler of the Hazell type [i.e. left-arm orthodox], a very punishing bat and very alert in the field.' A separate report informs us that 'this excellent all-rounder has a great future if he can get the necessary experience in higher grade cricket'. Unfortunately, there were few opportunities to nurture any talent on the first-class stage.

After featuring in county trial matches from 1948 onwards, he made appearances for Somerset Second XI and continued to knock on the door without being selected for the First XI. He was eventually selected for his solitary first-class game in May 1953 at the County Ground, taking one wicket at a cost of 44 runs and completing knocks of 18 and 1. A report in the *Somerset County Gazette* informs us that '[R. E. C.] Pratt launched an onslaught on newcomer Stenton which considerably quickened the scoring and loosened the bowlers' grip on the situation' but that there was redemption when 'eight runs short of saving the follow on, Stenton came in for his first innings in county cricket. He played excellently for twenty minutes and by the time he was taken at extra cover all follow-on dangers had been averted.' If the county were pondering whether or not to give John further opportunities to build on this start, the matter was resolved when he left Queen's College in 1954.

He had played a very active role in the life of the school. Married in 1951 at St Joseph's Roman Catholic church in Bridgwater to Louie Nellie Dorothy Shellard, a dental nurse whose father was a corporation water inspector, he had a son and daughter, both born in Taunton. The Queen's College magazine (*The Wyvern*) recorded that 'Mr Stenton contributed much hard work and enthusiasm to the successful effort in raising the standard of rugby and cricket'. In the *History of Queen's College*, H. J. Channon observes that 'Mr Stenton paid constant attention to the physical fitness of the [rugby] players'. He had also taken a party of nineteen boys on a skiing trip to Zermatt in Switzerland in 1954, one pupil noting admiringly his teacher's astonishing ability to enjoy a nap in the noisiest of carriages. Parenthood and consequent sleepless nights had perhaps played their part.

John's work would take him briefly to Kingston before he was employed for three decades in Sussex, continuing to pursue a career in the field of Physical Education as an administrator and advisor. He and Louie were divorced in 1961 and he was later married in Chichester to Ethel Mary Richards, who worked as a Physical Education advisor. After his second marriage was dissolved, John was married for a third and final time on his sixty-first birthday in 1985 to Mary Jane Pellett, a headmistress in Brighton and a fellow divorcee, aged thirty-five. It would prove an eventful time for Mary. Shortly after her marriage she would be called to give background evidence in the harrowing 'Babes in the Wood' tragedy when two young pupils, aged nine and ten, were brutally murdered and their bodies found in nearby Wild Park, Moulsec-oomb. Two years later she was appointed headmistress of the Balfour County Junior School in Brighton, where she remained until 2001, taking up a similar appointment in Cuckfield. She and John have lived for a number of years in Worthing and continue to reside there at the time of writing.

392
Brian Anthony Langford
6 June 1953 v. Lancashire, Bath

Brian Langford's name will be forever linked with a feat of cricketing parsimony never likely to be matched and certainly unable to be bettered. His eight overs in the 40-over match against Essex in the inaugural 1969 season of the Sunday League yielded eight maidens as Brian Ward resolutely refused to allow his wicket to be taken, regardless either of run-rates or the booing of the crowd at Yeovil. So focused was he on decisions required of him as captain that Brian Langford was unaware that he was about to accomplish the feat until the umpire, John Langridge, quietly pointed out at the end of the seventh maiden that glory awaited. Essex compiled a total of 126 and Brian Ward looked set to be vindicated with Somerset at 82 for 8, until a spirited rally by Peter Robinson and Graham Burgess saw Somerset home.

Brian was born in Birmingham on 17 December 1935, the son of Alan Langford, a machine tool setter, and his wife Florence (née Orme). With the family having moved to Bridgwater when Brian was four, he was educated at Dr Morgan's Grammar School in the town. Although Brian remained an unshakeably loyal follower of Aston Villa FC as a result of his Birmingham roots, he grew up a huge fan of Somerset cricket. He travelled to watch the team at every opportunity, doing what most cricket-mad schoolboys do – collecting the autographs of his heroes and spilling onto the pitch during the lunch interval, playing with a tennis ball, looking askance at the pavilion, praying that an authority figure was watching and hoping that he stood out from the crowd. Alas, no one tapped on his or any other boy's shoulder.

On leaving school at the age of fifteen, he went to work for British Cellophane, a major employer in Bridgwater, but he was soon making waves, not as the off-spinner he would become but as an opening batsman who bowled medium pace. Wally Luckes, that stalwart of Bridgwater and Somerset cricket, knew that here was a special talent and brought Brian to Somerset's attention whilst reassuring his near-neighbour that the life of a pro would be a fine idea. Offered the opportunity to play professionally, Brian threw in his lot with Somerset. Given an airing but little chance to shine in the Second XI in 1952, none could have predicted the

Brian Langford – took 1,390 wickets for the county he had supported as a boy.
SOMERSET CRICKET MUSEUM

impact he would have in 1953. Invited to join the side at Bath in June, he made his first-class debut in the infamous Bertie Buse Benefit Match against Lancashire, when, having posted a total of 158, Lancashire won by an innings and 24 runs. The match had finished in less than a day and groundsman Cec Buttle, when asked by Club Secretary Air Vice-Marshal Taylor what he was planning to do replied, 'Hang myself, Sir.' Cec had in fact worked tirelessly with the assistance of Johnny Lawrence to improve the pitch.

Brian set to work and astonished everyone (possibly himself included) with a total of 25 wickets for 290 runs in the games against Kent and Leicestershire. He had been guided through the process by Harold Gimblett and Maurice Tremlett who had passed on all their experience – two men with reputations for cussedness whose ire was generally only ever directed at the men they considered the amateurish fools running the club. In the interests of fairness, it should be pointed out that one of those supposed 'fools' – Air Vice-Marshal Taylor – had sent Brian into Bath after the Bertie Buse Benefit fiasco to buy himself a new pair of cricket boots to replace the existing ones that had failed to pass muster. At the end of the Bath Festival the seventeen-year-old off-spinner bestrode the national first-class averages. Not since the days of the youthful

Jack White, shortly before the First World War, had such a thing happened. It heralded the beginning of a remarkable career – interrupted in 1954 and 1955 by his National Service at Woolwich – that encompassed a total of 504 first-class matches for the county, a record as untouchable as his Sunday League clean sheet.

In the winters he found local employment, working for a while as a car salesman at Marshalsea Brothers in Taunton. During the summers he took 1390 wickets for Somerset at 24.89, a fine achievement for a spin bowler asked to complete a goodly proportion of his bowling on the benign County Ground tracks that at least instilled in him the need for a precise line and length when containing rather than taking wickets. Indeed, such was his metronomic consistency that when he was hauled out of retirement as an emergency measure by Brian Close in 1974, he immediately slotted into his rhythm as if he had never been away, as if off-spin bowling at the first-class level were as easy as shelling peas. His parsimony as a bowler is reflected in the fact that over the course of his career, he conceded runs at only 2.34 per over. His batting was sound but not spectacular as an average of 13.58 and fourteen half-centuries in a long career attest.

In 1969 he was offered the captaincy of the club and would remain in that role for three seasons before handing the reins to Brian Close who had by then acclimatised to his new surroundings and was ready to take under his wing a group of youngsters who each, in their way, would shine as brightly as the teenage Brian Landford had done. Brian would play alongside the likes of those knights of the realm Sir Vivian Richards and Sir Ian Botham and – as a supporter of and student of Somerset cricket – was happy to be able to report that he had batted both with Harold Gimblett and Viv.

Having retired from the game, he worked for a while for Barclaycard, continuing to live in Taunton and increasingly turning to golf as his favoured pursuit. He was invited to become Chairman of the Cricket Committee in 1986. The timing was unfortunate as the county were about to be plunged into a civil war when the contracts of Viv Richards and Joel Garner were terminated. Even Brian's emollient approach to everything in life and the esteem in which he was held were insufficient to bring together the warring factions.

He was married in 1958 to Kathleen (née Stone), with whom he would have five children and in 1982 to Patricia Maureen Liscombe (née Gardner), known as Maureen or Mo.

He died in Taunton on 12 February 2013 at the age of seventy-seven. Cricket historian, Stephen Chalke, writes of Brian that he was 'an outstanding off-spin bowler, accurate at all times, with teasing flight and, on responsive pitches, probing turn'. He adds that 'up and down the land he was respected by everyone in the game'. Perhaps that was some sort of compensation for never having gained the Test cap many felt he merited. The competition had been strong, though, throughout his career and Brian was not one to have worried unduly about being overlooked.

Brian Langford – after a sensational start as a teenager he became in time captain and elder statesman of Somerset CCC. SOMERSET CRICKET MUSEUM

393

Clive Frederick Davey
10 June 1953 v. Kent, Bath

In a similar vein to Brian Langford, who also made his first-class debut at the 1953 Bath Festival, Clive Davey had cut his cricketing teeth with the Bridgwater club side. Unlike Brian, he would not have a major impact on proceedings.

Clive was born on 2 June 1932 in North Petherton, where his father, Roland Henry Davey, worked as a wicker chair and basket maker and was married to Olive Mary (née Owens). While Clive was still an infant, the family moved to Bridgwater, where he attended the Somerset Bridge School. Although he never played cricket whilst a schoolboy, he watched the matches at The Parks, the home ground of Bridgwater CC and in time was invited to join the club. It came as no surprise that he took to cricket, given that he was blessed with natural sporting ability and hand-eye coordination that would later see him play hockey, table tennis, billiards and snooker for Bridgwater. He even represented the town at chess.

Clive developed into a technically correct batsman, primarily by observing others and by heeding the advice of the club's more experienced members such as former Somerset player Wally Luckes and Wally's replacement as Bridgwater CC's wicket-keeper, Fred Moore. He was also quick to enlist the help of Somerset's Johnny Lawrence, who for a while kept his caravan at The Parks during the cricket season, using the facilities in the pavilion. A condition of the arrangement was that Johnny would make an occasional appearance for the club – usually the first match of the season – and would undertake ad hoc coaching while in residence. Clive must have impressed his mentor as he was invited to pre-season coaching at Johnny's indoor cricket school at Rothwell in Yorkshire on a regular basis. Clive was never asked to pay for the additional coaching, which lasted for one or two weeks each year.

During the late 1940s, he began to prove his worth, performing consistently for Bridgwater CC as a right-handed batsman and leg-break bowler. With Johnny Lawrence and Wally Luckes singing his praises, it was inevitable that Clive would attract the attention of the Somerset authorities. He turned out regularly for the county, firstly with the Colts in 1950 and then in the Second X1 from 1951 onwards. After completing his National Service with the RAF he accepted a three-year contract in 1953 to become a professional at the County Ground. During his time with Somerset he played in thirteen first-class fixtures. Never quite hitting the heights – his top score being 46 – he mustered an average of 12.42. He was not asked to bowl in any first-class matches. He was offered a further one-year contract for the 1956 season and

Clive Davey – offered a professional contract after establishing his reputation with Bridgwater CC. SOMERSET CRICKET MUSEUM

Clive Davey – 'I had to be honest
with myself: I was never going to make
the grade in first-class cricket'.
SOMERSET CRICKET MUSEUM

also received an approach from Sussex – through the auspices of Harry Parks – but in Clive's own words: 'I had to be honest with myself: I was never going to make the grade in first-class cricket.'

It was a brave and eminently sensible decision not to prolong his professional cricketing days but he had to find new employment, especially as he was about to be married. He chose to start a business making picture frames and this would provide him with a rewarding living for the remainder of his working life. He was married at the beginning of 1956 to Joan (née Purcell). Joan was the daughter of Edgar Purcell, a commercial traveller, whose family lived in Park Road directly opposite the entrance to The Parks cricket ground. The connection was coincidental as Clive and Joan met at a dance in the town on Christmas Eve 1953. They would have two sons and two daughters, all born in Bridgwater.

Clive remained part of the fabric of the Bridgwater social and sporting scene, continuing to play for Bridgwater CC well into his forties and captaining the Second X1 in later years. He had still been playing for the First X1, though, in 1973 when he was invited to tour the West Indies with the Mendip Acorns CC, a tour best remembered for having spirited the young Viv Richards into the UK.

Clive's business – H&D Photomounts – was well-known in the environs of Bridgwater, for many years operating from a property off Wembden Road and employing five people. As he looked towards retirement, one of his sons gradually took over the day-to-day management. At the time of writing, Clive and Joan continue to live in the town they have called home for more than eighty years.

394
John David Currie
13 June 1953 v. Leicestershire, Bath

J Currie (signature)

John Currie was a colossus, standing 6 feet 3 inches tall and strongly-built, weighing 15 stone in his prime. Not for nothing did he go by the name of 'Muscles'. His main claim to fame would be his twenty-five international appearances as a rugby player rather his cricketing exploits, which were creditable though less noteworthy.

Born in Clifton on 3 May 1932, he was the only child of James Scott Currie, a Scottish medical practitioner, and Kathleen Edna Sharman (née Rooke), a vicar's daughter born in Cambridge.

Educated at Bristol Grammar School, John was already a member of Clifton RFC while still a teenager. The club is able to claim a surprising number of internationals but he remains the most capped among them. On leaving school to go up to Wadham College, Oxford, to study Geography, he would gain rugby blues in four successive seasons and would also play nine times for Oxford University at cricket, although not in the Varsity match, so that a blue eluded him.

He was first invited to play rugby for England while still an undergraduate, having already declined the opportunity to play for Scotland, for whom he qualified via his father. Unusually, John was not only an imposing lock-forward but also a place kicker. In most of his twenty-five internationals he was partnered by fellow lock R. W. D. (David) Marques of Cambridge University who, at 6 feet 5 inches was an equally impressive specimen. Feared in the line-out, Marques would stand at the back and Currie at the front of the line, the latter adding his skill at the maul to his armoury. John would joke when challenged after a trial match over why he had failed to make much of an effort to leap for the ball during line-outs in front of the Twickenham West Stand that 'I only jump at the other side of the field. Then the selectors can see my number on my jersey when I go up.' He became something of a poster boy, making an unlikely appearance in 1956, for example, on adverts for Roberts Original Brown Windsor Toilet Soap. *The Times* was not referring to his complexion, however, when it later wrote that he and David Marques had 'illuminated English rugby union' in the late 1950s, leading their country to their first grand slam in three decades. The pair also teamed up for Harlequins. Having begun his career at Clifton, the course of John's rugby playing career was charted by his business career. Employed by Imperial Tobacco, he would play for Bristol before appearing for Harlequins and then enjoying spells for Northern, while based in Newcastle, and then West of Scot-

John Currie – an imposing international lock-forward who 'illuminated English rugby union'. SOMERSET CRICKET MUSEUM

land, while working in Glasgow.

His one match for Somerset CCC yielded a batting average of 8.50 in a low-scoring match dominated by the young Brian Langford. John would also play for Somerset Second XI on a number of occasions and would also later play for Gloucestershire Second XI. He was still enjoying companionable games of cricket for The Forty Club in Scotland in the 1970s.

He was married in 1962 to Patricia Williams with whom he had two sons and a daughter. One son, David Scott Currie (born in Newcastle in 1969) would go on to play rugby for Harlequins. John was in fact on his way to Loughborough University, on 8 December 1991 – by then a Recruitment Manager by profession, although more relevantly undertaking parental chauffeuring duties, collecting David for the Christmas break – when he was taken ill and had to be rushed to hospital in Leicester. He was pronounced dead on arrival. His death at the age of fifty-nine spawned a number of tributes from those who had remembered the feats of a man who had been in more ways than one a giant of rugby union.

395
George Herbert David Evans
20 June 1953 v. Glamorgan, Swansea

G.H.D. Evans

David Evans won international honours though, sadly from a Somerset cricketing perspective, for hockey. John Harris, a contemporary of David's in the Somerset fold, recounts a tale that reinforces the courage of this successful club cricketer who never quite made the grade at the first-class level. John recalls that in a so-called friendly fixture in which Somerset were pitting their wits against the RAF at Taunton, David Evans came out to bat. John describes him as 'an amateur from Weston-super-Mare and he looked like an amateur, too'. A glance at David in certain Weston-super-Mare team photographs in his billowing shirt reinforces the point. John relates that as David walked to the crease, Fred Trueman told the incoming batsman in an expletive-laden aside that he looked like a clown. Unperturbed, David told Trueman to shut up and get on with the game, at which point Fiery Fred demanded the ball from his skipper (Alan Shirreff, who would later play for Somerset) and 'told all around him that he was going to plant Evans on the sight screen. But Evans stood up to him, didn't back away and stuck around. He didn't score many runs … but he wasn't afraid to square

up to Trueman.' In fact, David had done more than hang around. He had made 34 in the first innings while Fred had caused carnage all around him with figures of 5 for 60 and in the second innings he had registered a half-century.

David Evans was born on 22 August 1928 in Westbury-on-Trym in the northern part of Bristol. His father, Samuel George Evans, a grain superintendent at Barry docks, was married to Evelyn Annie (née Rogers). David was educated at Wellington School perhaps because his maternal grandparents resided in the West Somerset town (Jacob Rogers having been the station

David Evans – played hockey for Wales.

145

David Evans – an inspirational captain for Weston-super-Mare and brave enough to square up to Fred Trueman.
SOMERSET CRICKET MUSEUM

master there). He proved an outstanding all-round schoolboy athlete and would continue to enjoy a number of sports during his adult life. As well as being a leading light in athletics meets in the Bristol area, he would also perform well at table tennis and golf and was a good enough hockey player to represent both Somerset and Wales. He played his club cricket for a strong Weston-super-Mare side and his performances as a batsman who was also able to bowl at medium pace brought him to Somerset's attention. A regular in the Somerset Second XI where he made a number of telling contributions, he played in eight first-class games for Somerset, all in 1953, averaging 12.85 and taking no wickets while conceding 22 runs. His greatest contribution to Somerset cricket is arguably his influence on a young Brian Rose, who would go on to lead Somerset to their first silverware. Brian relates that 'I started as a fifteen-year-old in the Weston-super-Mare First XI when David was still captain. He was always very competitive at any sport, very similar in many ways to Brian Close, and I felt privileged to have learned about captaincy from two great mentors.'

A chartered accountant, David was married in 1955 to Margaret May Turner, who also lived in Weston-super-Mare at the time and with whom he would have two daughters. He remained for many years with Butterworth Jones, with whom he became a senior partner. When many of the Somerset team led by Brian Rose formed a marketing company in the late 1970s, Brian asked him to become Treasurer of the enterprise. David continued to reside in the town of Weston-super-Mare after his retirement. A fitness fanatic, he stayed in shape by running and it therefore came as a shock when he died on the way to the Weston General Hospital after suffering a heart attack at his home at the age of sixty-two on 20 June 1991.

396

Boris Esmond Collingwood

12 August 1953 v. Nottinghamshire, Weston-super-Mare

[signature: Boris Collingwood]

Writing in the *Somerset County Herald* in 1950, H. J. Channon observes that 'one very good player overlooked in the selected team ... was Maurice [sic] Collingwood, a master at Taunton School. His fielding at cover point would inspire any team and he is a first-rate aggressive batsman who only just missed his blue at Cambridge.' If H. J. Channon had a notable weakness beyond his memory for names it was his exuberant claims to greatness for anyone associated in any way with Somerset cricket.

Born in Hither Green, Lewisham, on 8 January 1920, Boris was the son of Cecil James Collingwood who ran an upmarket clothing shop along with his wife Mildred (née Rogers) whose father was also a local businessman, a licensed victualler. An only child who arrived when Mildred was in her thirties and Cecil in his forties, Boris was educated at Dulwich College where he played for the First XI in four successive seasons, latterly as captain and in sides including Trevor Bailey of Essex and England and Alan Shirreff, a widely-travelled first-class cricketer whose final appearances were for Somerset. The school magazine, *The Alleynian*, notes in 1938 that 'he scored over five hundred runs during the season, and easily headed the batting averages'. The following year, it is reported that as a captain he was 'over-cautious at times' with the 'responsibility making him anxious'.

He left Dulwich College in 1939 and went up to Clare College, Cambridge, where he read Modern Languages. His studies were interrupted in 1940 when he served in the Intelligence Corps, spending time in Nigeria, the Middle East, Orkney and Eritrea. He returned to Clare College in 1946 to complete his degree and was married in 1949 to Octabrena Hilda (née Silin), known as Brena, the daughter of a merchant seaman from Riga, the capital of Latvia, at the time an outpost of the Soviet Union. Brena's family owned three nursing homes in Kent by the time of her marriage and she had lied about her age in order to serve as a nurse in the war. She and Boris would have two daughters. A resourceful woman, Brena would later open a school in Marbella while also serving as a tour guide and finding time to gain a pilot's licence before emigrating to the United States, where her daughters also resided.

Boris began his teaching career at Taunton School in January 1950. He taught French and Geography, also taking charge of cricket. The newspaper report of his arrival announces that he was accompanied by 'Mr G. W. S. Smith who is in charge of shooting'. For a while, Boris lived in residence as an assistant housemaster but he and

*Boris Collingwood as a member of the
Dulwich College XI (top) and as a
teacher at Taunton School (above).*

Brena later chose to live some distance from the school at the Manor in Waterrow. He would remain at Taunton School until 1957, assisted in his final three seasons by a professional coach, former Sussex cricketer, Harry Parks. The school magazine notes of Boris that 'he never spared himself in service of the school generally and the cricket in particular'. Among his charges had been Somerset players John Baker and Peter Eele, and Warwickshire and England's John Jameson, who racked up seven centuries in his final season as a schoolboy cricketer.

A right-handed batsman, Boris also bowled on occasions but never in a first-class match. He made one appearance for Cambridge University and then, alongside his appearances for the Second XI, played once for Somerset, averaging 8.00. He enjoyed rather more success with the Somerset Stragglers side. In his history of the club, P. C. Lennard Payne writes that:

> *Boris was a batsman who ate runs and who in his fairly short career with the club hit twelve centuries between 1951 and 1954 and by so doing became the member with the third highest number of centuries in the club's history. He was very athletic and an excellent cover point and when he discovered that he had a knee joint problem which was effectively incurable, he gave up playing cricket. It was a great loss to the club and a great sadness for him.*

Boris left Taunton School to take up a post at Dartford Grammar School in 1958 but was forced to retire early owing to a serious problem with phlebitis, an inflammation of the veins in his legs. He and Brena separated and in 1962 he was married in Wood Green to Elsie Don (a divorcee who was four years his senior and whose maiden name was Storey). Brena changed her name by deed poll the following year from Collingwood to Serra. Although Boris was not always the easiest of companions, perhaps in part because he was dogged by ill health, he retained cordial relations with his ex-wife and children, who would note that, when it came to being difficult, their stepmother would show Boris to be a mere novice.

When his father died in 1965, Boris moved to Storrington, West Sussex, to be near to his widowed mother. With the son now in an increasingly poor state of health, it is not clear who was caring for whom. Although he had ceased playing cricket, his interest in the game remained undiminished. Sparked by his lifelong passion for philately, he had also become a stamp dealer, generating a steady but limited income. Boris died of heart disease at his home in Storrington on 18 November 1968 following two separate blood clots. He was only forty-eight and was survived by his mother, by both wives and by his daughters.

397
Philip Hillier Fussell
12 August 1953 v. Nottinghamshire, Weston-super-Mare

Former teammates describe Philip Fussell as 'a lively character' or similar. None of them accuses him of having ever been a blushing violet. Philip himself writes that 'for as long as I can remember, I've never been happier than with a gun, rod or cricket bat in my hand'. His life is detailed in his autobiography, *The Sportsman: I Should Have Been Born Under a Hedge*, published in 2015. A brief précis could perhaps read: all play and no work makes Philip a crack shot. Certainly the book makes uncomfortable reading for lovers of wildlife. Philip delineates his successes with relish – 500 dead wood pigeons here, another 500 slaughtered there. There's a telling statement when he laments a shortage of rabbits to bag and observes that 'myxomatosis was a disaster for me', with no acknowledgement that the disease might have been an inconvenience for the rabbit population. In Philip's world, sparrows offer target practice rather than a tuneful adornment to the countryside, ancient hedgerows are not seen as an invaluable wildlife habitat but as an obstruction that must be grubbed up. A row of venerable trees beloved by generations of locals is a source of profit to be sold to the highest bidder and felled, rather than a stately landmark. Philip is nothing if not single-minded.

Born in the village of Rode on 12 February 1931, he was the fourth child of Henry Sidney Fussell and his wife, Ada (née Hillier). Ada's family owned quarries in the region and Henry's family, having started out as bakers, had set up the Fussell's Brewery, run by three brothers. The business benefitted greatly from Henry's contacts during the First World War, when he managed to retain continuity of supply of malt.

Philip Fussell – 'for as long as I can remember, I've never been happier than with a gun, rod or cricket bat in my hand'.
SOMERSET CRICKET MUSEUM

The enterprise grew to the point that besides the brewery, the company would own sixty-four pubs and four hotels. In addition, Henry owned Church Farm, where Philip was brought up. A tearaway from the off, Philip recalls that he required fifty-five stitches when falling through the French doors of their home at the age of five. He had soon recovered sufficiently to bag his first kill, an unsuspecting moorhen. Thereafter he graduated onto rabbits, which he shot for the pot or for money, or sparrows, which he shot simply to hone his skills as a marksman. At the age of ten, he was sent to Monkton Combe School near Bath. Here he gained the moniker 'Fisty' after he floored a seventeen-year-old prefect who had had the temerity to slap him on the back of the head for a misdemeanour. A teacher wisely encouraged him to channel some of his energy into boxing lessons. By his own admission, Philip was one of the least academically-minded pupils at the school, although he was at least able to demonstrate an ability to outwit wood pigeons, whom he had learned to ensnare by mimicking their call and then knocking them with a stick as they approached. Seemingly unmanageable, he was at one point threatened with expulsion and summoned to appear before the headmaster on the ensuing Sunday morning. On the Saturday he took 8 for 22 against King's School Bruton. The following day, Fisty was informed by the principal that he had earned a reprieve.

After leaving school with little or nothing in the way of qualifications he was exempted from National Service while he undertook farm work as an intern at a farm in Salisbury. This would prove one of the few periods in his life when work took precedence over leisure but, unable to resist a money-making venture, he shot rabbits in his spare time and sold them to the manager of the Cathedral Hotel at Salisbury, owned by the Fussells.

Philip was by now making a name for himself as a marksman and had begun to enter competitions and usually won them with his unerring eye. Wood pigeons would remain his speciality and over time his telephone number would become the first one that farmers near and far would dial when their crops were threatened by an invasion. He tells many a tale of coming away with his car packed to overflowing with dead birds that were sold on to restaurants or butchers. Some of them he of course ate himself. Philip notes that he is partial to pigeon testicles although apparently approximately twenty of them are required to create something resembling a meal.

He retained his interest in balls of a different variety, playing as a forceful batsman and forsaking his leg-breaks for fast-medium deliveries. His speciality was the in-swing but this would come back to bite him when he required an artificial hip in later life as a result of all those times he had planted his foot unnaturally across the line of his body to impart the desired swing. He would carry on playing for Frome into his early forties at which point he transferred his allegiance to Bath. He played regularly as a young man for Somerset Second XI and cites Horace Hazell and Eric Hill as two important influences who helped him with technique. He played in two first-class fixtures for Somerset. After a trouncing at the hands of Nottinghamshire, he was asked by Ben Brocklehurst to make further appearances but was needed

Philip Fussell – a brilliant marksman. COURTESY OF PHILIP FUSSELL

for the harvest. He appeared once more in 1956. Philip came away with an average of 2.50 and took one wicket at a cost of 71 runs. Unlike his shooting, his first-class cricketing exploits had been a little wide of the mark.

Philip's father installed him as a tenant farmer at Church Farm, a 229-acre holding that adjoined the family brewery. It was another example of the Fussell family's nose for a good business deal and meant that when Bass bought the company in 1958, they could not oust him and he was able to negotiate a favourable price for the farmhouse and surrounding land, which he subsequently sold for housing. In a similarly profitable deal, he purchased a further eleven acres and promptly covered his costs by selling sixteen impressive elm trees for their timber. Ever the wheeler-dealer, he purchased Shawford Farm and employed a manager so that he could get on with the business of shooting. Further money fell into Philip's lap when he was given compensation for land when a road passed through his farm.

His wisest decision, though, was perhaps to settle down when he reached the age of thirty-five and propose to Jane (née Ardley) who was sixteen when they met and brought youth and vitality into his life. She would prove his rock. As well as raising two sons, Jane ran a popular restaurant, known as *The Sportsman*, which was sited in a converted barn. While Philip continued to live a self-confessed hedonistic lifestyle, Jane was left to hold the fort until her untimely death as a result of cancer in 2007. She had been happy for Philip to pursue his interests which, as well as shooting –

where he would win a world championship at clay pigeon shooting in 1988 – included squash, which he took up in his forties, and salmon fishing at which his expertise was widely respected.

Country sports divide opinion, but there is no doubting that Philip Fussell has been a skilled practitioner. 'I'm still enjoying my sporting life and every day I think how lucky I've been,' he confesses. The many hundreds of thousands of birds who have fallen within his purlieu and met their untimely deaths were less fortunate. Nor can those birds who have survived the carnage sleep easily in their nests just yet. Well into his eighties at the time of writing, there is still life in the old sportsman.

398
Peter Bernard Wight
22 August 1953 v. Australia, Taunton

Although he came from a family of talented sportsmen, it was pure chance that Peter Wight opted for the life of a professional cricketer and a stroke of good fortune that he came to play for Somerset. He brought artistry to the team. He may have been waif-like (although at 5 feet 10 inches not short) but such was his exquisite timing that when the ball left his bat it cut through the fielders more often than not like a rapier thrust. Graham Atkinson would say of him in conversation with writer Stephen Chalke that 'there was a lovely ring to his bat … if he'd gone out with an old chair leg there'd have been a nice ring to it … I used to stand at the other end and drool at the shots he played.' Praise indeed from another fine batsman.

Peter was able to boast an interesting cocktail of Portuguese and Scottish ancestry and cricket was certainly in his genes with a brother and cousin who both represented the West Indies. Born in Georgetown, British Guiana, on 25 June 1930, he travelled as a young man to Lancashire by cargo boat, hoping to qualify as an engineer, in the words of Stephen Chalke 'a twenty-year-old shivering in his tropical clothes and shocked by the rationing and outdoor toilets'. When his employer in Burnley reneged on a prior agreement to release Peter for a motor mechanic's exam, he emigrated to Toronto, perhaps unaware that the weather there was even less clement. He soon returned to Burnley, working in a factory and playing as an amateur for Walsden CC in 1951 before being offered a professional contract in a strong Burnley CC side which included his compatriot Bruce Pairaudeau. It was at that time, while visiting his sister, who lived in Bridgwater, that his brother-in-law suggested that he should play for

Somerset, noting that 'they've got no players', a statement that was regrettably not too far from the truth.

Peter showed up for a trial and within a short space of time he was selected to play against the Australians. After scoring a duck in his debut innings, he was offered reassurance by Richie Benaud who breezily told him he would probably make a century in the second innings. He did. Although he eschewed the more ribald aspects of post-match celebrations and changing room banter, 'Rajah', as he became known, was liked and admired by his teammates and opponents alike. In common with the other great run-maker who preceded him – Harold

Peter Wight – 'there was a lovely ring to his bat ... if he'd gone out with an old chair leg there'd have been a nice ring to it'. SOMERSET CRICKET MUSEUM

Gimblett – he was cursed by perennial hypochrondria, claiming a bewildering number of ailments. It was also said that he was in fear of fast bowling but the facts do not bear this out. In truth, only Fred Truman appeared consistently to unsettle Peter, but, then again, Fred engendered fear in the vast majority of his contemporaries.

By the time of his marriage in 1957 to Joyce (née Pickup), whom he had met in Burnley, he had settled into his adoptive county. In every season between 1954 and 1963 he would top 1,000 runs and twice he would exceed 2,000 runs, becoming the leading run-maker in County Championship cricket in 1960. He would retire as a player in 1965. Over the course of 328 matches he had accumulated an impressive 16,965 runs at an average of 32.75 with twenty-seven centuries to his name. His occasional off-spin had yielded 62 wickets at 33.24 apiece.

In other circumstances he might have been called on for international tours but,

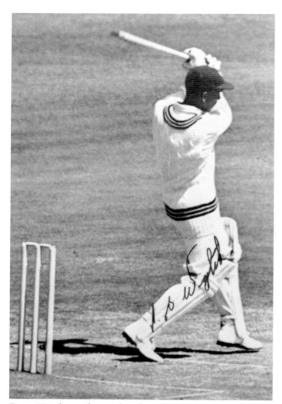

Peter Wight – 'fours of such perfectly timed speed as to charm even those who played against him'.
SOMERSET CRICKET MUSEUM

obliged to find off-season work, he found employment locally with the likes of Hawkes & Son, a sash window maker based in Bath. In 1963-64 he spent a winter at Christchurch in New Zealand, coaching and playing, and it was perhaps this experience that encouraged him to invest the proceeds of his benefit year (1963) in an indoor cricket school in Bath, completed in 1964. Peter was very committed in particular to the idea of girls' and women's cricket and was generous in offering his facilities to advance the cause. In 1969 he helped to found Somerset Wanderers Ladies CC and became President of the club. The cricket school would not demand all his time though, as he would go on to stand as an umpire in 567 matches, retiring as a first-class official in 1995, meaning that with his combined appearances as a player and official, he had been involved in more first-class fixtures in England than any other player post the Second World War. It remains an oddity that he should never have appeared in a Test Match in either capacity. Having retired to Ross-on-Wye, he died there on 31 December 2015 at the age of eighty-five.

John Arlott is always worthy of the last word. He wrote that 'Post-war English cricket has seen few men who have made runs so prolifically and so charmingly as Peter Wight ... He will be remembered as long as those who have watched him remain alive to talk about cricket. He has made many runs elsewhere, but he has never been happier than at Taunton where the ball has bounced true and fast and he has strolled almost negligently towards it and, with a flick of those thin, steel-strong wrists, flicked it away ... for fours of such perfectly timed speed as to charm even those who played against him.'

399
Yawar Saeed
22 August 1953 v. Australia, Taunton

Yawar Saeed was born into cricketing aristocracy. His father, Mohammad Saeed – later afforded the prefix Mian as a respected elder statesman, as indeed Yawar would be – had captained Pakistan in their first unofficial tests. Yawar was born in Lahore on 22 January 1935 and after having been raised in Northern India prior to Partition and the formation of Pakistan, he became the unfortunate victim of political wrangling on the part of his father's successor as Pakistan's captain, Abdul Hafeez Kardar. Yawar was advised by his father to extend his cricketing education in England, offering his services as an amateur. An imposing figure, he was very popular with the Somerset faithful. We are left with a description of his approach to the game, reported in August 1953 in the *Somerset County Gazette* and written by Eric Hill:

> *And then we have the breezy approach of Jawar {sic} Saeed, the massive eighteen-year-old Pakistani. A delightful fellow off the field ... he really does hit the ball ... It seems to me that he considers it an affront to everyone involved not to provide something in the way of entertainment. And the person he entertains most is quite obviously Jawar himself ... Fast bowler, big hitter, character on the field enjoying himself.*

Eric then concludes his feature with a summary that shocks the modern reader into the realisation that overseas players were likely to need the resilience to cope with the racism – even racism unsullied by ill-intent – that was endemic at the time.

> *How nice to see the younger population jumping to their feet as he comes to the wicket and shouting 'Good old Sambo' the way they used to cry 'Good old Arthur {Wellard}'.*

Nice? Yawar perhaps saw it as patronising at best but bore it all with great fortitude. The cultural difficulties did not end there. Teammate Roy Smith would later relate that when Yawar was served bacon at mealtimes and was obliged as a Muslim to avoid it, Roy volunteered to undertake the bacon-eating duties with great enthusiasm.

Yawar first played for Somerset in 1953 and there was then some discussion before MCC agreed that two appearances for Punjab would not impact on his eligibility to play for Somerset in 1954. He was a regular team member throughout 1954 and 1955, taking part in fifty matches and averaging 15.60 with the bat (including six half-centuries) and taking 78 wickets at 35.73. It was noted a propos his medium-pace bowling that 'if he can iron out his delivery stride he may be really quick one day'.

He left after the 1955 season as 'business commitments were too pressing'. He was married in Lahore in April 1956 to Parveen Sadiq, returning to the West Country for his honeymoon in Torquay and playing for an MCC XI at Lord's while in England. Yawar would enjoy a successful career employed by the Pakistan Tobacco Company (a subsidiary of British American Tobacco), rising to the level of director.

He continued to play first-class cricket in Pakistan for a short while but was never selected for the national side. He would, however, later become an influential figure in the administration of Pakistani cricket as a member of the Pakistan Cricket Board. Through his commanding presence, powers of diplomacy and easy manner with the press he was able to bring the best out of a team notorious for factionalism and in-fighting. He played his part from the 1970s, serving variously as a selector, board member and tour manager and among his notable achievements was the management of the national side when they won the Carlton & United (50-over) Triangular Tournament in Australia in 1996-7. In 2003 he served as the Chief Operating Officer of the PCB and six years later managed the Pakistan team who lifted the 2009 T20 World Cup. The following year, while he was managing the 2010 tour of England, three members of his team – captain Salman Butt and bowlers Mohammad Amir and

Yawar Saaed (centre) enjoys a glass of milk at a reception for the Somerset team as those around him, including Peter Wight (right) and the club's scorer, Tommy Tout (facing camera), opt for sherry. SOMERSET CRICKET MUSEUM

Mohammad Asif – had succumbed to pressure or temptation from a spot-fixing cartel. It should be added that at no stage was Yawar implicated in the scandal. His daughter, Tehzeeb, remembers it as a time of intense stress. On asking her father why he was shouldering the burden, his response was: 'It's my team and I have to stand by them through thick and thin'. Ironically, he had earlier led an enquiry into the workings of the national team after suspiciously inconsistent performances in Australia and this had led to the jettisoning of seven players. Yawar resigned a month after the scandal broke. At the age of seventy-five, he was ready to step down.

He died on 21 October 2015 in Lahore at the age of eighty as a result of a brain tumour, having lived

Yawar Saeed – a charismatic man and in later life a leading figure in the management of the Pakistan national side. SOMERSET CRICKET MUSEUM

and breathed Pakistani cricket for so many years and done much for the country he loved, often in trying circumstances and against a backdrop of factionalism that continued to dog the national team. The Chairman of the Pakistan Cricket Board, Shahryar Khan, was present at Yawar's quiet family funeral, acknowledging the debt the country owed him.

1954

"Somerset County Cricket Club, say what you will, is regarded as a laughing stock. The way to arrest this is to avoid being beaten so often – and then set about winning matches."

Eric Hill in the *Somerset County Gazette*

Championship Position: 17 of 17

The peasants' revolt had been quashed at the second time of asking after an acrimonious meeting in Weston-super-Mare. One of the rebels, former player Bill Andrews was elected to the committee and another, Eric Hill, was made captain of the Second XI and charged with bringing on young talent. Not that any of the changes elicited any discernible improvement, with Somerset sitting at the bottom of the County Championship for the third season in a row. Most depressing of all for the supporters was the departure of Harold Gimblett who after two matches could take no more and suffered a breakdown. He worked for the remainder of the season as cricket coach at Queen's College in Taunton, a tonic that restored his equilibrium. On summoning the courage to visit the County Ground at a later date, he was asked to leave on the orders of the club Secretary, Air Vice-Marshal Taylor. The man who had adorned Somerset cricket to breathtaking effect for thirteen seasons and racked up forty-nine centuries had been summarily dismissed.

Despite the mood of despondency and frustration, there were the first stirrings of reform. The new indoor school had been opened with the club's President, Dr Bradfield, the Bishop of Bath and Wells, bowling the first ball to Harold Gimblett, who had curbed his instincts and resisted the urge to smite the ball to oblivion. The *Yorkshire Post* reported that 'Somerset, bottom of the County Cricket table for three years are to sponsor a senior cricket league ... in the hope of encouraging local talent'. The idea would be undermined by stronger clubs such as Frome CC who declined the offer of involvement. Arguably more important was the agreement that the Second XI would take part from 1955 in the Minor Counties Championship, allowing young fringe players to engage in competitive fixtures on a regular basis. Pleasing, too, was the arrival of a group of seasoned pros expected to offer some solidity to the side, with Geoff Lomax, Jim Hilton and John McMahon all given their first airing. The emergence of the youthful opening batsman Graham Atkinson would in time prove a tremendous investment.

Peter Wight, playing in his first full season, amassed the most runs in a generally indifferent season for the batsmen. Johnny Lawrence took 93 wickets and narrowly missed out on the double. John McMahon offered useful support with 85 victims, but the bowling attack lacked any teeth on all bar the most spin-friendly wickets. In truth, there was little to cheer the supporters.

This was also Johnny Lawrence's benefit year. His principled stand against allowing any Sunday fixtures to swell the coffers sparked a national conversation. Typical among the responses is a letter in the *Banbury Advisor*:

> SIR – *This Methodist Gentleman makes it quite clear that he does not wish to benefit financially from any sources contrary to his Christian principles ... I would strongly suggest we show our appreciation and thanks by sending a donation to the fund at Somerset County Cricket Club.*
>
> *Your etc.* CECIL WATTS *of Rugby*

The Somerset team who played Middlesex at Lord's in May 1954.
Back row: *J. Hilton, J. W. J. McMahon, J. G. Lomax, P. B. Wight, D. L. Kitson, R. Smith, Y. Saeed.* Front row: *M. F. Tremlett, J. Lawrence, B. G. Brocklehurst, H. W. Stephenson, F. L. Angell.* SOMERSET CRICKET MUSEUM

400
James Geoffrey Lomax
8 May 1954 v. Nottinghamshire, Nottingham

A willing, wholehearted and popular cricketer, Geoff Lomax was a useful all-rounder, very good on occasions but never threatening greatness. He was born on 20 May 1925 in Rochdale. His father, James Richard Lomax was a Rochdale man to his very bones: a labourer, married to Doris (née Bassett), he was born, lived and died in the town.

Along with fellow Lancastrian Jim Hilton and Australian-born Surrey player John McMahon, Geoff came to Somerset having already gained experience of first-class cricket as the county tried to shore things up after a succession of poor seasons. Unlike the others, he would forsake his roots and choose to make Taunton his permanent home.

Geoff had begun to make a name for himself in club cricket at the age of sixteen, opening the batting for Castleton CC. Among his excellent innings was a century against Flixton CC and he was soon playing for Rochdale CC in the Central Lancashire League, appearing for them for three seasons from 1942 until 1944 before representing Milnrow CC in 1945. The *Rochdale Observer* notes in 1942 that he 'has a grand style and only requires a little more experience to become a sound opening batsman'. By 1945 he had developed into an all-rounder, bowling at something between medium and fast-medium pace.

After the war, he became a member of the Old Trafford ground staff and began to appear for Lancashire Second XI on a regular basis. Between 1948 and 1953 he also made fifty-seven first-class appearances for Lancashire. By now considered more a bowler than a batsman, he took 81 wickets at 31.09

Geoff Lomax – 'figures cannot illustrate all the in-filling he did and his unselfish response to whatever the situation demanded'.

SOMERSET CRICKET MUSEUM

apiece and averaged 14.96 with the bat. His contract was not renewed after an indifferent season in 1953 when his appearances were sporadic.

He had by now established himself as an electrician, finding work between the cricket seasons. He was married in 1949 to Norah Mary Fisher, who also lived in Rochdale and worked in a factory where card tubes were made. The couple would have two daughters.

With Lancashire's blessing, he came to Somerset on a special registration with no lengthy residential qualification required. He proved a worthy but not stellar addition to the ranks, his main contribution being his versatility and a preparedness to 'muck in' and deliver what was required of him, including performing as anything from opener to lower-order batsman and opening the bowling as and when required. Over the course of 211 appearances between 1954 and 1962 he

Geoff Lomax – 'whichever difficulty arose he met it with a ready smile'.
SOMERSET CRICKET MUSEUM

would take 235 wickets at 35.02 each and would average 20.76 with the bat. On occasions, he would enjoy a day in the spotlight. He completed two centuries, including one where he withstood the terror that was Frank Tyson, despite that fact that he was batting with an injured elbow. Perhaps his finest moment came against Nottinghamshire in 1958 when, in the words of the *Somerset County Gazette*, 'a brilliant all-round performance by Geoff Lomax helped Somerset to a nine-wicket victory'. The report details his first innings knock of 80, followed by an inspired spell of bowling where he took 4 for 15, including a hat trick. He then pulled off a brilliant diving slip catch to end the Notts second innings before rattling off 53 runs in less than an hour with eleven boundaries. The report concludes that 'for a man who spent most of last season in the wilderness of the Second XI, this was the commencement of a fine comeback for the amiable Geoff'. The role of Dennis Silk deserves acknowledgment. Following a mix-up and recognising that Geoff was the man in form, he sacrificed his own wicket, run out.

By 1959 Geoff was fully into his stride with just shy of 1,300 runs and 43 wickets.

He suffered a fracture in his left arm while batting against Northamptonshire in May 1960, although he was unaware of the fact at the time and had stayed at the crease for twenty painful minutes. Consequently he was unavailable for most of the season but came back with some useful contributions until his release at the end of 1962. Peter Roebuck would later write of Geoff that 'whichever difficulty arose he met it with a ready smile, a pint or two (or several) and a twinkle in his eye suggesting that, fun as cricket could be, it was not quite so attractive as a day's fishing over at Lyme Regis where, in time, he kept a boat. Deservedly he was given a benefit in 1961 and a year later departed, without an enemy, not even amongst those critics who mourned his want of aggression, but without truly leaving his mark, either.'

He was offered employment by the brewers Hall & Woodhouse, who were managed by former Somerset captain George Woodhouse. Having made Taunton his home and raised his family there, he died on 21 May 1992 at Frenchay Hospital on the outskirts of Bristol, at the age of sixty-seven. His obituary in *Wisden* sums up his contribution by observing that 'figures cannot illustrate all the in-filling he did and his unselfish response to whatever the situation demanded, or the fact that he was a real gentleman'.

401
Jim Hilton
8 May 1954 v. Nottinghamshire, Nottingham

Jim Hilton was born in Werneth, near Oldham, on 29 December 1930. His father, James was a master decorator and restorer, married to Ivy (née Jameson). Sporting ability ran in the Hilton genes, with Jim's older brother being an England cricketer and Jim an all-round sportsman who not only played first-class cricket but was also a good enough footballer to be offered trials with Accrington Stanley and Torquay United.

His brother, Malcolm, was ten years Jim's senior and won the first of his four England caps in 1950. Given that Malcolm's spin partner in the Lancashire side was Roy Tattersall, also an England player, Jim, as a right-arm off-break bowler, was always destined to be on the fringes of the county side.

He cut his cricketing teeth with his local team, Werneth CC, with whom Malcolm had also started out. From 1948, still not yet eighteen, Jim was taken on by Manches-

Jim Hilton of Lancashire and Somerset. SOMERSET CRICKET MUSEUM

ter CC and became a member of the Old Trafford ground staff. In 1950 he became a regular in the Lancashire Second XI and as part of his cricketing education was allowed to appear as a stand-in pro for a variety of Lancashire League sides such as Colne CC (where he played as a substitute for Bill Alley in 1951), Lowerhouse CC (in 1952) and Neston CC (in 1953). Not every assignment went swimmingly. A report of his appearance for Colne in the *Barnoldswick & Earby Times* praises his 'tireless effort' and ingenuity but informs us that 'he bowled fastish, he bowled slowish, he sent down leg-breaks and off-breaks but it was not his lucky day out and he failed to claim a single wicket'. By 1952 he had seen the writing on the wall and would begin the process of qualification with Somerset, being offered lodgings while continuing to ply his trade in Lancashire at club and county level. He would in fact play eight times for Lancashire.

Once he had made the move to Taunton he played seventy-one times for his adoptive county, taking 133 wickets at a respectable 26.48 apiece and averaging 10.68 with the bat. The return of Somerset off-spinner Brian Langford from National Service meant that Jim was likely to be marginalised yet again. His imminent departure was reported in the *Somerset County Gazette*, with Jim stating that 'I have been in and out of the side for the past two seasons and feel I must find some security for my family. I am going home to find a job and play league cricket for which I have had several offers.'

He had been married in 1952 to Hilda (née Walmsley), the daughter of a shoe maker and repairer. They would have four children together, including twins. After leaving Somerset he was offered a coaching appointment in South Africa but Hilda was pregnant at the time and wished, as did Jim, to return to their roots in the North of England. He therefore accepted a contract as the pro at Fleetwood CC before being employed first at Kelburne CC in Paisley, Scotland, and then by Werneth CC, where he saw out his days initially as a pro but then for a number of years as an amateur. Having attained the MCC Advanced Coaching certificate, he invested much time and effort in bringing on the local cricketers and would become something of an institution at Werneth CC, acting for ten years as their President.

At the end of his professional career, he became the licensee of the Falconer's Arms in Oldham for thirteen years before being employed by the Wild Leisure Group as a manager and head of maintenance.

Still retaining his links with nearby Old Trafford, he was President of the Lancashire Ex-Players' Association for three years until he suffered the first of two serious strokes that resulted in his suffering ill-health for the last years of his life. He died in the Royal Oldham Hospital on 26 November 2008 at the age of seventy-seven.

402

John William Joseph McMahon

8 May 1954 v. Nottinghamshire, Nottingham

[signature: Jn M Mahon]

Known to teammates as Digger or Mac, John McMahon was born in Balaklava, a small town in South Australia, on 28 December 1917. He was in fact registered as John William with the Joseph added in later life. Known in his youth as Dookie or Jack, it seems that few people referred to him as John, although given the bewildering number of alternatives we shall do so, here. His father, James Lawrence McMahon was a black-smith and amateur boxing champion, married to Ellen (née McEvoy), a policeman's daughter. Both parents were of Irish descent, John's paternal grandfather having emigrated to Australia in 1863 to work as a storekeeper in Hammond, South Australia, until tragically falling from his horse a mere 'two chains from his door' and thus meeting his end in 1882.

John was educated at Balaklava High School before completing his secondary education at Adelaide High School and going on to train as a teacher at Adelaide University. His first teaching appointment was at the Rostrevan College in Magill, South Australia. A keen cricketer from an early age, he graduated through the Metropolitan Leagues but his breakthrough into Grade A cricket in Adelaide resulted from a period of being coached that coincided with his teaching appointment in 1938. He enlisted in 1940 with the 13 Field Brigade of the Royal Australian Artillery who were deployed in Papua New Guinea until 1943. On returning to Adelaide, John was married to his childhood friend, Irene May Richman. They had a son, Brendan John, who was born in Calvary, North Adelaide, in 1944, by which time John had joined the RAAF. He would have only two months to become acquainted with his son before being stationed in England. He was demobilised with the rank of corporal in 1947 and never went home. His desire to become a professional cricketer in England may have been a contributory factor but he had also met his future second wife, Marion Thornborough. Irene divorced him in 1953 on the grounds of his desertion. Brendan, who never saw his father again, died in the Northfield Hospital, Port Adelaide, aged twenty-five, leaving a widow and two young children. John and Marion were married in 1954 and would have a daughter together.

A left-arm orthodox spin bowler, John had come to the attention of Surrey while playing club cricket for Southgate CC in North London. Having appeared in the county Second XI in 1946, he was drafted into the First XI the following season. He would make eighty-four first-class appearances for Surrey between 1947 and 1953 and

John McMahon – a successful left-arm spin bowler with Surrey and Somerset.
COURTESY OF TRACEY McMAHON

take 234 wickets for the county, but with Jim Laker and Tony Lock operating in tandem, he realised that the opportunities would be limited and agreed to an amicable separation after Somerset's Harold Gimblett recommended him as a replacement for slow left-armer, Horace Hazell. John was a popular member of the Somerset side and immediately became part of the clique of players who rallied around their figurehead, Maurice Tremlett. In addition to John and Maurice, the boisterous group – noted for their wholehearted commitment both to cricket and to post-match refreshment – included the likes of Bill Alley, Harold Stephenson and Jim Hilton.

John proved a useful addition to the bowling attack. Capable of varying flight and extracting substantial turn in the right conditions, he took a steady stream of wickets. In 1956, when Johnny Lawrence had retired, John stepped up to the plate as the lead spin bowler with a haul of over 100 wickets in the season. Indeed he was such an important member of the side that he would appear in 108 consecutive fixtures until he fell out of favour in August 1957 for reasons unrelated to on-field performance. Described in *Wisden* as 'a man who embraced the antipodean virtues of candour and conviviality' he had raised eyebrows when stories emerged of his having beheaded an arrangement of gladioli with an ornamental sword at the *Flying Horse Inn* in the centre of Nottingham. John also upset the powers that be on another occasion by having the temerity to ask for a pay rise. The club's patience ran out after what *Wisden* would later report as 'an embarrassing episode at Swansea's Grand Hotel' that also involved captain, Maurice Tremlett. Both were dismissed, although the latter was quickly reinstated. Maurice – inspired both by loyalty and a pragmatic awareness of John's value to the team – then orchestrated a peti-

John McMahon – 'a man who embraced the antipodean virtues of candour and conviviality'.
COURTESY OF TRACEY McMAHON

tion for his return to the side. The committee washed their hands of the matter and left the decision to him but the moment had passed. In conversation with Barry Phillips, John would later reveal: 'I had already agreed a contract with Milnrow in the Central Lancashire League by then, though I would have preferred to have stayed at Somerset'.

In 115 first-class matches for the county, he had taken 349 wickets at 26.11 apiece. With no claims to being anything other than a tail-ender, he had averaged 6.14 with the bat. He played for Milnrow CC for three years, having been recommended to them by George Tribe. He then played for Leek CC in 1961 before representing the now defunct Castleton Moor CC side during the 1962 and 1963 seasons. While living in Rochdale he worked for David Bridge & Co, an engineering firm who ran the Castleton Moor iron works. He also took to writing articles, many of which appeared in the *Manchester Evening Chronicle*. His style of writing was bright, direct, unpretentious and engaging. Just like the man himself. He had a lifelong passion for literature with a particular love – surprising in a hard-drinking Aussie - for nineteenth century poetry. Having ceased playing cricket, he relocated with his wife and daughter, Tracey, to Crouch End in London, working for the local council in the Borough Engineer's office. He also helped with coaching at Alf Gover's cricket school in Wandsworth. After retiring from the council in the early 1980s he continued to coach and was about to take up the post as Head Coach at Highgate Boys' School when an aneurism put paid to the idea in 1993.

He died in Crouch End on 8 May 2001 at the age of eighty-three, having – since the Second World War – refused all invitations to return to his native Australia. Like his grandfather before him, his end was sudden and close to his home. In John's case, he had collapsed on the pavement after a massive heart attack when visiting the local library. His wife, Marion, and daughter, Tracey, were left to grieve an open-hearted man of contrasts, an easy-going roisterer with an abiding love of literature and a man who forsook his native Australia but whose passion for the game of cricket was never diminished.

403
Graham Atkinson
28 July 1954 v. Pakistan, Taunton

One of the many players to have been recommended to Somerset by Johnny Lawrence, who had watched him in action at his cricket coaching school, Graham Atkinson is arguably the one exceptional talent who would have been welcomed into the First XI of his native Yorkshire had he been minded to play for the county.

Born in Lofthouse on 29 March 1938, Graham was the younger of two sons of William Atkinson, who was a gravel extractor, married to Grace (née Gordon). From a young age he demonstrated the technique and ability to build an innings that set him apart, although he was inclined to play a high percentage of shots to the leg side. Having been given a number of outings in the Somerset Second XI as a fifteen-year-old, he made his debut first-class appearance at sixteen and demonstrated steady but unspectacular progress before being obliged in 1957 and 1958 to undertake his allotted period of National Service at RAF Locking, near Weston-super-Mare. Able to continue in the first-class game with appearances for the RAF and Combined Services, he made

Graham Atkinson – 'started slowly and deliberately until he had bowling, wicket conditions and light completely summed up. And then he cut loose with shots rich and dazzling'.
SOMERSET CRICKET MUSEUM

intermittent appearances for Somerset while on leave, most tellingly in the game against Warwickshire at Taunton in 1958, when he scored an impressive 164.

Returning to the bosom of the Somerset fold, he enjoyed consistent success and would amass nearly 2,000 runs both in the 1959 and the 1960 season before finally achieving the feat in 1961. At twenty-three, he was the youngest Somerset player to have done so and he would go on to repeat it the following year. Writing in his auto-biography, published in 1961, the seasoned campaigner Colin McCool would observe that 'the partnership of Virgin and Atkinson will be the brightest thing in Somerset cricket for the next ten to fifteen years. They are already an established pair, and they will get better and better. So far, no other county has a pair of such promise.' With

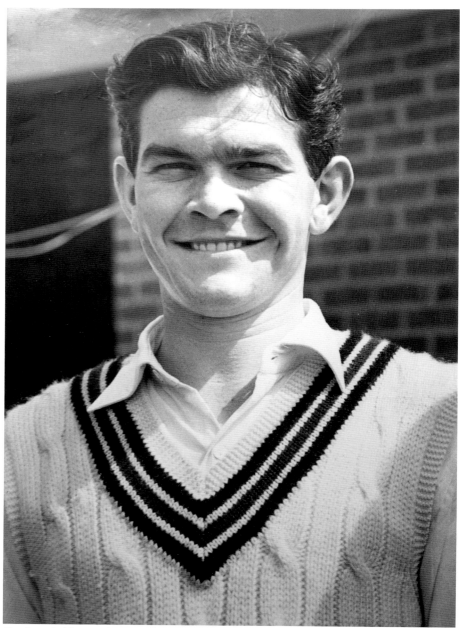

Graham Atkinson – '*a man of great integrity, probably the best captain Somerset never had*'.
SOMERSET CRICKET MUSEUM

Roy Virgin primarily an off-side player and Graham Atkinson the reverse, they often posed problems for opposing opening attacks. Colin McCool goes on to provide a summary of Graham's knock of 190 against Glamorgan at Bath in 1960.

He started slowly and deliberately until he had bowling, wicket conditions and light completely summed up. And then he cut loose with shots rich and dazzling to build a memorable innings.

Although 1962 would prove a turning point, he would continue to exceed 1,000 runs each year. Over time – perhaps aware of the responsibility of holding innings together – he became more reticent in his shot selection. It nevertheless came as a surprise to many when in 1966 and at the age of twenty-eight, he was overlooked for the captaincy and only offered a one-year contract while most of his teammates were offered the security of two-year contracts. Roy Virgin would later explain the committee's doubts, stating that 'it was supposedly because of his fielding – although I always thought he was quite good'. Roy also said of his opening partner that 'he was a man of great integrity, probably the best captain Somerset never had'. In 271 games for Somerset he had averaged 32.07 and scored twenty-one centuries. His occasional off-breaks had yielded four wickets at 59.00 apiece. Having declined the contract offered, Graham was granted permission to talk to Lancashire and joined them for three seasons, averaging 27.42 in sixty-two games. At the age of thirty-one, he left the first-class arena.

He was married in 1959 to Sheila Margaret Bracey, a bank clerk in Downend on the outskirts of Bristol. They would have three children. While working as a pro, Graham had found employment during the winter months, working for a while for Stansell Ltd, a building company based in Taunton. Obliged to now find a career post-first-class cricket, he was appointed Secretary of Salford Rugby League Club and remained in that post for twelve years before going on to manage the University of Manchester's sports facilities.

He died at the age of seventy-seven on 12 November 2015 in Bath, where he had returned with Sheila. He had made many telling contributions for his adoptive county and perhaps a later generation of supporters is unaware of just how highly regarded he was by the players and the public alike. Journalist John Mason wrote that 'Graham Atkinson was the epitome of the professional batsman – calm, assured, capable, obstinate, aware of his particular ability and not easily diverted from a chosen path.' Teammate Ken Palmer observed that 'Graham was one of the best ... I've always said that if I wanted someone to bat to save my skin on a rough pitch then he would be the one.'

1955

"This supposed spring of 1955 had begun with a public row over whether or not it was right to call players by their Christian names. Elders from Weston-super-Mare called this 'a serious breach of discipline', while Rex Frost, now serving as Treasurer, dismissed such criticisms as scandalous."

Peter Roebuck in *From Sammy to Jimmy*

Championship Position: 17 of 17

Another miserable season and another year spent propping up the table. With no need for a trophy cabinet, perhaps the club should have considered investing in a kitchen cupboard to house a burgeoning collection of wooden spoons. A trawl through press reports of the time yields up the words 'dismal' and 'disappointing' with depressing regularity. There was a heated debate over whether or not professionals should continue to be addressed by their surnames. The tide was turning inexorably. Given leave by the Royal Navy, Gerry Tordoff agreed to captain the side but for one season only. Others such as Trevor Bailey had declined the poison chalice, despite a mouthwatering offer of £2,000 per annum to take up the combined duties of captain and secretary. Infectiously enthusiastic and not entirely without talent, Tordoff had the good sense to consult the more experienced pros and the team eked out four wins. The captain was among five players who topped 1,000 runs, foremost among them being Maurice Tremlett.

The wicket-keeping skills of Harold Stephenson shone brightly and he was now adding a significant number of runs. At the end of the season, Johnny Lawrence decided to call it a day. He had brought runs, wickets, jollity and a number of recruits from his cricket school in Rothwell but had decided that his future lay in his native Yorkshire. A caravan pitched at various times at the County Ground or Bridgwater was not the place to continue bringing up his young family, but his strong links with Somerset would continue.

Among the new-joins, Ken Palmer would in time become a linchpin of the club and Bryan Lobb would bring genuine pace to the opening attack and 90 wickets in his debut season for Somerset.

The Somerset Second XI, captained by Eric Hill and coached by Bill Andrews. Terry Clements is the only member of the group who never appeared in a first-class fixture. Standing left to right are: P. H. Fussell, G. M. Tripp, L. Pickles, J. Baker, K. D. Biddulph, B. A. Langford, J. D. Currie, E. Hill, T. Clements, W. H. R. Andrews, R. Smith. COURTESY OF GRAHAM TRIPP

Somerset Past XI who lost to Somerset Present XI in September 1955 in a Benefit Match for groundsman and former player, Cec Buttle. All bar Herbert Hopkins had played first-class cricket for the county. Back row: M. V. Spurway, G. H. Rowdon, W. H. R. Andrews, J. Baker, G. W. L. Courtenay, H. O. Hopkins (Oxford University & Worcester-shire). Front row: C. F. D. Buttle, S. S. Rogers, H. D. Burrough, H. Gimblett, R. J. O. Meyer. SOMERSET CRICKET MUSEUM

173

404
Bryan Lobb
7 May 1955 v. Warwickshire, Birmingham

Bryan Lobb.

Bryan Lobb would prove a great favourite with the Somerset supporters. His fielding was woeful and his running between the wickets calamitous and the Somerset faithful loved it. They embraced his eccentricities and an approach where his ungainliness was matched only by his irrepressible enthusiasm. His errors were deemed forgivable in one with such a sunny disposition. He was born on 11 January 1931 in Bournville, the son of Charles Lobb, a Devonian who was a police constable at the time in the City of Birmingham force, married to Myfanwy (née Williams). Myfanwy died when Bryan was only eleven years old and he would spend time with his uncle and aunt in Ruthin, Denbyshire. His father was remarried in 1945 to Myfanwy's younger sister, Gwladys.

Before joining Somerset, Bryan had been with Warwickshire but had failed to establish himself in the First XI, playing only one first-class match in 1953. He was sounded out while acting as twelfth man in Warwickshire's fixture with Somerset at Coventry. At the time, Somerset were without a pace bowler worthy of the name. Tall and rangy and bowling fast-medium with a pronounced swing in the right conditions, Bryan fitted the bill.

He was married in Birmingham in 1953 to Jean Brown, with whom he would have three daughters, the second and third being born in Somerset. Although he struggled to make an impact on debut against his former county, his importance to Somerset soon became apparent. Sadly, with a lack of support with the new ball, it was insufficient to turn around his adoptive county's fortunes. In 1955 he took 90 first-class wickets and he followed this with hauls of 82 and 110 wickets in the following seasons. Injury would curtail his efforts in 1958.

Thereafter, he would become a more occasional player as he opted for a career as a schoolmaster. After completing his teacher training at St Luke's College, Exeter, he was offered a job teaching Geography and supervising games at Edgarley Hall, the Millfield Preparatory School in Street. He would remain there for thirty years. A convivial host, he would retain a stash of cans of beer in the scorebox in order to entertain visiting schoolmasters while their charges enjoyed a more traditional tea break.

David Foot has left us with a vivid and jocular first-hand account of Bryan Lobb's efforts for his adoptive county in *Sunshine, Sixes and Cider*. He writes:

He smoked a pipe and good-natured sceptics were surprised that it ever reached his mouth because of his singular lack of co-ordination. It was evident in his fielding as he changed

Bryan Lobb – his fielding was woeful and his running between the wickets calamitous.
SOMERSET CRICKET MUSEUM

Bryan Lobb – ungainly and uncoordinated and yet an effective fast bowler.

course a dozen times while the ball trickled straight to him at long-leg. He turned ungainliness into an art form. He was all arms and legs and gargantuan groans as he missed the ball. His batting was stunningly grotesque; the surprise was that bat and ball ever found a meeting point.

The batsman himself would delight in telling the tale of his attempt at a single from the non-striker's end when he was caught unawares by the man at deep mid-on who, having fielded the ball, sprinted past a surprised Bryan Lobb and ran him out. Over the course of 115 games he would indeed average only 5.20 with the bat, astonishing everyone, himself included, with a highest score of 42. He was also able to lay claim to a six over extra cover off the bowling of the great Brian Statham, although, as he later admitted, he was trying at the time to heave the ball to leg. He took a total of 368 first-class wickets for Somerset at a respectable 23.72.

After leaving Edgarley Hall, he retired to nearby Glastonbury and continued to offer his services as a cricket coach at a local junior school. He died in Glastonbury on 3 May 2000 at the age of sixty-nine.

405
Lewis Pickles
14 May 1955 v. Surrey, Oval

Lewis Pickles was born in Wakefield on 17 September 1932, the son of Joseph Pickles, who was married to Ivy (née Wharam) and subsequently moved to Huddersfield to work as a millwright.

From the outset, cricket became Lewis's overriding passion and as young as eight years old, he declared that he planned to become a county cricketer, though no doubt he had his native Yorkshire in mind at the time. Having left school he played Yorkshire League cricket and attended Johnny Lawrence's cricket school in Rothwell, Leeds. He would enjoy two outings for the Yorkshire Second XI but realised that his chances of establishing himself in the First XI were slight, given the county's strength in depth.

His burgeoning career was interrupted when he was called up for National Service in 1953 as part of the Royal Army Service Corps and was stationed outside Taunton. The *Somerset County Gazette* noted erroneously that 'Pickles, an eighteen-year-old [sic] Yorkshire lad at present stationed in the area carries a strong batting recommendation from J. Lawrence and also bowls off-spinners'. He appeared for the Somerset Second XI on a number of occasions. Having sought the advice of Johnny Lawrence, he applied to become a pro at Somerset and, after a successful trial, was offered a three-year professional contract, initially playing for the Seconds.

His breakthrough came in 1955 after he had made an attractive 49 in a friendly fixture against the RAF, but it was not until the 1956 season that he became a regular in the Somerset First XI, scoring 1,136 runs that year, with a highest score of 87. In that match, against Lancashire, he had been at the crease all morning and had scored little more than 30 runs, at which point, England selector and Lancashire great, Cyril Washbrook, when asked by the local reporter what he thought of Lewis's potential, had replied that 'Yes, he's pretty useful but why can't he play any shots?' The report in the *Somerset County Gazette* adds that 'the remark got back to the lad who proceeded to 87 with the full range of shots'. Elsewhere there are accounts of his watchful start to each innings and then a later preparedness to produce more attacking strokes once he was established at the crease. There was, however, some criticism of his running between the wickets and his speed in the field. By 1958 his form had fallen away and he and Malcolm Walker were not offered new contracts. Over the course of forty-seven matches he had averaged 20.50 and had taken one wicket at a cost of 65 runs. Eric Hill, who had captained Lewis and Malcolm in the Second XI was vociferous in his opposition to the decision, which he had been told was down to 'attitude'. Conceding that 'Pickles is a dreamy character who rarely shows any special reaction to any set of circumstances', he asserts that 'talent is here in abundance'.

Lewis Pickles - 'talent is here in abundance'.
SOMERSET CRICKET MUSEUM

Lewis went on to play as a pro for Fife, based in Dunfermline, before returning to Yorkshire League cricket. Over the years he would appear for Pudsey St Lawrence CC, Lightcliffe CC and East Brierley CC. He continued to play the game until the age of fifty-two. Always happy to dispense his accumulated wisdom to young hopefuls, he patiently demonstrated the art of

Malcolm Walker (left) and Lewis Pickles (right) opening the innings against Yorkshire at Bath in 1958. COURTESY OF BARRY PHILLIPS

batsmanship to any club members willing to learn.

He had begun working in the winter months as an accountant in Bradford but became involved in computer systems and programming in the early days of computer technology. He rose to become Systems Manager with responsibility for the design of efficient production methods for R. S. Crooke, a manufacturer of paper and plastic bags.

He had been married in 1958 to Jane Celia Burkinshaw, with whom he would have a daughter and son. At the time of writing, Lewis still resides in Yorkshire but retains fond memories of his time at Somerset, making an annual trip down to the County Ground for reunions of former players, accompanied by his good friend and fellow former Somerset cricketer, Graham Tripp. Lewis confesses that cricket has always been an overriding passion and that he remains delighted to have fulfilled the ambition he had harboured as a primary school boy to play first-class cricket. He retains the friendly, phlegmatic demeanour that made him an unruffled opening batsman but was perhaps mistaken for a lack of energy and enthusiasm by those who opted to terminate his contract at Somerset.

406
David Garfield Hughes
21 May 1955 v. Nottinghamshire, Taunton

Perhaps only in Somerset could a young man receive a telephone call on the evening before his twenty-first birthday and be asked to appear in the morning in a first-class game, having rarely made it into the school First XI and having only been keeping wicket for four years.

David was born in Taunton on 21 May 1934. His father, Brynley, hailed from the Rhonda Valley in South Wales and had come to work in Taunton on the sales floor of the Fifty Shilling Tailor shop sited on The Parade in the town. He was married to Mary (née Collis) who was born in Orange Free State. A schoolmistress and the daughter of a businessman in the leather industry, she had arrived in England at the age of sixteen.

As a child, David was severely knock-kneed and unable to walk with the result that at the age of two he was required to have an operation in Worcester where his legs were broken and reset. He would continue to receive orthopaedic care until the age of sixteen. He would later joke that the problem stood him in good stead when he went to Exeter for tests ahead of his National Service and was rejected as 'physically incapable', despite the fact that he was playing cricket and rugby for Taunton, the latter as a 'nippy wing forward'.

David Hughes as captain of Taunton CC. COURTESY OF DAVID HUGHES

Educated at North Town Junior School, he won a scholarship to Taunton School. He was clearly a member of a bright family, his brothers both being awarded places at Wellington School. He stresses that his parents would have been unable to afford the school fees. Given his medical history, it is perhaps unsurprising that he played only the occasional game of cricket for his school First XI. He left to become an apprentice chartered surveyor with Venning, Hope & Partners based on The Crescent, in Taunton, and while working there played for the Somerset County Gazette team. At the time he was an all-rounder, bowling medium pace and batting high up the order but in a match against Taunton CC,

David Hughes – offered professional terms by Somerset and Glamorgan but opted for a 'proper profession'.
COURTESY OF DAVID HUGHES

the team's wicket-keeper failed to appear and David volunteered his services. Taunton were so impressed that they immediately offered him the chance to join them. With their matches played at the County Ground, it was an offer too tempting to refuse.

When Harold Stephenson suffered a bereavement, his father dying during the week, David was called up as a last minute replacement. It would prove his only first-class appearance as Ken Day, unavailable on this occasion at short notice, was considered the county's number two to Stephenson. David's major obstacle was the gateman who attempted to make him pay to enter the ground and greeted his revelation that he was playing with disbelief. In the event, after initially spilling a leg-side chance in the second over, David acquitted himself well with a catch and a stumping in a tight match where Somerset's Gerry Tordoff and Nottinghamshire's Reg Simpson engineered a competitive finish. David relates that 'when I went in to bat only twenty runs were needed, but Somerset ended up losing by eight'. He had made two runs in his only first-class innings.

He was in fact offered professional terms both by Glamorgan and Somerset, although his father persuaded him that a 'proper profession' was a wiser option, given that he was likely to be cast in the role of reserve keeper, a tenuous position at best. He would go on to work for Somerset County Council as a surveyor before enjoying a period with Hampshire County Council. During that time, he was living in Salisbury and appearing for Wiltshire. He states that his enjoyment was diminished by what he regarded as the woeful captaincy of fellow Somerset cricketer Ian Lomax. He regarded Lomax as arrogant and unlikeable and states that the last straw was a match against Oxfordshire in 1968 in which his captain had thrown in the towel but David hung around to build a recovery and salvage a draw. There were no thanks. Given Ian

Lomax's reputation, David's captain had no doubt been anxious to get off to the races and had been frustrated that he was unable to do so.

David was married in Staplegrove in 1960 to Gwynneth Phillips, who worked on the counter at Debenhams and later for the jewellery retailer H. Samuel. He and Gwyneth would have two daughters. After taking early retirement from Hampshire County Council, he returned to his home town and was offered a job as a consultant by Venning, Hope & Partners, returning to the place where he had embarked on a career after leaving school. One of his major projects was working with Somerset County Council in the construction of a substantial section of the M5 motorway.

He continued to play club cricket for many years and was a familiar figure in local cricketing circles until the late 1980s, turning in later life first to golf and then to lawn bowls. At the time of writing, he was still residing in Taunton, still able to recall the pleasure of playing for the county he loved and loves, though the memories are fading fast and harder to retrieve these days.

407
Graham Malcolm Tripp
15 June 1955 v. South Africa, Taunton

Graham Tripp was born in Clevedon on 29 June 1932, the son of Charles Tripp, who worked for a furniture removal company and was married to Muriel (née McGrath). Graham cites former Somerset county cricketer and footballer E. J. 'Son' Hack as a guiding influence in his younger days. Son was regarded as a hero in Clevedon and had played for Somerset both at football and cricket. Having established a reputation in club cricket, Graham was approached by Somerset and invited to join the ground staff in 1952 as a fledgling pro, his duties including everything from time in the nets to the selling of scorecards. He was also blooded into the Second XI and performed strongly enough for Somerset to retain him.

At the age of twenty-one he completed his National Service with the RAF, based at Merrifield, Ilminster, and during that period represented the RAF at cricket. With his service completed in September 1954, he returned to the County Ground and was given his initial taste of first-class cricket against South Africa. Immediately after this he appeared in a County Championship game, enjoying a baptism of fire at Lord's. Talking to Graham, it becomes apparent how overwhelming an experience coming out to bat can be for a novice: the intimidating atmosphere of the Long Room, infused

Graham Tripp – 'he could be tense about his batting'. COURTESY OF GRAHAM TRIPP

Graham Tripp – a stylish and correct batsman who scored freely for the Second XI but never imposed himself on the first-class stage.

COURTESY OF GRAHAM TRIPP

with the charisma of great players, some of them seated there, the walk down the steps, brushing past childhood idols such as Dennis Compton and taking guard in front of the packed crowd, praying that he would not be humiliated. In the end, he eked out eight runs.

Modest, gently spoken and conscientious, he was initially expected to enjoy a long and productive first-class career but perhaps his diffidence or nervousness limited the performances in the Championship of a man whose batting is described as stylish and correct and whose cuts could be exquisite. Teammate Roy Smith would write of their time together in the Somerset Second XI, noting that 'Graham Tripp and I roomed together on away games and I spent time trying to calm him. He could be tense about his batting and I appreciated how that could affect a player.'

Short of stature, Graham was dependent on a sound technique. Although he continued to score very heavily for the Second XI, topping the batting averages twice in the late 1950s, his first-class average over thirty-four matches between 1955 and 1959 was 12.72 including two half-centuries. His performances as an athletic out-fielder were never in question, though. Released by Somerset at the end of the 1959 season, he threw in his lot with Devon until 1964, continuing to enjoy club cricket for Clevedon CC and later for Bristol Optimists CC.

Graham also played football for a number of seasons for Clevedon AFC and was in the town's hockey team. He also reached county standard at badminton. In later life he would turn to golf.

His working life was spent with the Brockley Timber Company, based in Clevedon. The raw materials for the saw mills were imported from a variety of sources including Europe and Thailand and the timber was sold on to the retail trade. The company was taken over by Rexmore, based in Liverpool, but, having risen to become a director, Graham remained with the company until his retirement.

He was married in 1958 to Ann Colman, a teacher in Exeter when they met, and they would have a son and daughter. At the time of writing, Graham continues to live in the small town he has been able to call home since his birth. He remains an active member of the Somerset Former Players' Association.

408
Kenneth Ernest Palmer
29 June 1955 v. Middlesex, Bath

Ken Palmer, who was awarded an MBE for his services to cricket in 2003, will be remembered by many as an umpire who stood for thirty-one years, including in twenty-two Test Matches, but those who saw him in his prime as a player will recall a fine all-rounder who in 1961 became, at twenty-four, the youngest ever Somerset player to have achieved the double of 100 wickets and 1,000 runs. The following year, Bill Alley would become, at forty-three, the oldest. They remain the only two Somerset cricketers to have done so since the Second World War.

Ken was born in Winchester on 22 April 1937 but he was to all intents and purposes a Devizes boy. His father Henry Ernest Palmer and his mother Cecilia (née Rhapps) had been married the previous year and worked at the County Mental Hospital in Roundway, near Devizes, Henry as a store man and Cecilia as a nurse.

On the basis of his birthplace, Ken went for trials with Hampshire but was not offered any terms. When he came to Somerset's attention as a seventeen-year-old, he was a batsman, noted for his doggedness and what Eric Hill, writing in the *Somerset County Gazette*, called 'unmistakeable signs of a cricket temperament'. Ken's development into a fast-medium bowler was gradual, as steady and purposeful as one of his innings. He hands the credit to Maurice Tremlett, who patiently taught him how to swing the ball. Former teammate Terry Willetts jokes that 'Ken was the best person I knew at picking the seam. Back then they took a more relaxed view but he had this ability to do it with one hand that was really impressive!'

Between 1955 and 1969 he would play 302 times for Somerset. His batting yielded an average of 20.67 and remained steady, with no discernible trajectory in performance. The fact that Ken was not out in approximately 18% of his innings is evidence of his technical correctness and determination to make bowlers work for his wicket. His bowling showed a marked improvement after a modest start. He would take over 100

Ken Palmer – the youngest Somerset player to achieve the double of 100 wickets and 1,000 runs. SOMERSET CRICKET MUSEUM

wickets in a season four times and narrowly missed out on another two occasions. In all, he took 837 wickets at 21.10. Although fast-medium, he had the ability to unsettle and surprise batsmen with the way the ball sometimes sped off the wicket and he came close to Test recognition on two occasions in 1963 when he was named in the twelve but not selected. He was arguably at the height of his powers at the time, winning the inaugural national Single Wicket competition. His chance, when it came, was unexpected and anti-climactic. Having in earlier seasons been on tours with a Commonwealth side and a Rothman's Cavaliers team, he had opted to ply his trade as the pro and coach for Johannesburg League side Old Marists when he was called up for the game in Port Elizabeth by an injury-ravaged England team for the Fifth Test of the 1964-5 series in South Africa. On a placid wicket he scored 10 runs and took only one wicket at a cost of 189 runs over two innings.

Peter Roebuck cites one-day cricket as having rung the death knell for Ken's career, observing that neither being hit around the ground by batsmen chancing their arm nor having to go in and slog for a few overs at the end of an innings appealed, so that he called it a day in 1969.

Ken had been married in 1962 to Joy Valerie (née Gilbert). Their son, Gary, would play fifty-four first-class games for Somerset and later become a respected coach, credited with turning around the form of former England Test captain, Alastair Cook. In the early years of his cricketing career, Ken had worked during the winters initially alongside brother, Roy, at Marshalsea's Garage in the car repair workshop and later at Dunn's Motors Ltd, managed by the Dunn family, who remain supporters of Somerset cricket. Coaching roles had followed and after his playing days were over, Ken went on to become a first-class umpire, invited onto the Test Match panel and standing for more than thirty years. With twenty-two Tests and twenty-three one-day internationals under his belt, he was a popular and well-regarded umpire though he once courted controversy with the Pakistan team when failing to give Graham Gooch run out, with replays showing that the Essex and England batsman was well out of his ground, demonstrating that even the more experienced among officials are capable of human error.

Following the sad loss of his wife, Joy, to cancer in 1988, Ken found love again and was married to Jacqueline Jotcham, known as Jackie, in 1994. In his eighties at the time of writing, Ken is a regular at the County Ground and a source of many an anecdote about his playing days. He arrived as a teenage batsman expected to sweep the stands after practice and allowed a break at lunch for sandwiches and a bottle of milk. He had developed into one of the County Championship's leading all-rounders by the mid-1960s. And then for many years he was a highly-regarded match official. He is now one of the elder statesmen of the club he gave sterling service to.

Ken Palmer (centre) as England's twelfth man in 1963, photographed with the Duke of Edinburgh and Fred Titmus. He played 302 times for Somerset and once for England.
SOMERSET CRICKET MUSEUM

409
Kenneth David Biddulph
13 July 1955 v. Worcestershire, Taunton

Born in Chingford, Essex, on 29 May 1932, Ken was the son of William Edward Biddulph, a travelling salesman who sold furniture and was married to May (née Williams). Ken had begun his working life in the Borough Treasurer's Department in Chingford and honed his skills as a bowler while an *Evening News* colt at Alf Gover's Cricket School. The London newspaper had set up a scheme whereby they sponsored promising local cricketers. Despite having no previous links with Somerset, he was invited to the County Ground – no doubt at the behest of Arthur Wellard, who coached with Alf – as the county searched for a quick bowler to help share the burden with Bryan Lobb. Assuredly a tail-end batsman, Ken would later recount the gruff words of encouragement he received from Fred Trueman. As David Foot reports, Fred's advice amounted to: 'Don't worry, Kenny. You'll get into that bloody team for your batting!'

He made his debut for the Second XI in 1954 and began playing first-class cricket in 1955, although it was not until Bryan Lobb's departure at the end of the 1958 season that he became a regular. Ken bowled at fast-medium pace and generally relied on in-swing, delivering the ball from wide in the crease. Not all quick bowlers are possessed of a mean streak but Ken Biddulph, described by Peter Roebuck as 'a chirpy Cockney' who 'surprised local Somerset players by using coat hangers for his clothes' was perhaps too pleasant and easy-going a man to bowl with enough venom. According to Roebuck, he was 'in the habit of stopping just before delivery' but he nevertheless enjoyed a bountiful season in 1960 when he claimed 83 wickets. His progress in learning how to exploit the new ball would have been hampered by the poverty-stricken county's reluctance to waste any resources. Having been given an already well-worn practice ball, Ken would relate that 'it was my ball and I was responsible for it. I'd take it home and polish it up every evening. By the

Ken Biddulph – 'The sports shop in Taunton had a cut-out of me in the window, bowling'.

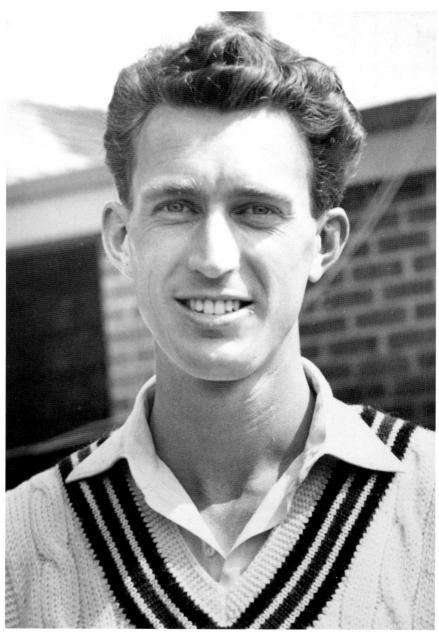

Ken Biddulph – an amiable opening bowler who hailed from Chingford in Essex.
SOMERSET CRICKET MUSEUM

middle of July it was getting a bit tatty, so I went to see if there was any chance of another one.' The response of the Somerset Secretary Dicky Robinson was: 'Another? You've only had that this summer.'

In total Ken would claim 270 wickets at 27.61 apiece over the course of ninety-one matches, at which point he departed to play league cricket for Hartlepool CC. He would reveal in conversation with writer Stephen Chalke that he quickly came to grips with the brutal finality of a terminated contract. In Ken's words: 'The sports shop in Taunton had a cut-out of me in the window, bowling. And the next time I walked past, it had gone.' At Hartlepool, he combined his club matches with appearances between 1962 and 1972 for Durham CCC, at the time a Minor Counties side.

Ken Biddulph – advised by Fred Trueman: 'Don't worry, Kenny. You'll get into that bloody team for your batting!' SOMERSET CRICKET MUSEUM

Married in 1958 to Norma McLaren, he would have a daughter. For a while he provided for his family by becoming a brewery rep and subsequently a publican, encouraged to make the switch by former Somerset teammate and fellow licensee, Malcolm Walker. Then in 1984 Ken took up a post as the cricket and squash coach at Wycliffe College in Gloucestershire, remaining there until 1992. Thereafter, while residing at Amberley, he worked as a coach for the Gloucestershire Cricket Association Men's and Ladies' XIs and for a variety of clubs and individuals on a freelance basis. He also organised Easter coaching weekends which drew customers from around the country. He was appointed chief coach of 3-D Cricket, fronted by Tom Graveney. The title was perhaps rather grander than the role, which involved Ken's offering his services on a freelance basis. He would continue to ply his trade, never likely to become rich, but eking a living inspiring others and doing what he enjoyed. Award-winning author Stephen Chalke recalls his conversations with Ken in his book *A Long Half Hour*. Stephen says of this amiable Somerset cricketer that 'he was the most perceptive of coaches with a great sense of fun. He was also a superb raconteur, with stories of his playing days that always seemed to end with him putting himself down. It was his storytelling that inspired me to become a cricket writer.'

After suffering a heart attack at his home in Amberley, Ken was taken to hospital in Oxford, where he died on 7 January 2003 at the age of seventy, still a popular character, fondly remembered by the many whose paths he had crossed and whose lives he had brightened as a player, a coach or a friend.

191

410
Gwynfor Lloyd Williams
10 August 1955 v. Surrey, Weston-super-Mare

G. Lloyd Williams

Born in Kidwelly, Carmarthenshire on 30 May 1925, Lloyd was the son of Thomas Lloyd Williams, a tax inspector, married to Gladys (née Williams). Lloyd was educated at Christ College, Brecon, before being offered a place at Brasenose College, Oxford, to study Classics but his entry was delayed when he joined the 24th Regiment of the South Wales Borderers in 1943. After the cessation of hostilities he took up his place at Brasenose and was invited to play for Oxford Authentics but never managed to break into the First XI. Although a good rugby player, he missed out on representing the Varsity team at that game, too, but had the compensation of playing table tennis for Oxford University.

After graduating, Lloyd would spend his working life as a Classics teacher, initially at Downside and then – after a two-year spell at Rendcomb College, near Cirencester – for a quarter of a century from 1961 until 1986 at Millfield School, following an invitation from R. J. O. Meyer, the school's maverick founder and headmaster.

While at Downside, Lloyd had turned out regularly for Bath CC and was appointed captain for their centenary season of 1959. He would also play occasional representative games for a Glamorgan XI. David Smith, who has written a history of Lloyd's alma mater, Christ College, and remained a close friend, says of Lloyd that he 'firmly believed in playing back to get a longer look at the ball' and adds that 'his style was correct and neat and he used his feet well against slow bowlers'.

Word of Lloyd's prowess reached Bill Andrews, who invited him to the nets at the County Ground in April 1955. He became an important member of the Somerset Second XI, and was averaging more than 50.00, after scoring 139 against Wiltshire, when he was invited to join the First XI. He had the misfortune to enjoy his brief experience of first-class cricket over a Weston-super-Mare Festival which proved an unmitigated disaster for Somerset. On a wicket not fit for purpose, Tony Lock and Alec Bedser both wreaked havoc as Somerset were twice skittled out. Lloyd had contributed no runs in a first innings total of 36. Things were no better against Glamorgan, who thrashed Somerset by an innings, although Lloyd had the satisfaction of top-scoring in the first innings with 24. Promoted to opener in the third and final game, he was not alone in failing in both innings. Hampshire and England bowler Derek Shackleton returned figures of 8 for 4 in the first innings and 6 for 25 in the second. As Lloyd would later remark with his usual droll wit, Somerset were a pretty poor side anyway, so that 'having to play on a loose fitting carpet' was only ever likely to end in tears. He came away with an average of 5.00, which was rather more than most of his teammates had mustered over the three matches. As he would later observe: 'I should have played at Taunton: I'd have got runs there!' As a footnote, in his next match, having returned to the Second XI for the fixture against Dorset, he played his part in the dismissal of Micky Walford when the ball was edged and Lloyd was rendered unconscious while the ball ricocheted off his head to the safe hands of John Baker at first slip.

His judgement was clearly not in any way impaired by the blow, given that he had the good sense to be married in

Lloyd Williams – his three games for Somerset were on an unplayable pitch at Weston-super-Mare.
COURTESY OF ANN WILLIAMS

1961 to fellow teacher Elisabeth Ann Read, known as Ann, whose father was an ecclesiastical sculptor, well known in the West Country. Ann was a successful sportswoman, being a county tennis player who would go on to play hockey for England. The couple, who would have two children, became an integral part of the Millfield School community and as well as teaching Classics, Lloyd was a housemaster for sixteen years and the master in charge of cricket in the 1960s. He was proud of the fact that during his eight years overseeing the First XI, the school produced ten first-class players, including the likes of Paul Terry, Peter Roebuck and David Graveney.

When not overseeing school cricket, he played for Somerset Stragglers and for a strong Morlands club side in Glastonbury, playing his part in mentoring up-and-coming youngsters such as Graham Burgess and Peter Denning, both of whom attended Millfield. He was also an accomplished squash player who represented Somer-

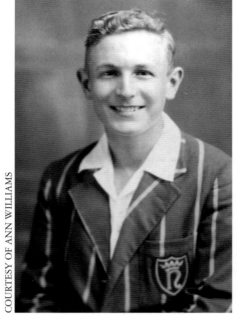

Lloyd Williams – a graduate of Brasenose, Oxford, he taught Classics and coached the First XI at Millfield School for many years.

set on a number of occasions from 1963 until 1967.

By 1986, when he had reached the age of sixty-one, he retired from the teaching profession. He would admit that he 'wasn't enjoying teaching any more'. Instead, he put his erudition and attention to grammatical detail to good effect by becoming a proof-reader for a number of writers, among them Leslie Thomas and Dame Barbara Cartland. It is not recorded whether or not he found the larger-than-life step-grand-mother of Diana Princess of Wales more difficult to handle than his charges at Mill-field.

Lloyd died on 18 July 2007 at Musgrove Park Hospital, Taunton, as a result of heart problems. He was eighty-two years old. An obituary issued by MCC (of whom he was elected a member in 1962) describes him as 'outgoing, but essentially a private man with high integrity' who would be 'remembered for his puckish sense of humour and quick wit'. Mick Hanna, who played with Lloyd on many occasions confirms that he was 'quiet and likeable, a great teacher and a fine club player'.

Lloyd's brief taste of the first-class game had been a double-edged sword: a night-mare at the time but, with the benefit of hindsight, a source of gentle, wry amusement for a wry, amusing and gentle man.

1956

"The man presented with the job was Maurice Tremlett, the county's first professional captain … I wouldn't have taken that job had there been a life pension to go with it. He led the side for four years. And in that time he achieved the next to impossible and turned Somerset into a cricket team. He was sneered at, moaned at, sniped at, but he shrugged it all off and got on with doing what I shall always rate as a magnificent job … He was never popular with those running the club, because he treated committee members in the same off-handed manner that they treated their players. I admired him for it."

Colin McCool in *Cricket is a Game*

Championship Position: 15 of 17

Professional and local boy Maurice Tremlett was appointed with some reluctance on the part of the club officials to the role of captain and thus the seeds of recovery were sown. The team no longer needed to carry a lame duck leader who inspired resentment rather than uplifting performances.

Despite having turned forty, Colin McCool, a seasoned Australian Test all-rounder, introduced class and discipline to proceedings and topped the batting averages with 1,966 runs. The *Northern Daily Mail* notes that he 'brought colour and dash to Somerset cricket that has been lacking since the retirement of Harold Gimblett'. Batting stylishly, Peter Wight was also beginning to demonstrate what an asset he would become. McCool's fellow Australian, John McMahon, exceeded 100 wickets and was ably supported by Bryan Lobb. The bowling of Brian Langford and Colin McCool also played its part and for the first time in what was beginning to seem like an eternity, the team had hauled themselves off the bottom of the table.

Apart from McCool, the only other debutant was Dennis Silk, a Cambridge blue and a teacher who appeared in seven matches during the summer vacation. As with Micky Walford before him, here was an amateur included in the team on the basis of merit.

411
Colin Leslie McCool
5 May 1956 v. Essex, Taunton

[signature: Colin McCool]

Colin McCool was born in the Paddington district of Sydney on 9 December 1916. He was the son of Neil McCool and Amy (née Blake) who had been married in 1902 in Gouldburn, a town in New South Wales. His five seasons with Somerset on the opposite side of the globe, some four decades later, would prove successful in cricketing terms, though he would later write that those years were not the happiest of his life.

An all-rounder who bowled leg-breaks with an unusual low-slung action and batted with a preponderance of shots square of the wicket – whether forceful cuts or hook shots – he was short, stockily-built and pugnacious. He attended Crown Street State School, whose most famed alumnus was Victor Trumper. Colin would recall that his school days were dominated by the memory of Trumper, but he developed his own style which by no stretch of the imagination could be compared to that of the master batsman. He was late to the first-class game, making his debut for New South Wales early in 1940 at the age of twenty-three and enjoying further appearances for them in the 1940-41 season in matches arranged to raise money for the war effort. Progress was then stalled by his involvement in the Second World War. Having enlisted in September 1941 he served with 33 Squadron in the Royal Australian Air Force. Stationed in New Guinea, he rose to the rank of flight lieutenant.

After the war he lived in and represented Queensland and made his first Test appearance against New Zealand. Having subsequently taken nine wickets against the England touring side ahead of the 1946-7 Ashes series, he was selected to play for Australia again that season. During the series he would perform strongly with bat and ball. A further personal triumph was that having been promised one pound by a Melbourne businessman for every run he scored in the Third Test at the MCG, he notched up a century and was thus able to pay the deposit for a house which he would share with the childhood sweetheart he had married in 1943, Dorothy Evelyn (née Yabsley). Colin remained an integral part of the Australian national side but although he was a member of 'The Invincibles' who toured England in 1948, he was not selected to play in the Ashes fixtures as a result of a torn spinning finger. He would remain saddened but philosophical about his omission. A successful tour of South Africa would follow but that marked the end of his Test career, despite continued success in Sheffield Shield cricket.

Knowing that his international playing days were behind him, Colin then decided that his prime consideration was to provide for his family. By the time he left Sydney

Colin McCool – came to Somerset after a distinguished career: he had been a member of the Australian 'Invincibles' who toured England in 1948. SOMERSET CRICKET MUSEUM

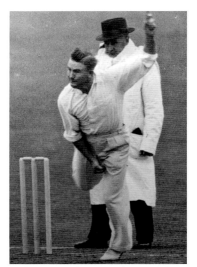

Colin McCool – a single-minded individual whose overwhelming motivation was to perform to the very best of his ability.

in 1953, bound for Tilbury Docks aboard the *Strathmore*, he and Dorothy had three young children with them. A fourth, Russ, would later be born in Taunton and would go on to play for the county. Colin played for two seasons with East Lancashire CC and was scheduled to play county cricket for Somerset when the rules for registration were tightened so that he was obliged to play league cricket for a further year. He was taken on by Stockport CC, replacing Bill Dean, who had made one cameo appearance for Somerset. Colin's one season there was a huge success, given that he completed the double of 100 wickets and 1,000 runs and turned around the club's fortunes.

He covers the frosty reception he received from some quarters down in Somerset in his autobiography, *Cricket is a Game*. The book is revealing in the sense of how little Colin reveals about himself. He comes across as a distant observer of those around him and there is no doubt that here was a single-minded individual whose overwhelming motivation was to perform to the very best of his ability and not to suffer fools gladly. Many in Somerset doubted the wisdom of offering a contract to an ageing Australian whom some felt had left his best days behind. But if he had regrets about the move to what was in cricketing terms a sleepy backwater, then these in no way affected his performance. Over five seasons he played in 138 first-class matches, averaging 33.81 with the bat, including twelve centuries, and he took 219 wickets at 28.05 apiece. Some thought him a mercenary but his loyalty was never in doubt. There were rumours that he planned to desert the county and return home but they were wide of the mark. He had indeed briefly considered a return to Australia in the winter of 1957 as his wife's mother had endured a major operation earlier in the year but as he pointed out to Eric Hill: 'Since the Suez crisis has put fares up 25% and [my daughter] Robyn is now classed as an adult, if you do bump into someone who would put £1,500 in the kitty we should be delighted to accept. I must add that never did I consider going home for the winter and staying there unless the club no longer wanted me.' The dogged and outspoken Aussie was indeed a man of his word.

Throughout his five seasons he set an unflinching example of dedication for the younger pros and undoubtedly takes much of the credit for helping to drag Somerset from the abyss after years of underperformance. He did so not by loud exhortation but by a quiet and considered approach allied to the confidence to point out when someone was not giving their all, while accepting that not every player would hit the heights.

After retiring from first-class cricket at the end of the 1960 season and glad to be back home in his native Australia, he went into business as a market gardener at Umina Beach in New South Wales. He also continued to enjoy club cricket until the age of fifty-five, when rheumatism rendered his spinning fingers ineffective. He died at the age of sixty-nine on 5 April 1986 in Concord, New South Wales.

412
Dennis Raoul Whitehall Silk
8 August 1956 v. Sussex, Hove

Dennis Silk was born on 8 October 1931 in Eureka, California. His father, Claude Whitehall Silk, was married to Louise Emelda Dumoret. Often referred to as Louisa, she had been born in Spain but had emigrated with her family to the USA at the age of fourteen. Claude had opted for a career as a minister in the Episcopal Church (the North American branch of the Anglican Church), working in Montreal and then California, where Dennis, his fourth child, was born. Claude's work was primarily with the Native American communities and, having trained as a priest, he had returned to university to study medicine once he realised that his flock required medical help more than they needed spiritual guidance. He was never in one place for long, crossing continents while ministering to the needs of parishioners and patients. Claude would become a widower while Dennis was still a child, although he would be remarried in 1941, to Frances Annie Wesley (née Binder), a widow. Dennis was sent to England as a five-year-old and brought up by his grandmother in Bognor Regis. His connection with Somerset began when his grandmother died and an aunt was appointed his new guardian. She had retired to Kingston St Mary, near Taunton, and Dennis would spend his vacations with her while an undergraduate. His father, Claude, emigrated to Northern Rhodesia in 1959 with his second wife, Frances.

If Claude left his mark around the globe then his son, Dennis, would bring his considerable drive and energy to bear largely within the confines of England, which he would

199

Dennis Silk – 'a man of gentle voice, charm and authority.'

make his permanent home. Educated at Christ's Hospital, near Horsham, he won a place at Sidney Sussex College, Cambridge, to study History. An accomplished batsman and occasional leg-break bowler, he played regularly for Cambridge University, completing five centuries for them and winning blues each season from 1953 to 1955. Two of his centuries came against Oxford in successive years, a feat that ensured near-legendary status among the Cantabrians. He also played rugby – variously at full-back or centre three-quarter – for Cambridge University and Bath and in 1951 for Sussex. He won a rugby blue and a half blue for rugby fives.

Dennis was committed to a career in teaching, appearing as an amateur for Somerset while a schoolmaster at Marlborough College. Not steeped in the class system as many amateurs were, but equipped for life as a leader of men, he enjoyed a rare positive reputation amongst both the starchier members of the committee and the undervalued and underpaid pros. David Foot would describe him as 'a man of gentle voice, charm and authority; and if he hadn't put education first, he'd have been unanimous choice as captain of Somerset'. His ability to bridge the divide came to the fore when Somerset sacked four players including captain Maurice Tremlett and wicket-keeper Harold Stephenson after their 'scandalous' behaviour at the Grand Hotel, Swansea. Used to handling seemingly intractable problems, Dennis was able to engineer Tremlett's reinstatement and, perhaps having been quietly informed that the onus was now on the skipper to make a point, the players performed out of their skins the following season.

Between 1956 and 1960 he would appear for Somerset on thirty-three occasions, averaging 33.54 with the bat and scoring one century but failing to take a wicket with his occasional leg-breaks. He would also take part in MCC tours, the first to East Africa in 1957-8 under the captaincy of Freddie Brown, another in 1960-61 when Dennis led a tour of New Zealand and his last in 1967 when he was captain on a tour to Canada. His was thus a voice of experience when he became a prominent figure in the heated debate when MCC stood firm over South Africa's refusal to play a side that included

Basil D'Oliveira. His stated position was that 'we do not stand as the social conscience of Great Britain'. He was of the view that economic considerations are sometimes paramount, that to sit on a high horse is to risk an unpleasant fall. The counter arguments were led by Rev. David Sheppard. Dennis would later serve as President of MCC, who had relinquished management of Test Matches to the TCCB shortly after the D'Oliveira Affair. He would also chair the TCCB from 1994 until 1996.

Able to articulate the complex with great clarity, Dennis would write two books aimed at encouraging young cricketers. *Sport for Schools: Cricket* was published in 1964 and *Attacking Cricket: A Coaching Manual* followed a year later. Pelham Books had the good sense not to have asked Dennis to complete a companion volume on *Defensive Cricket*.

It is perhaps for his career as a teacher that he has gained most renown. Having established his reputation as an inspirational teacher at Marlborough College, he left in 1968 to take up his post as Warden of Radley College (his official title as headmaster). Many of his fellow head teachers regarded him as the finest principal of his generation and there is near-universal agreement that he transformed the school from a moribund institution to a public school of the first rank. In a history of the school, his twenty-three-year reign is recounted in glowing terms. After an unpromising conversation with the senior prefect on day one, where he was told that 'You're not going to find this school very easy, Sir,' we are informed that:

His energy blew away the country-club complacency of the past, and his dedication to hard work and all-round excellence proved infectious to masters and boys alike. If he remained formidable he was also approachable, and boys became used to the summons to a drink and a one-to-one chat on their birthdays. Academic standards rose; the arts flourished and so did rugby, cricket and rowing; parents queued to enter their sons.

Throughout his sojourn, his wife, Diana Merylin (née Milton), whom he had been married to in 1963, would prove a tower of strength. A market research assistant and the daughter of a company director, she would have four children with him.

For a great leader to be so judged, what follows him is as much a part of his legacy as his achievements during his tenure and Dennis played his part in securing Radley's future by setting up the Dennis Silk Foundation to fund or subsidise the education of talented pupils from poorer backgrounds who would not otherwise be able to attend the school. In 1995 he was awarded a CBE for services to cricket and education and he was made an Honorary Life Vice-President of MCC in 2000. At the time of writing, he is also President of the Siegfried Sassoon Fellowship, having enjoyed a long friendship with and written widely about the poet. He retains an active interest in his beloved Somerset CCC and is an Honorary Life Member. Dennis is able, at the age of eighty-five, to look back on a full and hugely fulfilling life in which he has brought vision and drive to everything he has turned his hand to and where personal success has been a bonus for a man who has endeavoured to enrich the lives of others.

1957

"While other teams fretted away worrying about the
destination of the Championships, we were content to
earn a reputation as the best social team in the country.
My word, how we enjoyed ourselves!"

Bill Alley in *Standing the Test of Time*

Championship Position: 8 of 17

Secretary Dicky Robinson acknowledged that the Somerset hierarchy had been complacent after a run of modest success in the immediate aftermath of the Second World War and 'now they are paying the penalty' and planned to address the lack of coaching and talent-spotting. He also acknowledged that although 'the aim must be to field a team of players who come from Somerset', there was a rider that 'as long as our players entertain, it does not matter where they come from'. In truth, captain Maurice Tremlett was in a tiny minority in being a local lad (born in Cheshire but brought up in Taunton) but the county was developing the knack of drawing on the experience of outsiders such as Colin McCool and now newcomer Bill Alley. 1957 must surely be regarded as the season when the corner had been turned.

Colin McCool was now giving solidity to the batting, although Dennis Silk, appearing for nine fixtures, topped the averages. Maurice Tremlett, Peter Wight and newcomer Bill Alley would all exceed 1,000 runs. Alley was the stand-out debutant. After successful careers in Australia and then the Lancashire Leagues, he came down to Somerset for what many thought would be his twilight years but surprised everyone with the runs, wickets and catches at gully that just kept coming, most spectacularly in 1961.

Among the other debutants, Tom Dickinson had come down from Lancashire and shaped well as a pace bowler but chose to pursue a teaching career instead. Roy Virgin would in time develop into an outstanding opening batsman. Chris Greetham – a dashing all-rounder – and Brian Roe – a dogged opening batsman – would make useful contributions. Alan Whitehead would find more fame as a Test umpire than as a player.

413
William Edward Alley
4 May 1957 v. Lancashire, Taunton

Bill Alley played cricket like a pugilist. When he batted, he smacked or thumped the ball with an ungainly but effective swipe. He never stroked it. When he took to the field he was unflinching in taking the fight to his opponents, though his stock-in-trade was the witty barb rather than any gamesmanship. And after the day's play, he would drink friends and opposing players under the table. As a young man, he had been involved in twenty-eight welterweight boxing bouts – all of which he had won – before having to retire from the sport when his jaw was broken in the nets at Sydney. He had taken the full force of a hook shot by Jock Livingstone that had left him in a coma, clinging to life.

He was brought up in Brooklyn, at the time a deprived part of Sydney, though he was born in hospital in the nearby town of Hornsby on 3 February 1919, the son of Edward Kempton Alley and his wife, Thelma Kathleen (née Foodey). The eldest of six children in a home too small for the whole family, Bill lived for much of his youth with his grandmother. Raised in a house with no electricity, he felt privileged to be one of the few children in his school whose parents could afford to buy him shoes. He would rise 'at the crack of dawn to chop wood and feed the chickens' and, by his own admission, struggled academically at school, finding himself often on the end of beatings from his teacher, 'a violent-tempered man named Newman'. If his childhood had hardened Bill, his experiences on leaving school at fourteen would toughen him further. He began work on an oyster farm before finding work drilling tunnels, employment that was deemed too important for him to join the war effort. Throughout it all, Bill had taken part in street games of cricket where his natural eye was apparent and his unorthodox, uncoached methods hugely successful. He was cricket-mad and recalled queuing for three hours to secure the autograph of Don Bradman, only to find on arriving at the desk that he was required to part with 7/6d. When not playing cricket, he was earning money to supplement his wages with boxing matches, which he later dismissed as mere local affairs.

Having turned sixteen, he subsequently shot up in height and blossomed as a batsman. Playing for his local town, who were sponsored by a retailer who offered a pair of shoes each time a player scored a century, he bagged eleven sets of footwear in his first season. Suddenly he had shoes aplenty. He continued to rise to the challenge

after he was spotted by Petersham CC and then at the age of twenty-six was invited to join the New South Wales side. With his unorthodox batting style, tending to play most balls to leg, wherever they pitched, and with no defence, he was obliged to make his critics eat their words at every stage. His success was such that he was tipped to play for Australia, though he narrowly missed out when his form fell away and he was then dogged by two seasons of injuries.

He was married by then to his first wife, Merle Irene Monica Fisher (known as Irene), a Brooklyn girl, but

Bill Alley – in 1961, at the age of forty-two, he astonished every-one with over 3,000 first-class runs: the following year he achieved 'the double'. SOMERSET CRICKET MUSEUM

tragedy struck when Irene died in 1946 during her second labour, two years after the birth of their son, Ken. His mother and his mother-in-law also died in the same year and Bill was in a quandary. He had gone from job to job during the winter months – blacksmith's striker, boilermaker's helper, cart-rimmer's assistant and even dance hall bouncer. Here he was, in his late-twenties, with time seemingly running out on his chances of making a living from cricket but he had a two-year-old son in tow. He had been approached by Leicestershire, whom he declined, and the Lancashire League side, Rawenstall CC, who were only prepared to offer a contract if he came alone. His sister and brother-in-law stepped in and offered to raise Ken, while Bill agreed a professional contract with Rawenstall CC. The journey to England was paid for by Australian cricketer Sid Barnes, a man famed for his generosity, who had earlier paid for the funerals of the three women in Alley's life.

Bill was about to confound any doubters who regarded him as in the autumn of his cricketing career and proved an outstanding success in Lancashire League cricket. He has written of the weight of responsibility that would fall on the shoulders of the pros as, pitted one against the other, they often carried their teammates. Whichever pro outperformed the other was in most cases on the winning side. Bill's experiences in the boxing ring had prepared him for these unflinching clashes and his natural ability, honed in Brooklyn, served him well. The ground collections each time he performed another match-winning feat were seeing off the threat of penury. The Australian selectors made it their policy to ostracise those men who had felt obliged to earn their living abroad. They were debarred from Test Matches. In Bill's case, he was even later refused entry to the Sydney Cricket Ground he had once graced until Keith Miller intervened and gave the authorities a piece of his mind in his own inimitable style.

If there was any doubt that England was now his home, this was extinguished when Bill was married in 1949 to Betty Cortman, a telephonist based in Rawenstall. They would have two children and Ken was welcomed into the family when Bill collected him from Sydney in 1949. A promising young cricketer, Ken would die in 1970 while serving in the Army in Germany when he was trapped in a tank as it caught fire.

Bill followed his time at Rawenstall with a five-year contract with Colne CC which he opted not to renew when he was denied the opportunity to earn supplementary income playing for a Sunday Australian XI. He was by now thirty-four but such was his outstanding success that six first-class counties (including Somerset) approached him. He rejected them all, opting instead to spend four years with Blackpool CC. Here, he continued to make the headlines with a series of match-winning performances. In 1957, Somerset came in with a renewed offer of a three-year contract and a testimonial. Bill would later admit that he had never been to Somerset but thought it the most evocative name of any English county and, not being one to dwell on a decision, went with the offer. He also admits to falling in love at first sight with the place and knowing that he would never wish to live anywhere else. Any thoughts that the thirty-eight year old was past his prime or not up to the demands of first-class cricket would prove groundless. Somerset had taken a calculated but inspired gamble. At the end of his initial three-year spell, both parties had reason to be pleased and his contract was extended. Over the course of 350 matches between 1957 and 1968 he would compile 16,644 runs at 30.48 and would take 738 wickets at 22.03

Bill Alley – a Test umpire regarded as a 'strong character, able to give firm, clear decisions at the big occasion'.

apiece. In his *annus mirabilis* of 1961 he amassed over 3,000 runs and took 62 wickets. He was named a *Wisden* Cricketer of the Year in 1962 on the strength of this performance and in that year, by then aged forty-three, he achieved the double with 1915 runs and 112 wickets. As was so often the case, Somerset later made a hash of things when offering him the opportunity to play only in limited overs games. The explanation was that the county needed to bring in some young blood. It was not a financially viable proposition for him and so he walked away. Bill would observe wryly in his autobiography *Standing the Test of Time* that the youngsters drafted over the subsequent years included Tom Cartwright, Jim Parks and Brian Close, whose combined age at the times of their arrival was approximately 116.

If he was a latecomer to the Championship stage, then his elevation to the top of the umpiring tree was in stark contrast. Bill was sought out as a 'strong character, able to give firm, clear decisions at the big occasion'. His tenure was not without controversy. In particular, his decision to award three LBW decisions against Leicestershire in the 1974 Benson & Hedges Final led to a hostile reception when he next umpired at Grace Road. He was, however, widely praised for his umpiring skills, his trademark 'That's out' giving authority and clarity to his decisions. He was finally retired from the umpires list at the age of sixty-five in 1984. For a while he was employed by Blundell's School, acting as the match day host for visitors to their private box at Somerset's County Ground. He also wrote his second autobiography (his first such venture, *My Incredible Innings*, having been published in 1969). This time, publication was delayed after the Secretary of the TCCB, Donald Carr, considered Alley's views too forthright. *Standing the Test of Time* is an appropriate double entendre for a player who defied the ageing process and then stood with great authority as a Test Match umpire. Donald Carr's judgement has stood the test of time less well in this instance, given that Bill's observations seem surprising polite with the passing of the years.

He retired to his 2-acre smallholding in Adsborough, not far from Taunton and purchased from the proceeds of his benefit year. He had called it 'Down Under'. His knees were troubling him by then and were replaced, but he still rose early to see to his chickens, just as he had done as a boy back in Brooklyn. In the intervening years he had derived pleasure and pounds aplenty from the game he loved. This larger-than-life personality had been embraced by the folks of Somerset as warmly as he had embraced his adoptive county. He continued to watch Somerset and towards the end of his life could often be found in front of the Stragglers Pavilion, with Betty by his side and Bill happy to venture opinions on the game. He died in Taunton at the age of eighty-five on 26 November 2004.

414

Roy Thomas Virgin
29 May 1957 v. Worcestershire, Taunton

Roy Virgin

Born in Taunton on 26 August 1939, Roy was the second of five children of Sidney Lawrence Virgin and his wife Gertrude Violet (née Ousley). Sidney worked for British Rail on track maintenance, in charge of a small group of men, and ran the British Rail Taunton cricket team for many years, occasionally roping in a young Roy and his brother. Educated at Huish's Grammar School, Roy confirms that he received no formal coaching until he was approached by Somerset, having shown early promise as a wicket-keeper batsman. Although he would become a slip fielder, his experiences behind the stumps proved beneficial when he reprised the role on a number of occasions in limited-overs cricket.

He was highly rated by Somerset but at this stage of his career, he was 'a prodder', rather than the attacking opening batsman he would become. Once he had reached the Under 15s, he was taken under the wing of Somerset pro David Kitson, who expressed horror at the bat Roy was using. It was 'heavy as hell, saturated in oil, and borrowed from the Railways', in Roy's words. It was immediately replaced. Progress through the ranks continued as he absorbed lessons from more experienced pros such as Colin McCool, who would write that 'he will be a good player, make no mistake about it, and with [Graham] Atkinson he forms a combination that will be the backbone of Somerset'. They were indeed a fine pair of openers who complemented one another - Roy strong on the off-side and Graham predominantly a leg-side player – but while Graham appeared in the latter stages of his career suddenly to become constricted and consumed by doubt, Roy's batting traced the opposing trajectory. Roy is convinced that the changes in fortune were primarily attributable to confidence. He cites an innings against Northants at Kettering in 1970 in the John Player League as the catalyst. He had made 77 not out and it was as if a switch had been flicked and thereafter he carried with him a new-found belief.

After a promising start to his first-class career and then having been given an extended and successful run after an injury to Geoff Lomax, he left for National Service with the Somerset & Cornwall Light Infantry, including time in Gibraltar, Germany and, perhaps less excitingly, in Bodmin. Having returned to civilian life he was consistently among the runs, regularly topping 1,000 each season until in 1970 there was a sudden full flowering of his talent with over 2,000 runs, seven first-class centuries and an average approaching 50.00. As *Wisden* noted, he was now scoring 'fifty percent

Roy Virgin – 'he will be a good player, make no mistake about it'.
SOMERSET CRICKET MUSEUM

more runs than usual, about fifty percent faster'. He was chosen as a *Wisden* Cricketer of the Year, the citation noting that he had 'emerged from worthy competence into a realisation of potential with a great deal more achievement yet awaiting him'. He was also spoken of as a potential England player but the competition for opening slots was intense at the time.

He grew disenchanted with the Somerset hierarchy during the 1972 season, feeling, with good cause, that his commitment and years of valuable service were being taken for granted. When more than one member of the Committee criticised him for a temporary loss of form rather than offering support, he knew the time was right to look elsewhere. He had amassed 15,458 runs in 321 appearances for Somerset at 28.52 and taken four wickets at 80.25 with his occasional leg-breaks. It remains a sad indictment of the powers that be that Roy should ever have left the county he had supported since childhood and served so well. His good friend Bob Cottam, who had already agreed terms with Northamptonshire, acted as intermediary and he joined them in 1973. After a steady start, 1974 would prove another wondrous season with nearly 2,000 first-class runs and an average of 56.94. He would remain with his new county

Roy and Ann Virgin on their wedding day in 1960. COURTESY OF ROY & ANN VIRGIN

for a total of five seasons until his retirement at the age of thirty-eight. His close fielding was noteworthy, too, with Roy demonstrating the fearlessness and reflexes that would become associated with his batsmanship. In 1964, in the days when the position of first slip was bagged by a senior pro or amateur, he was fielding at short-leg when he took the full force of a hook shot by former teammate Geoff Keith and suffered a broken nose. He was back at short-leg after missing only one match. His 415 first-class catches are as lasting a testament as his thirty-seven centuries to his value as a player who made incisive contributions.

Roy Virgin – 1970 saw a full flowering of his talent with 'fifty percent more runs than usual, about fifty percent faster'. COURTESY OF ROY & ANN VIRGIN

He had been married in Taunton in 1960 to Margaret Ann (née Thresher), known as Ann, whom he had first seen at a YMCA dance in Taunton in 1957. Ann and Roy would enjoy a long and happy marriage and would have three sons. Always aware that a career as a professional would be insufficient in itself, he found winter work, firstly at Pearsall's of Taunton, who were silk throwsters, and then for ten winters at the County Hall in the town, in clerical work, undertaking a Diploma in Municipal Administration. He was also a successful footballer and regular goal scorer in local club matches in his younger days. Having made Northamptonshire his new home, he was offered part-time work with engine manufacturers Blackwood Hodge and joined them on a full-time basis in 1977 as Parts Manager before heading the export side of the business. He remained in the role until the company was taken over in 1990. He retained his interest in cricket, playing for Walsall CC in the Birmingham League for six years and later joining the Northants committee, acting as Cricket Chairman for five years.

Roy still follows the fortunes of his two clubs and looks back with fondness and a wry sense of humour at his time as a first-class cricketer, smiling at the memories. He recalls the time in 1972 when he strode out to bat against Worcestershire minus the all-important bat. Having retrieved it, he heard a spectator call out 'You won't be needing that'. After leaving his first three deliveries, all out-swingers bowled by Vanburn Holder, he shouldered arms to Holder's fourth delivery, which swung back and removed his off stump. 'Told you so', came the voice from the members' enclosure as Roy walked disconsolately back to the pavilion. Or there was the match against Gloucestershire where Roy and Merv Kitchen were opening together. Both by then stockily built and normally reliant on boundaries to save their breath, they had unusually built up a partnership as sizeable as their combined waistlines in singles and twos when opposing skipper Tony Brown remarked: 'We won't need the heavy roller with these two running up and down the track.' Roy chuckles at the memory, as vivid as the glorious moments when he delighted the Somerset faithful with centuries — peppered with drives bisecting the off-side field — that will linger long on the minds of those who witnessed them.

415
Christopher Herbert Millington Greetham
8 June 1957 v. Gloucestershire, Taunton

His surname is pronounced Greet-ham. Born on 28 August 1936 in Wargrave, Berkshire, Chris was the son of Albert Hector Greetham, known as Hector, a garage manager married to Phyllis Maxine (née Smith), the daughter of a poultry farmer. Hector, who would later retire with Phyllis to Devon, was able to use his contacts to provide his son with a supply of the sports cars that became his trademark accessory. Chris would cut a dashing figure arriving at the County Ground in his Red Jaguar XK 140 or his Austin Healey.

Educated at Maidenhead College and then Reading Collegiate, he was late to grow, possibly as a result of childhood asthma, and as a schoolboy played as a wicket-keeper batsman, never bowling at that stage. Even before he shot up in height in his late teens, he was an aggressive batsman with tremendous strength in his wrists and forearms and by the age of fifteen he was appearing for the Berkshire Under-19s. An all-round sportsman, Chris excelled at tennis, table-tennis and football and would also later go on to win a boxing medal while undertaking his National Service. He had been a regular at the Chiswick Indoor Cricket School and was recommended to Somerset by them. In the summer of 1953, aged sixteen, he began to play for Somerset

Second XI, initially as a forceful middle-order batsman and occasional wicket-keeper, although in time he forsook the keeper's gloves and developed into a genuine all-rounder, bowling at medium pace.

He broke into the First XI in 1957 but, like so many other pros, was obliged to find off-season work where he could. In the winter of 1958 he worked as a handyman at the Bray Film Studios and once stepped into the breach as an extra, playing the part of a prisoner of war in the film *Camp on Blood Island*. The story became embellished over the years with the handsome, fair-haired cricketer being talked up as a regular film extra. David Foot refers to him as a 'diamond sorter and a teacher and – much more appealing to us journalists – a film extra'. The reference to his having been a diamond sorter is equally an exaggeration in that he spent a very brief period working for the Diamond Corporation, as did his sister. In truth the only other career that Chris had considered was as a footballer. After trials with Bristol Rovers, he made it into their Reserves and later played for Wycombe Wanderers as a midfielder. For a while he was also offered off-season employment by the West Somerset Bacon Company as a sales representative. More predictable, perhaps, were winter stints coaching students while based at Cape Town and Stellenbosch Universities from 1961-2 until 1964-5. On the last two occasions he was accompanied by his wife, Wendy (née Wilday), the

Chris Greetham coaching in 1961 at Sea Point Boys' Junior School in Cape Town.
SOMERSET CRICKET MUSEUM

Chris Greetham – 'he moved with the grace of a thoroughbred'. SOMERSET CRICKET MUSEUM

daughter of an ophthalmic optician from Taunton. Chris and Wendy had been married in1963 and would have a son and daughter, enjoying fifty-four years of happy marriage.

Between 1957 and 1966, by which time his form had deserted him, he would play in 205 first-class matches for Somerset and average 21.97 with the bat, always looking to push the score along and completing five centuries. Of particular delight to supporters were his cleanly-struck sixes. He would frequently despatch the ball to the River Tone or the St James's Cemetery beside the County Ground and other examples of his prodigious six-hitting were the time he cleared Father Time at Lord's and the occasion a huge blow landed on an open-topped bus outside The Oval. 195 wickets were claimed at 28.35 and he was also regarded as a superb fielder in the covers with the arrow-like throw of the naturally athletic. There is a sense that Chris never quite fulfilled his potential. Colin Atkinson would write that 'he moved with the grace of a thoroughbred and sometimes batted (especially) and bowled like a world-beater'. One such moment had been his part in a record ninth-wicket stand of 183 with Harold Stephenson against Leicestershire at Weston-super-Mare, all the more laudable given that Somerset were reeling on 145 for 8 at the time. Peter Roebuck was of the view that Chris's figures were adversely affected by having to play second fiddle to Bill Alley and losing out in the choice of when to bowl and from which end. It has been noted that at the sight of a green track, Bill would insist on being handed the ball.

After leaving Somerset, Chris was employed for a season by Torquay CC as their pro, leading to an invitation to play for Devon. Perhaps he felt that he had a point to prove in his last game for Devon when he scored 92 against Somerset Second XI.

If cricket was his first love as a young man, he turned increasingly to golf, both as a player and an administrator. He took up the sport in the 1960s, becoming a member of the Taunton & Pickeridge Club before joining the Stover Club near Newton Abbot, where he was appointed captain in 1976. He became Secretary of the Exeter Golf and Country Club at Topsham from 1984 and after ten years in the role, he enjoyed a similar stint at La Moye Golf Club in Jersey. After returning to the mainland following his retirement, he became a familiar figure playing as a senior for East Devon Golf Club.

Having retired to Wrington, he died at home at the age of eighty on 13 March 2017 after suffering for a while from melanoma. He is survived by his wife Wendy, and their two children. His lifelong friend, Trevor Tollerfield, says of Chris that 'he was a charming fellow, the nicest person you could wish to meet. He was aggressive on the field of play but passive off it and well-liked.' Journalist and broadcaster, John Mason, also contrasted the uninhibited adventurer at the batting crease to the man himself who was 'modest to the point of self-effacement'.

416
Brian Roe
24 July 1957 v. Kent, Taunton

Teammates and opponents alike all knew Brian as 'Chico'. Diminutive and with boyish looks, that, in the words of David Foot, led 'older ladies on the West Country boundaries to feel they wanted to mother him', he was a dogged rather than a watchable opener whom bowlers respected for his tenacity. Bob Cottam, Hampshire's opening bowler while Brian was a first-class player and later a respected coach, observed that 'Chico ... was fiercely competitive and wouldn't give his wicket away' noting of his style that there was 'nothing fussy or flash, and when you looked at the stats at the end of the season he always had a stack of runs'.

Brian was born on 27 January 1939 in Cleethorpes, Lincolnshire, the eighth and last child of Geoffrey John Cyril Sinclair Roe and his wife Nora (née Clarkson). Having inherited a surfeit of Christian names, Geoffrey also took on a watch and clock repair business, following in the footsteps of his own father. He had retired to Barnstaple in North Devon by the time Brian reached his teens. Something of a schoolboy prodigy, Brian came to Somerset's attention as a fourteen-year-old when he was sent down to the County Ground for a trial by his headmaster, a Mr Heppenstall. He would make his debut in the Somerset Second XI at the age of fifteen. Always an accumulator of runs, Brian is described by Peter Roebuck as 'a bubbly, cheerful fellow utterly unprepared to give his wicket away easily, however witheringly a fast bowler might stare at his tiny frame'. Sadly, bubbly was not an adjective that could ever be applied to his batting. Limpet-like would be more apt. Brian's erstwhile coach Bill Andrews would recount a tale (which merits the usual warnings that Bill's tales sometimes grew taller with each telling) of a friendly fixture played in bitterly cold conditions when umpire Alec Skelding was officiating and Brian was determined to see out the day's play, giving nothing away but making few if any runs, until he was given out LBW. Brian is said to have later remarked to Skelding that he felt he wasn't out, whereupon he was told: 'Maybe, lad, but I was worried that if you'd stayed out there any longer you'd have caught pneumonia.'

Over the course of 131 first-class matches for Somerset between 1957 and 1966 – interrupted by two years of National Service with the RAF in 1959 and 1960, when he appeared for Combined Services – Brian averaged 22.39, scoring four centuries. He also made valuable contributions as a fine and fleet-footed outfielder. Although offered a contract extension in 1967, he declined on the basis that he needed greater job security. Married in 1964 to Marlene (née Miller), with whom he would have two children,

Brian Roe, Somerset's baby-faced opening batsman – he was dogged rather than watchable. COURTESY OF JOHN LEE

Future England Captain Mike Denness (fists clenched) acts as the main cheerleader as Brian Roe prepares to bowl in a game of ten-pin bowling between the Kent and Somerset teams at Gillingham in 1963. Among the Somerset players watching are Roy Virgin (left), Ken Palmer, Chris Greetham and David Doughty (right). SOMERSET CRICKET MUSEUM

he had worked for a period for Jantzens of Barnstaple (who make swimwear) but in 1966 he was offered a job working for an Insurance Agency, run by a friend and club cricketer from Barnstaple, Mike Snell.

The job afforded Brian a degree of financial security but also allowed him to satisfy his gargantuan appetite for cricket. Playing club and county matches for Devon, he was a prolific run-maker, apparently compiling 222 centuries over a period of nearly sixty years. In one particular year – 1980, when he was forty-one years old – Brian notched up an impressive 4,034 runs in all games.

Divorced by the time of his death, he had been enticed out of retirement at the age of seventy-two and scored an unbeaten half-century for Barnstaple and Pilton Third XI after a seventeen-year absence, demonstrating the same old unpreparedness to yield his wicket. He died at the age of seventy-five on 28 June 2014 in Bickington, close to

Barnstaple, having been a virtual invalid for some months and looked after by friends.

Brian is quoted as saying: 'Out in the middle, if a bloke can get my wicket then good luck to him. I'm there to stop him.' Former Somerset skipper, Roy Kerslake, who had been best man at Brian's wedding, felt that his teammate's great virtue was that he kept things simple, noting that 'Brian knew his limitations as a player and always made sure he played within them. His defence was solid and he had the temperament to bat and bat'. 'The darling of the River Stand', as he had been known in his days as a Somerset player, was a popular figure. His employer and team captain at Barnstaple and Pilton CC, Mike Snell, observed that 'cricket was in his soul: he loved the game and I think it loved him.'

417
Thomas Eastwood Dickinson
10 August 1957 v. Glamorgan , Taunton

[signature: T. G. Dickinson]

Tom Dickinson's forebears had set up a thriving builders' merchants business in Coppull, Chorley, but his father, William, recognised that as a younger sibling he was destined to play a supporting role. In Tom's words 'he was fed up with being bossed about by his older brother'. William Dickinson began a new life working for Goodyear Tyres in Australia, accompanied by his wife, Margaret (née Eastwood), and their daughter. Tom was born in Parramatta, Sydney, on 11 January 1931 but the family soon returned to Coppull when his paternal grandmother became ill. Tom's father then made the decision to remain in Lancashire.

Tom is a Lancastrian through and through, despite having spent his earliest years and the bulk of his adulthood elsewhere. Educated at Queen Elizabeth Grammar School, Blackburn, he proved an outstanding schoolboy cricketer, bowling at a hostile pace and first appearing in Lancashire League cricket for East Lancashire CC at the age of only fifteen. On leaving school he went to Manchester University where he gained a BSc in Maths. While still an undergraduate, he made his debut for Lancashire as an amateur. England captain Peter May notes in his autobiography that he had felt when facing Brian Statham and Tom that the future of Lancashire cricket was assured. Whereas Brian Statham of course went on to enjoy enormous success, Tom's priorities lay elsewhere. Peter May concludes in *A Game Enjoyed* that 'one would have thought then that he had a very bright future in the game but he scarcely played any first-class cricket afterwards'. Unable to make himself available on a consistent basis, he played for Lancashire in only four first-class matches taking 3 wickets at 32.66 apiece. A silver

Tom Dickinson — 'a very bright future in the game' was predicted but he opted instead for a teaching career.

casket commemorating Tom's cameo role as a member of the Championship-winning team of 1950 remained a treasured possession.

After his National Service with the Royal Engineers, during which time he played for The Army, Tom went on to become a Maths teacher at Bristol Grammar School, remaining there for three years. This was followed by a four-year spell at Arnold School, Blackpool.

His next career move was to Queen's College, Taunton, where he was appointed Head of the Maths Department and where he would remain for twenty-nine years, also taking on responsibility for coaching the cricket First XI and later the Second XI. His commanding presence and gruff Lancashire accent may have added to his reputation as a strict disciplinarian, but he was in fact a modest, gentle man, encouraging those who needed a helping hand. For many years he held a pastoral role as head of the Day Boy contingent at the school, a job he undertook with quiet efficiency. He also introduced the Duke of Edinburgh Awards to Queen's College and found ways to ensure that less able pupils were not left out of the sporting life of the school, orchestrating, for example, an annual 'village cricket' tournament for the 'also-rans' based very loosely on the local geography, with competing teams such as the 'Corfe Clouters' or the 'Blagdon Bashers'. The teams competed for the Hyland Trophy, presented by Tom's predecessor as Head of Maths.

For many years he was a chief examiner for the Joint Matriculation Board. He was also a member of the Oxford Examination Board, overseeing the setting and marking of papers. Interestingly, a fellow member of the board and a good friend was Colin Dexter, who later found fame as the writer of numerous 'Morse' novels.

In 1953 Tom was married to Frances Mary Lord who also hailed from Lancashire and taught Chemistry at Weirfield School (later merged with Taunton School). With such a pedigree, it is unsurprising that their three sons were academically gifted or that one of them - the youngest, Philip – should be awarded a hockey blue while at Oxford.

Having qualified by residence, Tom's cricket for Somerset was limited to two summer vacations. In 1957 he announced himself in the Second XI with two strong bowling performances against Wiltshire and then Cornwall, the latter including figures of 7 for 17. He was fast-tracked into the First XI where he continued to bowl impressively, commencing with some devastating bowling against Glamorgan on his debut when he took 5 for 36 in the first innings, playing his part in setting up a ten-wicket victory. He would take a total of 17 wickets at 18.88 apiece over his five appearances.

He was nominally a fast-medium right-arm bowler and a left-handed tail-end batsman but was ambidextrous, able to bowl or bat left- or right-handed. Tom gained a reputation for adopting a fluid and pragmatic approach to his guard while batting. Former teammate John Harris recalls a match for Somerset Second XI where, with the clock ticking down and the need to secure an additional over to knock off the required runs, Tom switched his guard to match his fellow tail-ender, denying Wiltshire the opportunity to slow proceedings and allowing Somerset to eke out a narrow victory. He only bowled left-arm when the need arose while coaching his charges at school.

Former teacher John Wade is full of praise for his colleague's achievements and describes him in his valedictory summary in the school magazine on Tom's retirement as 'a man of principle and integrity … and above all a schoolmaster with a sense of humour and fairness'. Many of his former pupils would have agreed.

After retiring from teaching, Tom and Frances embarked on an extended tour, including a visit to Tom's native Australia, before moving to their home in Edwalton, close to where another son, Matthew, is Professor of Plant Pathology at Nottingham University.

418
Alan Geoffrey Thomas Whitehead
21 August 1957 v. Sussex, Bristol (Imperial Athletic Ground)

By the age of twenty – a time when some players are about to embark on their careers – Alan Whitehead had already retired as a player after five seasons of first-class cricket. He would, however, continue to enjoy a fulfilling life involved in the game.

Born in Butleigh on 28 October 1940 but brought up from a young age in West Pennard, he was the son of Francis Thomas Whitehead, known as Tom, who was married to Emily (née Dunkerton). He was part of closely-knit family. Tom managed a farm and next door lived his brother, Fred, who was a cowman and married to Emily's sister, Winifred. Alan's father was already serving with the Royal Artillery by the time

Alan Whitehead – ended his career at the age of only twenty after five seasons as a first-class player. SOMERSET CRICKET MUSEUM

of his son's birth. At Dunkirk, standing up to his neck in sea water, he had eventually been rescued by a small boat. He had been back in action with his tank regiment among the troops who landed in the first fortnight after D-Day and was one of the first men on the scene at the liberation of Bergen-Belsen. For the duration of the war, Alan's uncle had acted as his surrogate father.

He enjoyed a happy childhood, able to indulge his passion for sports of all kinds. By the age of ten he was already making occasional appearances alongside his Uncle Fred – a keen club cricketer – in the West Pennard CC team. Educated at West Pennard School, he left at fifteen to become a member of the junior ground staff at the County Ground. A left-arm orthodox spinner, he was offered a full contract the following season and at the age of sixteen he was given his initial taste of first-class cricket in a friendly fixture against Sussex. Writing in the *Somerset County Gazette*, Eric Hill would state that 'he bowls ... with plenty of air, a measurable amount of turn and a good control of length'. There was always competition for places from the likes of Eric Bryant and John McMahon but in 1959 he was selected on a more regular basis and responded with 44 wickets, although he notes that when Harold Stephenson took on the captaincy he tended to favour other bowlers and rarely called on his services. At this stage Alan was approached by Nottinghamshire and offered a contract but declined, preferring to take his chances with the county team he had supported as a boy.

He played a major part in the success of the Second XI in 1961, topping the bowling averages with more than 80 wickets. He recalls vividly his final first-class appearance for Somerset against Glamorgan at Weston-super-Mare. Having not been selected for any of the previous first team matches in 1961, he was awoken by a knock on the door from Peter Wight who informed Alan that the pair of them were playing in the match in two hours' time. Given Peter's importance to the side, Alan told him to go on ahead and that he would catch a train. He arrived at 12.30 but made useful contributions, taking 3 for 25 on the third day and then holding out valiantly for a draw with fellow tail-ender, Ken Biddulph. He was nevertheless released at the end of the season. In thirty-eight first-class appearances he had taken 67 wickets at 34.41 apiece and had averaged 5.70 with the bat.

During the winters, he had found temporary work where he could, either working on the farm with his father or for companies such as Snows, a Glastonbury-based timber merchant. At the age of only twenty he needed to opt for a new career. He therefore took the Advanced Coaching Course at Lilleshall and was offered a job as sports coach at Wells Cathedral School, where he was employed for eight years. Among his charges was Malcolm Nash of Glamorgan, a fine player whose career will forever be defined by the over in which Garry Sobers despatched him for six sixes.

By 1969, Alan was ready for another change of career and made the decision to try his luck as an umpire. After standing on a trial basis in a Minor Counties fixture, he

was added to the umpires list and between 1970 and his retirement in 2005 at the age of sixty-five, he would stand in 609 first-class fixtures. In addition, he was asked to officiate in five Test Matches between 1982 and 1987 and would stand in numerous List A and international one-day matches. He also stood at a World Cup semi-final.

A resolute and undemonstrative man, he was well-regarded and refused to be intimidated by the aggressive tactics of some of the more head-strong bowlers. His calm demeanour – crucial in the role both of umpire and spin bowler – stood him in good stead in later years when he was diagnosed with the throat cancer from which he is now steadily recovering.

Alan Whitehead – a resolute and undemonstrative man, he became a Test Match umpire. SOMERSET CRICKET MUSEUM

At the time of writing, Alan lives in the city of Wells with his wife Marion (née Poulsom) whom he was married to back in 1963 and with whom he had three daughters. A gentle man entirely at ease and happy in his own skin, he feels blessed to have spent over fifty years with a wife he treasures, more than half a century – from the ten-year-old club cricketer to the experienced umpire – involved in the game he has loved, and a lifetime in the county he has always fondly called home.

1958

"Having studied all the great captains from Bradman down to Brearley and watched them at close quarters, I reckon Maurice was the best of the lot ... and it was a miracle when in 1958 he led his happy band of jokers to third place."

Bill Alley in *Standing the Test of Time*

Championship Position: 3 of 17

There had been a clear-out after a drink-fuelled incident at the Grand Hotel in Swansea that had brought shame on the club. Despite having scored nearly 1,500 runs in 1957, Maurice Tremlett was among those sacked. John McMahon was also given his marching orders, despite his haul of 86 first-class wickets. In the end, after Dennis Silk in particular had interceded, Tremlett was reinstated but McMahon had by then committed himself to Lancashire League cricket. Tremlett proceeded to answer his detractors by leading the county to third place in the County Championship with twelve wins. In the absence of a penetrative bowling attack, the heady position was engineered with a series of adept declarations.

Graham Atkinson announced his arrival as a player of genuine class with a superb century against Warwickshire, while Peter Wight and Colin McCool amassed the most runs. With 116 wickets, Brian Langford topped the bowling averages, nearly a third of his wickets coming during the Weston Festival at which Somerset recorded comfortable wins in each of their three low-scoring fixtures.

Alan Shirreff arrived with a distinguished career behind him and the promise that he would captain the club, an offer rescinded when Maurice Tremlett was reinstated. Instead he was asked to act as coach, which required the sacking of Bill Andrews – a man whose love of the club was unquestioned but whose outspokenness won him friends and enemies in equal measure, though sadly it was his enemies who had more influence. Shirreff was asked to play in two matches but was shoddily treated by his captain and not asked to bowl. Accustomed to life in the military, he had too much pride and too much good sense to hang around at a place as shambolically run at that time as Somerset County Cricket Club.

419
Peter James Eele
31 May 1958 v. Sussex, Taunton

Peter Eele was born in Taunton on 27 January 1935, the first of three children of James Robert Eele, a teacher at Huish's Grammar School, known to generations of schoolboys as 'Bomber'. James was married to his cousin, Hilda Eleanor (née Eele). Their son, Peter, won a scholarship to Taunton School where he was coached by two first-class players. Former Sussex batsman, Harry Parks, had taken on a coaching role at the school following his retirement from first-class cricket and Boris Collingwood, who played once for Somerset, also taught and coached at the school.

Short and slight, Peter was a useful wicketkeeper and a left-handed batsman watched by Somerset from a young age and appearing for the Under-19s. But he was destined to live in the shadow of first-choice wicket-keeper, Harold Stephenson. His introduction to the senior game began well when he came home from leave during his National Service and was asked by Somerset Second XI coach Bill Andrews to step into the breach in a friendly match against their Gloucestershire counterparts. Peter responded by taking part in a double-century opening partnership with Graham Atkinson and going on to score 139, before returning to what he jokingly refers to as his 'overseas posting' with the RAF on the Isle of Portland, Dorset. Bill Andrews was determined to retain the services of the promising young keeper and a letter would land regularly on the desk of Peter's commanding officer, signed off by Bill but always beginning with the words 'Air Vice-Marshal Taylor would be pleased if you would release...'. It is not known whether or not Somerset's distinguished Honorary Secretary was aware that his name had been taken in vain.

On the basis of his performances, Peter was offered a professional contract in 1957. The sum of £325 remains etched in his memory. Between 1958 and 1965 he would stand in for Harold Stephenson on fifty-four occasions, taking 87 catches and effecting 19 stumpings. In addition he averaged 12.24, his one century coming in the match against the Pakistan Eaglets in 1963. Former Test captain and commentator Tony Lewis would later compare the two men who held the Somerset wicket-keeping berth, noting that Harold had 'lovely balance, beautiful hands, and a few thick Geordie curses' but that 'the conversation rose many decibels when Peter Eele was deputising'.

When he was overlooked and Harold Stephenson was replaced by Geoff Clayton,

Peter realised that his moment had passed and he would spend seven happy seasons keeping for Devon. His links with Somerset's neighbouring county had begun when at the end of his first professional season he went to the Labour Exchange and was directed to Whiteways Cyder Company Ltd in Whimple and told to 'ask for Mr Dick'. It transpired that the gentleman in question was the owner, Richard Whiteway, a Somerset cricket supporter who was happy to take on Peter and fellow Somerset cricketer Haydn Sully for the winter break. Peter was charged with paying apple suppliers in the accounts department and both players would return to the company each winter. Whereas Haydn remained and rose to become a

Peter Eele – Harold Stephenson's patient understudy, 'the conversation rose many decibels' when he was deputising.
SOMERSET CRICKET MUSEUM

director of the company, Peter sought permanent employment with the brewery firm of Hall & Woodhouse in Blandford Forum, managed by erstwhile Somerset captain George Woodhouse. Peter states with characteristic understatement that he 'failed to settle'. Indeed he left after two months and having eschewed the world of brewing he opted instead for banking and would work at the Tiverton branch of Lloyds Bank for fifteen years.

His return to cricket was not premeditated but followed a conversation with John Harris, at the time Chairman of the Umpires' Association. Having qualified, Peter was retained on the umpires list for two spells, retiring from the role at the end of the 1990 season.

Thereafter, he found work as Assistant Secretary of the Taunton Vale Golf Club, which was later closed. No longer in possession of the slight, elfin frame that made him suited to the role of wicket-keeper, he remains an affable man, never married but with a long-term partner. He was never one to rush to a decision.

His primary interests are golf and orchestral music, which he describes as 'something of a passion'. Since the 1970s he has supported the Bournemouth Symphony Orchestra. Having finished conducting an interview, he looks askance when asked if he has retained any photographs that might be used in a book about Somerset cricketers. He confesses to never retaining any photographs and adds that 'if you come across that one of me in the sweater coming down to my knees, I'd had to borrow one and the only teammate with a spare was Paul Dunkels [of Harrow School and Devon]. He was a QC and 6 ft 10 in tall.'

We have spared this likeable, amusing man the indignity of its inclusion.

420
Leonard Eric Bryant
31 May 1958 v. Sussex, Taunton

Eric Bryant's brief career was a controversial one, cut short when his action as a left-arm orthodox spinner was called into question. Born in Weston-super-Mare on 2 June 1936, he was the son of Leonard Stanley Bryant, a railway fireman, married to Doris Ada (née Thomas), the daughter of an assistant grocer.

Eric came to Somerset's attention having been watched by Bill Andrews in club cricket for Weston-super-Mare and he first played for the Somerset Second XI in 1957. Having been offered an annual contract, he graduated to the First XI in 1958 after a useful performance against Gloucestershire Second XI. In conversation with Barry Phillips in the early 1990s, Eric cited Somerset's Horace Hazell as his role model in the art of spin bowling. There were, however, some issues. Somerset wicket-keeper Peter Eele (who was given his debut in the same match as Eric) reveals: 'I knew Eric was a 'chucker' and you could tell which ones he'd thrown when they smacked into your gloves – usually about one an over.' The problem came to a head in the match against Gloucestershire at Bath in 1960 when umpire 'Hugo' Yarnold called him for no-balling five times. Gloucestershire batsman Arthur Milton had the good grace not to exploit the situation, making no attempt to score from the deliveries. As reported by Eric Hill in the *Somerset County Gazette*, 'I gather there was a long net at Bath on

Eric Bryant – dogged by controversy over his bowling action.
SOMERSET CRICKET MUSEUM

Eric Bryant – 'you could tell which ones he'd thrown when they smacked into your gloves'.

the day after the affair and that Richard Robinson [the Secretary] and George Lambert with the Chairman E. F. Longrigg watched Bryant's action and suggested amendments.' Eric would later reveal that when he appeared in a subsequent friendly fixture, he was umpired by Sid Buller who could now see nothing untoward in Eric's delivery. More than forty overs were filmed and sent to MCC who agreed that any problems had been resolved. When he departed at the end of the season, his contract not having been renewed, Eric was quietly handed the film as a memento by Tommy Tout, the county's scorer. Perhaps one member of the side particularly sad to see Eric leave would have been Bill Alley. Drawing on a cigarette as he chain-smoked, Eric would confess in conversation with Barry Phillips that he perfected the art of signing Bill's autograph and was delegated the role when Bill tired of the many written requests to send his signature. Collectors of Somerset memorabilia have been warned.

Eric was married in Taunton in 1960 to Sylvia Thorne and a year later the couple had a son. After leaving the first-class stage, Eric found work at Brentwood School in Essex, as a coach. He would recount, more than thirty years later, that after approximately two years of marriage he came home to find his son crying and Sylvia unable to cope with the pressures, waiting to leave them. There is of course more understanding in the modern age of the nature of post-natal depression. Left quite literally holding the baby, Eric was obliged to abandon his coaching role and return to his parents' home in Weston-super-Mare, where his son, Paul, was brought up.

He returned in time to club cricket and played for many years for Weston-super-Mare, captaining the side for three seasons, although he felt that the no-ball controversy had followed him and was conscious that his action was being scrutinised. He was remarried in Weston-super-Mare in 1966 to Margaret Perry and worked in a variety of jobs but for seventeen years up to his retirement he made quilted headboards for a local firm. Increasingly he turned to golf as a leisure pursuit and became a member of the Worlebury Golf Club.

He died at the age of sixty-three in Brent Knoll on 28 November 1999. Although he felt to the very last that he had been treated unfairly, any bitterness was not directed towards the county team he continued to support, and he felt privileged to have had the opportunity to have been employed as a professional in the first-class game.

421

Alexander Campbell Shirreff
16 August 1958 v. Sussex, Eastbourne

Alan Shirreff

Alan Shirreff, as he was known, was born in Ealing on 12 February 1919, the son of an electrical engineer, James Arthur Shirreff, and his wife Eleanor Alice (née Longden). Alan was educated at Dulwich College, where he captained the school team in a 1938 season in which they remained unbeaten. His master in charge of cricket, former England international C. S. Marriot, would later describe Alan as 'the best of the sixteen captains I have had under me at Dulwich: he raised the team spirit of the 1938 XI to a height that I have never seen surpassed'. At the end of the season he was sent a letter of congratulation by former Dulwich pupil P. G. Wodehouse who included a £5 note, describing it as 'a purse of gold'. Alan was later able to joke that he used the windfall to treat the whole team to a dinner and a show but opted to pocket the change.

He went up to Pembroke College, Cambridge, where he played twelve times for the Varsity side in 1939, gaining a blue. After serving in the Second World War with the RAF as a fighter pilot and instructor, Alan would observe that he 'didn't pick up a bat between the summer of 1939 and 1946', but thereafter, his would be a peripatetic first-class career. After appearing for a variety of sides over a number of years, he would confess that his happiest times were those when he was captaining the Combined Services team. Tight military discipline and responsibility for leadership both held their appeal. Alan found the professionals on the county circuit less inclined to obey orders than their counterparts in the Air Force, demonstrating a tendency to see an amateur as a threat to their livelihood. His three experiences of county cricket each left him disappointed in various ways.

Alan Shirreff – captain of Dulwich College: 'he raised the team spirit of the 1938 XI to a height that I have never seen surpassed'.
COURTESY OF DULWICH COLLEGE

Having gone straight from Cambridge into the RAF, he would remain with them until 1958, rising to the rank of squadron leader. Throughout his time with the RAF, his various managers were generous in allowing him time off to play cricket and he would amass 119 first-class appearances over a nineteen-year period. Sandwiched between

Cambridge University and his spell at Somerset were games for Combined Services and the RAF, Hampshire, Kent and MCC. His career statistics – a batting average of 21.71 and 304 wickets at 31.49 apiece (bowling medium pace) speak of a competent all-rounder who brought much beyond his leadership skills.

He was married in 1946 to Jean Fountain, with whom he would have two sons. In 1948, with his parents based in Boscombe, he was invited to come to Hampshire's County Ground and be interviewed as a potential captain. Also on the shortlist was Freddie Brown, but the role was offered to Desmond Eagar, already well-connected, his father at the time an influential figure in Hampshire cricket. Alan would play sixteen times for Hampshire under the captaincy of Eagar and the relationship between the two men was never entirely harmonious. Sensing Alan's unhappiness, the Kent captain, David Clark, invited Alan to join him, given that he resided in the county by then. In conversation with Barry Phillips, Alan would observe that 'it wasn't easy being an amateur: Tich Freeman had a go at me for keeping [Peter] Hearn out of the side and depriving him of a living'. The RAF continued to be generous in allowing him time off to play both for Combined Services and in the County Championship. Then, in his own words, 'by the time Somerset approached me I had been in the RAF for nineteen years and was about to take up a promotion and flying refresher course. The invitation with the offer of a three-year contract came out of the blue. I was thirty-nine at the time, had just got my MCC coaching qualification and it seemed like a good career move.'

The new appointment proved a disaster from the outset. In Alan's own words, 'I turned up in April to find a rabble in grey trousers, not fit, and there was a total lack of discipline.' For a man steeped in the ways of service life, the shock was enormous. To add to his woes, there was no clarity about the role, which had been presented to him as Assistant Secretary and coach with the possibility of being appointed captain. The truth of the matter was that Maurice Tremlett had been sacked at the end of the previous season but had then been reinstated. The promise that Alan might be made captain was then withdrawn and a more dedicated coaching role created by the enforced departure of Bill Andrews. Alan explained that 'I got no support from the committee, which was too big, and [Richard] Robinson the secretary was incompetent. When it became clear what the job really was I should have made a stand. There was a clique of senior players who were drinking pals. They made my job impossible and the players generally resented me for taking Bill Andrews's place. Tremlett made it clear they didn't need coaching and so I ended up as the Second XI captain and coach where Bill Andrews would turn up unannounced and undermine everything I did. I went to the committee and asked to be released from the contract. It was a traumatic time for me.' When Alan was drafted into the First XI for two matches, Eric Hill used his column in the Somerset County Gazette to lead the chorus of disapproval, believing it had been a retrograde step to bring in a player in the autumn of his career, rather than one of his young charges who were 'bursting at the seams for a go in the Championship'. Eric added that, with the Second XI having a tough time of it, 'this was the last time on earth to put their captain and coach into the First XI'. In the event, Alan averaged 15.66 with the bat and did not bowl.

After half a year spent looking for new employment, Alan found work as a salesman for Schweppes and he would remain with the company for two decades, rising to the level of Sales Director. After having retired he would take up two directorships in the charity sector, helping to support young people in London and the South East. He also derived pleasure from watching the progress of his grandsons as accomplished schoolboy and club cricketers.

He died in West Wickham, London, on 16 December 2006 at the age of eighty-seven.

Alan Shirreff – 'they made my job impossible'.
SOMERSET CRICKET MUSEUM

1959

"This was to be Peter Wight's first truly great year.
He missed seven games because he had double vision ...
and yet managed to hit six hundreds, score 1,874 runs
and strike 222 against Kent."

Peter Roebuck in *From Sammy to Jimmy*

Championship Position: 12 of 17

With new rules allowing pitches to be covered, there was a marked increase in the side's batting averages, headed by Peter Wight, with 55.11. He would undoubtedly have made many more runs, but for a blow to the head while fielding at short leg that put him out of action for several weeks. Others – in particular Colin McCool, Bill Alley and Graham Atkinson – made the most of the improved wickets. The bowlers enjoyed the changes rather less. Brian Langford amassed 83 wickets and the next most successful wicket-taker was a steadily improving Ken Biddulph, who was now regularly leading the opening attack, although relying on swing rather than outright pace. After the triumphs of the previous season, Maurice Tremlett appeared to have lost his love for the game. Troubled by his failing eyesight – the result of having previously taken the full force in his face of a well-struck cricket ball – and worn down by the attempts by certain committee members to undermine him, he often 'lost himself' at third man and allowed Harold Stephenson to run proceedings.

Although they joined the newly-formed Second XI Championship for first-class counties, Somerset Second XI also remained participants in the Minor Counties Championship. It made commercial sense to continue their rivalry with neighbouring or nearby counties in the South West and afforded an opportunity to keep an eye open for any emerging talent.

Four debutants were introduced to the side – one of them Miles Lawrence, the son of Johnny Lawrence – but none of them left any lasting mark on the game.

422
Geoffrey Leyden Keith
13 May 1959 v. Cambridge University, Cambridge

Geoff Keith was born on 19 November 1937 and his place of birth is variously given as Winchester or Portsmouth. As a baby, he was adopted by Gerald Leyden Keith and his wife Marjorie (née Handley), who lived in Dewsbury. Gerald's adoptive parents hailed from Dublin and his father's work as a travelling salesman for W. R. Jacobs, famed for their cream crackers, had brought him initially to Leeds. Gerald had followed his father into the company but subsequently joined his father-in-law, William, who was a woollen rag merchant. With Gerald aged forty and Marjorie thirty-two at the time of Geoff's adoption, the event proved a godsend for parents and child alike as they brought him up in Dewsbury as 'a Yorkshireman by early adoption' in the words of Eric Hill, writing in the *Somerset County Gazette* in 1959.

Another in the production line of young cricketers to come out of that county, Geoff was taken on as a member of the ground staff at the age of eighteen but was released for his National Service with the RAF at Yatesbury in Wiltshire in 1956. He returned to the County Ground and was introduced into the Second XI in 1957. Described as 'a tidy, stylish batsman' who also bowled off-breaks, his chance for first-class cricket finally came in 1959 but he would play only fifteen times for Somerset, averaging 12.76 with the bat and taking one wicket for 9 runs in the only three overs he bowled. Eric Hill, writing in the *Somerset County Gazette*, describes him as 'a watchful batsman who can also drive with great power', adding that 'he is the longest thrower on the staff and a beautiful outfielder'. Alan Whitehead reveals that 'Geoff threw the ball higher and harder than anyone in fielding practice until he dislocated his shoulder launching it into the air and after that he struggled to throw it ten yards'. Teammates express the view that it was diffidence rather than talent that held Geoff back as a cricketer. Peter Eele suggests that 'Geoff's temperament wasn't quite right for the first-class game' and Mick Hanna says that Geoff was 'a bit hesitant and lacking in self-belief'. Both agree that he was a likeable and popular member of the squad. He was also a dapper figure, described by John Holder of Hampshire as 'a man with style', who cut a glamorous figure in his MGB GT sports car.

Having departed from Somerset on an amicable basis at the end of the 1961 season, he threw in his lot with his birth county of Hampshire, whom he appeared for on sixty occasions between 1962 and 1967. His moment in the sun – quite literally so, on a balmy day in 1965 – came when he scored his only century, an unbeaten 101 against

Geoff Keith – 'a watchful batsman who can drive with great power'.
SOMERSET CRICKET MUSEUM

South Africa. Having put Hampshire in a strong position, Geoff was then called on to hold out for a draw with his unbeaten 21 in the second innings after Graeme Pollock had launched a blistering assault on the Hampshire attack with 94 runs in 66 minutes. South Africa's Eddie Barlow was sufficiently impressed to invite him to represent the Western Province team he captained in 1968, but Geoff would only appear in two Currie Cup matches for them.

He returned to Hampshire in 1971 as coach and captain of the Second XI. A fitness fanatic, he was also charged with improving the speed and stamina of the Hampshire squad as a whole and some observers attribute Hampshire's winning of the Championship in 1973 in part to the team's superior athleticism. In September 1974, Geoff was married at the Southampton Register Office to his partner, Annya Maria Snell, an air hostess, known as Ann. His marriage certificate records that a previous marriage of his had been dissolved. Geoff already knew that he was suffering from a brain tumour and, on the day of his wedding, wrote his will to ensure that Ann and his new step-daughter, Zoe Maria Samantha, would be provided for.

He died in Southampton at the cruelly premature age of thirty-eight on 26 December 1975. At his request, his ashes were scattered on his beloved Hampshire County Ground.

423
Terence Ian Barwell
8 July 1959 v. Combined Services, Taunton

J. Barwell.

Terry Barwell was born of English parents in Bloemhof, Transvaal, on 29 April 1937. His father, Charles Arthur Barwell was an officer in the General Service Corps of the South African Forces, married to Kathleen Lillian Joan (née Thompson). Terry was only seven years old when his father died in a tragic accident in Cape Town as he grappled with another man who was struggling to break free: he fell against a pillar, fracturing his skull.

Educated at Rondebosch Boys' High School, he captained the First XI and went on to play for the Western Province Nuffield XI. Having arrived in the UK, Terry began his residential qualification in May 1959 and was invited to play in his debut first-class fixture against the Combined Services two months later as a wicket-keeper batsman. He would continue to be selected on an occasional basis behind the stumps but increasingly appeared as a batsman only, garnering a reputation as a good player of spin bowling. He was also soon integrated into the rugby scene, playing as a centre

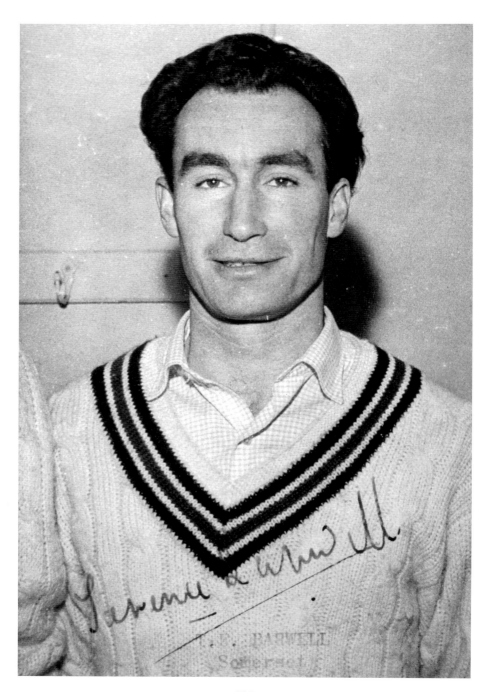

three-quarter for Taunton RFC and Somerset.

In 1961 he left to enter St Luke's College in Exeter in order to train as a teacher but made himself available during the summer school holidays and sometimes during term times. In 1964 he would add another string to his bow when he gained the MCC Advanced Coaching Certificate at Lillieshall, improving his effectiveness as a school cricket coach.

He began his teaching career at Dr Morgan's School in Bridgwater and was married in 1965 to Judy Anne Clifford (née Rice), with whom he would have two daughters and two sons. He played for Somerset and Somerset Second XI until 1968, appearing in forty-three first-class matches for the county and averaging 19.47, including nine half-centuries. A highlight was his appearance in the Gillette Cup Final of 1967, an occasion marred by his run out for 24 after a terrible mix-up with Graham Burgess at a time when the pair had given Somerset the glimmer of a hope of victory. Having left the county to teach at Marlborough College, he would represent Wiltshire between 1971 and 1975 before leaving to take up a teaching post at Blundell's School. He would remain with Blundell's for many years until his retirement and enjoyed outings in club cricket with Heathcoat CC, at Knightshayes, near Tiverton.

Quietly-spoken, affable and with a fine sense of humour, Terry has remained in his adoptive West Country. Sadly, he was widowed when his wife, Judy, died in 1998. He is still an active member of the Somerset Former Players' Association.

Terry Barwell receives his Runners-Up medal (presented by Sir Alec Douglas-Home) at the 1967 Gillette Cup Final, with Roy Palmer behind him.

Opposite page: A youthful Terry Barwell - born and raised in South Africa, he became a teacher and remained in his adoptive West Country.
COURTESY OF JOHN LEE

424
Haydn Sully
8 July 1959 v. Combined Services, Taunton

Born on 1 November 1939 in the village of Sampford Brett, near Williton, Haydn was the only child of Arthur John Sully and Dorothy Edith (née Bulpin). Dorothy hailed from a family of farm carters, while Arthur was employed by the Great Western Railway and well-known locally as a footballer and a cricketer for Watchet CC before becoming a respected umpire in club cricket.

Although there were secondary schools closer to home, Haydn chose to be educated at Huish's Grammar School in Taunton, where he was a contemporary of Roy Virgin. He remained there until he was eighteen and, were it not for his success in landing a contract as a professional cricketer, would in all likelihood have trained to become a History teacher. Having come to Somerset's attention as a successful right-arm off-break bowler, he had the misfortune to arrive on the scene when fellow off-spinner Brian Langford was already establishing his reputation as a match-winner. Haydn would remain in Brian's shadow during his time with the county of his birth. Between 1959 and 1963 he made only twelve first-class appearances, taking 12 wickets at 46.41 apiece and averaging 14.00 with the bat. Over that period he was a regular in the Second XI but, recognising that opportunities would continue to prove few and far between, he made discreet enquiries with other counties. This led to his amicable departure for Northamptonshire in 1964. He became a first team regular there by 1966, when he claimed the prized 100 wickets in the season. His form then fell away and Haydn and Northants parted company in 1969 when the county failed to renew his contract. He had taken 314 first-class wickets in total at 27.66 apiece.

Having embarked on his professional cricketing career back in 1959, Haydn had been offered work in the off-season by Richard Whiteway, known to all and sundry as Dick and a cricket fanatic and supporter of Somerset cricket who adopted a benevolent approach towards the poorly-remunerated pros. Haydn and teammate Peter Eele joined the Whiteways Cyder Company Ltd, based in Whimple, Devon, Peter to work in the accounts department and Haydn overseeing the inflow of harvested apples. Once this operation was completed, Haydn would work alongside Dick Whiteway in the export of finished product. He would stay with the company for the remainder of his working life.

The West Country retained its appeal and he never put down roots in Northants, not just because of his burgeoning career at Whiteways but also because he was married in 1965 to Margaret Joan Perry, whom he had met whilst making a guest appearance for Sidmouth CC. It was common practice for pros to supplement their pitiful wages with such guest appearances, although Margaret's own attendance at cricket matches had until that moment been rather rarer. She had been persuaded to go along by a female friend. The chance meeting would prove serendipitous. The couple were based in

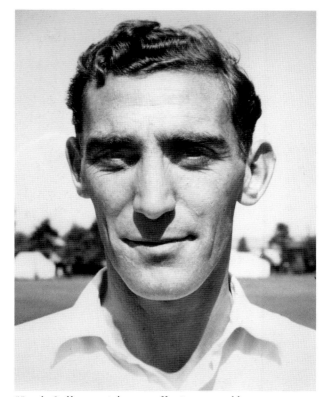

Haydn Sully – a right-arm off-spinner: unable to secure a regular place in the side, he left to join Northants.
SOMERSET CRICKET MUSEUM

Taunton until 1969 when, with Haydn's professional career coming to an end, he was offered permanent employment by Dick Whiteway and purchased a house in Honiton.

Over time, he was given increasing responsibility for the company's export business. When Dick died in a car crash in 1980, Haydn was handed control of exports. He was made a director of Whiteways and was also listed as a director of Shepton Mallet-based Showerings – the manufacturers, among other products, of Babycham – who had merged with Whiteways back in 1961. His work entailed a great deal of travel to places as far afield as Africa and the USA. Also within his ambit were the West Indies, where together with their love of cricket, the locals demonstrated a love for Cydrax, a brand whose sales had nose-dived towards oblivion in the UK while the drink remained hugely popular in the Caribbean.

He continued to play cricket for Sidmouth CC, whom he captained for several years, and he also represented Devon in 1970 and 1971. Later, he turned out for Whimple CC where there were midweek, weekend and touring matches to be played. The regular requests from club captain Dick Whiteway had proved difficult to turn down.

Haydn and Margaret had no children and, on his retirement, he was encouraged by his wife to become involved in the local community in a way that he had been unable to during a busy working life. He was soon appointed President of the local Rotary Club and became a director of the Honiton Music Festival. His other great interest was History and he took an active part in the Local History Society. He died at the age of sixty-seven at Exeter Hospital in Wonsford on 14 December 2006, a life foreshortened by childhood illnesses that had weakened his lungs and by a lifetime of smoking. It was nonetheless a contented and fulfilled life, enriched by a chance meeting with the woman whose wellbeing he cared for above all else and who in turn describes him as 'a kind man who loved his cricket and loved his work'.

425
John Miles Lawrence
22 August 1959 v. Surrey, Bath

Born in Rothwell, Yorkshire, on 7 November 1939 (and not 1940 as stated in some sources), Miles was the son of Somerset cricketer Johnny Lawrence, who was married to Mary (née Clarkson). His name was chosen as a result of Johnny's close friendship with fellow Somerset cricketer, Miles Coope.

Miles Lawrence was blessed with huge talent but blighted throughout his short life with health issues that barred the way to his ever making it to the top of the game he loved. As a child, he suffered from a twisted bowel (volvulus) that resulted in serious illness and although he would develop into a technically excellent cricketer, he would remain a frail-looking figure in adult life. Educated at Rothwell Grammar School, he was able to hone his skills as a batsman and leg-break bowler at his father's coaching school at Rothwell. Also attending the nets was a young Geoffrey Boycott who was heard to say that he wished he could bat like Miles. Sadly, raw talent was not enough. Geoffrey Boycott had the additional qualities required to take him to the top of his profession whereas Miles was never able to make the mark that those watching his development had anticipated. They had included Millfield School headmaster and former Somerset cricketer, R. J. O. Meyer, who offered Miles a place at the school in

Miles Lawrence (left) also shown (standing, far right) at Millfield with his sister, Pauline, Jack Meyer, and Miles's father, Johnny Lawrence. COURTESY OF STEPHEN LAWRENCE

order to bolster the cricket team. Sadly, within a year of joining the school, Miles contracted pneumonia and was obliged to return to the family home in Rothwell.

He persevered, though, and Somerset continued to believe in him. Having broken through into the Somerset First XI as a nineteen-year-old in 1959, he would play eighteen first-class games over three seasons before departing the scene in 1961. He had averaged 15.50 with the bat and taken 9 wickets at 40.33 apiece. Miles was at times a fragile and troubled soul, but was also possessed of the inner strength to stand up for what he believed in. Like his father, Johnny, he played no part in the bacchanalian post-match indulgences that some teammates revelled in. Prayers and The Bible were more to his taste. As teammate Alan Whitehead observed: 'Miles just quietly went about his business and never tried to foist his beliefs on the rest of us.'

Miles had dreamed of a career in the first-class game commensurate with his natural ability and was hugely disappointed when he failed to make the hoped-for breakthrough at Somerset. Some were of the view that it hung over him thereafter like a dark cloud. Having gained his coaching qualification, Miles was appointed coach at Leeds Grammar School in 1965. He continued to play League cricket in Yorkshire, initially as an all-rounder but later as a wicket-keeper where his natural talent allowed him to adapt to the new role more or less immediately. He appeared for Castleford CC

Miles Lawrence – hugely disappointed when he failed to make the breakthrough with Somerset.

and Heckmondwike CC – where he was said to have been perhaps the best player of his father's bowling – before joining Johnny for a season at Wakefield CC in 1966. Later, Johnny and Miles were united once more at Honley CC. In the mid-1970s, opponents of Bilton CC in the Airedale and Wharfedale League would encounter four Lawrences – Johnny, his brother Sam, and two of Johnny's sons: Miles and Stephen. By now able to read his father's bowling like a book, Miles was as successful at keeping to him as he had been when batting against him.

Miles also assisted Johnny at the family's cricket school at Rothwell until the enterprise was sold to Johnny's eldest daughter, Pauline, and her husband in 1976. Miles was by now clearly suffering from what is now more clearly understood as depression with the additional burden of schizophrenia. His mother and father were determined to help their son by retaining his interest in coaching and Johnny began to pursue a dream of starting a cricket boarding school, including an outdoor cricket field in the grounds of their large house just outside Tadcaster. Johnny completed the construction of a new indoor cricket school in 1981 – the facility now being run by his son, Stephen.

Miles was never married and was only forty-nine when his life was extinguished by a cardiac arrest at his home in Toulston near Tadcaster on 16 April 1989 just four months after his father, Johnny's, death, also from a heart attack.

1960

"The summer's results made it painfully clear once
more that the county badly needed another fast bowler."

David Foot in *Sixty Summers*

Championship Position: 14 of 17

Seasoned campaigner George Lambert of Gloucestershire was brought in as the new coach and set about trying to instil discipline and fitness with a regular morning rifle drill. In the absence of any available weights, a crate of rifles (sans ammunition) had been deployed. Desperate times called for desperate measures. Harold Stephenson was awarded the captaincy after his years of outstanding service behind the stumps but, as with his predecessor, Maurice Tremlett, he was hampered by the absence of any bowlers above medium pace. Very rarely was it possible to winkle out the opposition twice. Brian Langford proved the main wicket-taker with 100 victims, with support from the persevering Ken Biddulph and the persistently accurate Bill Alley. Peter Wight was again the outstanding batsman, creating a new club record of 2,316 runs, surpassing the landmark set by Harold Gimblett. Graham Atkinson also enjoyed an excellent season and local boy Roy Virgin came into his own with 1,453 runs. The presence of Oxford blue Abbas Ali Baig added class to the batting line-up for sixteen matches, but this was only ever going to be a temporary arrangement.

It was widely acknowledged that Head Groundsman, Cec Buttle, was not averse to preparing a peach of a batting track when he knew one or two well-heeled amateur batsmen were in evidence and likely to slip him the odd five pound note as an expression of their gratitude for bolstering their averages. Perhaps that had been the case when Cambridge University came to the County Ground and four century opening partnerships and a total of seven centuries ensued in a run-fest.

Behind the scenes, there were problems. An appeal to increase the cost of membership was rejected at the Annual General Meeting and the Supporters Club felt moved to bail out the county with a donation of £3,000. Highlighting the underlying issues, Peter Roebuck cites two examples of the wrongheadedness of the powers that be. The club decided not to approach Tom Graveney – who could have shored up the team and was in dispute with Gloucestershire – on the basis that 'he was the sort of chap committees did not want'. They directed their energies instead into creating a sixth area committee to give mid-Somerset a greater voice. As Roebuck states, their efforts may have been well-intentioned but by creating layers of officialdom they were 'compromising the decision-making process but assuaging those who felt that all was not well'.

Among the debutants, Merv Kitchen would become an integral part of Somerset cricket for a number of years and Colin Atkinson would make important contributions as a captain and an administrator.

Somerset XI at Lord's in 1960.
Back row: *C. H. M. Greetham, K. E. Palmer, A. G. T. Whitehead, B. Roe, G. L. Keith, R. T. Virgin.* Front row: *G. E. E. Lambert, C. L. McCool, H. W. Stephenson, P. B. Wight, B. A. Langford.* SOMERSET CRICKET MUSEUM

426
Colin Ronald Michael Atkinson
7 May 1960 v. Nottinghamshire, Nottingham

Born on 23 July 1931 in Thornaby-on-Tees in North Yorkshire, Colin's name was registered as Ronald Colin Atkinson although he would later come to be known as 'C. R. M.' His father managed a fish, game and poultry business and was married to Elizabeth May (née Smith).

An able pupil, Colin was educated at St Mary's Grammar School in Hummersknot, Darlington, before going on to Durham University to study History, Latin and English. He then studied for a Dip Ed at Loughborough College but, his thirst for learning as yet unsated, he took further degrees in Education at Queens University, Belfast, and in Psychology, again at Durham. Essentially a shy but a very driven man, he played as a pro in league cricket in order to fund his studies and would also make appearances on a regular basis for Northumberland and for Durham in Minor Counties fixtures. In 1956 he appeared for The Army while serving with the Royal Northumberland Fusiliers in Ireland and Kenya before returning to civilian life. He was married in 1957 to Shirley Angus, with whom he would have three children, one of whom – Jonathan or Jonny – played in fourteen first-class matches for Somerset.

As an all-rounder who bowled leg-breaks, Colin had been able to hone his skills in the hot house of league cricket where the pro is expected to take on the weight of responsibility for the team's successes and failures. Further experience as an amateur while he taught at Great Ayton and Darlington added to his know-how. He was invited to join the staff of Millfield School in 1960, teaching English and Latin and helping with Games.

Having been recommended to Somerset by Harold Stephenson, he played as an amateur during the school holidays but his effectiveness was limited when he began to suffer the early effects of arthritis and had to reinvent himself as a medium-pace bowler, relying primarily on line and length. His enthusiasm as an outfielder remained unbounded and he played as captain of the Second XI.

It came as a pleasant surprise when he was asked to lead the First XI in 1965, having already captained the Somerset Hockey XI in 1962. Inevitably, he was faced with resentment from those team members who felt that the appointment of an amateur was a retrograde step. In truth, Colin was an amateur in name only. An arrangement whereby he was paid by Millfield and the school were then paid by Somerset satisfied the traditionalists that the role was not being tarnished by professionalism. He certainly divided opinion. He was undoubtedly single-minded in pursuit

Colin Atkinson – played a major part in the development of Millfield School and Somerset CCC. SOMERSET CRICKET MUSEUM

of his goals and some found him an inspirational leader while others felt – and still feel – that he rode roughshod over those who did not fall readily into line. Despite initial resistance, Colin harnessed the skills of the team with his quiet but unflinching determination and led them to third place in the County Championship in 1966 and to their first one-day final in 1967 – an event in which the Somerset supporters, starved for eighty-four years of any hopes of winning anything, brought a carnival atmosphere to Lord's, though of course any triumph was still a long way off. Colin was a firm believer in traditional values and once threatened to dismiss Geoff Clayton when his wicket-keeper was deliberately slowing down play in an attempt to eke out a draw against Warwickshire. To bring a recalcitrant Geoff Clayton into line required leadership skills of a higher order.

Colin's performances as a player were worthy, but of less value than his contribution as a skipper. In 163 matches he averaged 19.05 with the bat and took 190 wickets at 31.01 apiece. In 1971 he was appointed Headmaster of Millfield after the founder, Jack Meyer, was deemed to have become too maverick for the taste of the governors. If R. J. O. Meyer is indisputably the man who made Millfield School, then Colin Atkinson is the individual who secured the school's future. In many ways, both of them moulded the institution in their own image. Jack Meyer planted the seed and grew it with a heady combination of inspiration, innovation and sheer chaos. Colin Atkinson brought order and planning. He had inherited a school still using the old corrugated iron Nissen huts but oversaw a transformation to brick-built structures. Colin embarked on his programme of improvement with great energy and vision until his retirement in 1990, one year after having been awarded a CBE for services to education. He might just as readily have been cited for services to Somerset cricket, having spent time as President and Chairman and having had to call on all his diplomatic skills. He was required to speak up for the players when Somerset were dumped unceremoniously out of the Benson & Hedges competition after an unsporting early declaration to preserve their run-rate and he was at the helm when the club was plunged into civil war at the time of the departure of Joel Garner, Viv Richards and Ian Botham. He also served for a while as Chairman of HTV West.

He died at the age of fifty-nine on 25 June 1991 in Glastonbury. The following year, his wife, Shirley, opened the impressive Atkinson Gallery at Millfield. Just as the gallery stands as a lasting memorial to his contribution to the development of Millfield School, so the Colin Atkinson Pavilion at the County Ground, refurbished in more recent times, serves as a reminder of all he gave to his adoptive county as a captain and administrator. As David Foot wrote, 'Atkinson balanced ambition with a down-to-earth streak and basic common sense'. Those qualities would play their part in Somerset's rise from a team of also-rans to the one that would dominate one-day cricket for a few heady years.

427
George Ernest Edward Lambert
25 May 1960 v. Surrey, Oval

Somerset supporters have traditionally seen Gloucestershire as their rivals although, for much of their history, Gloucestershire have regarded their neighbours with a degree of condescension, considering them 'noisy neighbours', to borrow a phrase from former Manchester United manager, Sir Alex Ferguson. George Lambert's arrival from across the county border in 1959 at the age of thirty-nine raised some eyebrows but he had been hired to bring discipline, fitness and improved technique to Somerset's promising band of young Second XI players as their captain and coach.

George was born in Paddington on 11 May 1919, the son of George Edward Lambert, a tailor's cutter and Ada Louise (née Constable). At seventeen, he was invited to join the ground staff at Lord's and although he was undoubtedly talented, the wheels may well have been oiled by the fact that Middlesex's coach, Archie Fowler, was his uncle, married to his father's sister, Georgina. (Sources suggesting that Archie was George's father-in-law are incorrect.)

George was also a talented footballer on the books at Arsenal FC for a while, but cricket was his first love and he was offered a contract by Gloucestershire in 1937 and would represent them in 334 matches between 1938 and 1957. In his prime a fast bowler, he inevitably slowed over the years to medium pace and although not quite an all-rounder was also a relatively successful lower-order batsman, notching up one century. David Foot notes in his *Who's Who* of post-War Somerset cricketers that in the late-1940s George 'was arguably the quickest bowler on the domestic circuit and was very near to a Test call'. Described as an ebullient character or the archetypal 'chirpy Cockney', his wit was often in evidence. David Foot cites elsewhere an incident where Arthur Wellard was 'taking the most outrageous liberties with Sam Cook's bowling', as was Arthur's wont, when George chipped in with the less-than-reassuring words to his teammate: 'Don't worry, Sam. He's been mishitting them so far.' If he continued to contribute to team morale, George's effectiveness as a bowler was blunted after Gloucestershire took the decision to play into the hands of their spin attack by applying substantial quantities of sand to the square at the County Ground in Bristol.

After leaving Gloucestershire and securing his coaching qualification, he answered Somerset's call and agreed to a five-year contract as coach and, initially at least, as Second XI captain. As needs must, he had shed some of his irreverence as he attempted to lick

George Lambert – a seasoned veteran by the time he arrived from Gloucestershire as coach and captain of the Somerset Second XI. COURTESY OF JOHN LEE

his charges into shape. Somerset batsman Graham Tripp recalls his and his teammates' surprise when, unable to find any weights, George managed to lay his hand on a crate of rifles and lined up the young players for their daily routine, intended to strengthen their wrists and improve flexibility. The request for George to join the First XI came in 1960 when he stepped up for three first-class matches after Ken Biddulph suffered an injury. He would average 10.66 with the bat and take 3 wickets at 53.33 apiece.

He had been married in 1939 to Phyllis Ann Sampson, who went by the name of Maud and with whom he had five sons and a daughter (who became the wife of crick-eter and umpire David Constant). After George's appointment by Somerset, he and Maud lived in Taunton until September 1963, leaving for Ross-on-Wye to manage the Prince of Wales public house until its sale by the brewery owners. Thereafter he returned to Bristol, where he worked for the Victoria Wine Company. Finally, in his sixties, he undertook clerical work for Abbey Life alongside a son, Paul.

As with so many of his generation who had been unaware of the perils of inhaling cigarette smoke, George suffered ill-health in later years, beset both by asthma and lung cancer. After having had a lung removed, his breathing became increasingly laboured until he died in his home in Bristol on 30 October 1991 at the age of seventy-two.

428
Frederick John Herting
4 June 1960 v. Gloucestershire, Bath

Fred Herting was born on 25 February 1940 in Ruislip. His father, William Paul Eugene Herting, oversaw amusement arcade machines and was married to Margaret Simon (née Purdey). Fred was only eleven when his father died in 1951 at the age of forty-one. A keen cricketer, William had encouraged a love of the game in Fred and had suggested, shortly prior to his death, that they should consider furthering his cricketing education at the indoor school at Harrow. Fred did indeed attend nets regu-larly and at the age of thirteen was told by the owner that 'there was a gentleman who wanted to speak with [him]'. The visitor was in fact from Millfield School and looking for young talent. Fred was invited to meet R. J. O. Meyer at the Café Royale in London to discuss a move to Millfield on the basis of a free scholarship. He subsequently spent five happy years as a boarder there and played for Somerset Second XI as an amateur from 1956 until 1958 while still at the school. After leaving Millfield in the summer of 1958 he signed a two-year professional contract. He was one of three Millfield boys

Fred Herting – a left-arm medium pace bowler whose skills were honed at Millfield School. SOMERSET CRICKET MUSEUM

who were offered terms at the same time. The others – J. Shaw and J. Taylor – failed ever to make it to the First XI. Bowling left-arm medium pace, Fred played regularly in the Second XI but a taste of first-class cricket finally came along in 1960 with a surprise call-up after Ken Palmer went down with tonsillitis. Fred did well on his debut with a four-wicket haul in Gloucestershire's first innings. Not among his victims was Tom Graveney, whom Fred describes as 'the best batsman I ever bowled to – he always had so much time'. Always broke and only getting by on his wages of three guineas a week plus free lodgings, Fred and some of the other young pros were dependent on the kindness of Tommy Tout, who oversaw the payment of bonuses for any wins or first innings leads and ensured that any money due was paid out instantly. Hearing that an international great such as Tom Graveney was only taking home £14 a week led Fred to the stark realisation that there might be more lucrative professions to be had. He would play in five first-class matches and take 7 wickets at 72.28 apiece. His batting average was 8.80.

In conversation with Barry Phillips in the 1990s, Fred confessed that his time as a pro was a sometimes unhappy one after his carefree days as a schoolboy amateur. He remained a well-liked member of the band of young men at the club but admitted that he found some of the senior pros stand-offish and a clique, although Maurice Tremlett was always approachable. Fred apparently had a prickly relationship in particular with George Lambert that was never quite resolved. Perhaps the generational differences, with George being in his forties, twice the age of the impish Fred, had some bearing. Peter Eele relates an incident on Fred's final day as a pro. He says: 'I was rooming with Freddy at the time Somerset parted company with him. George Lambert's room was done over by some prankster the same day and George was convinced that it was Freddy, but it wasn't.' Peter discreetly avoids identifying the true culprit.

Fred confirms that prior to this incident and towards the end of the 1960 season he talked over his concerns with Maurice Tremlett and representatives of the committee and it was agreed that his contract would be terminated. 'I was all for going immediately,' he confesses, 'but the secretary [Dicky Robinson] insisted I play out the last few Second XI games. At the end of the season I dumped my kit bag under my mother's stairs and didn't play again for years.'

Fred was married in 1963 to Heather Sanger, with whom he would have two sons, born while they resided in Chatham. The family left for East London, Johannesburg, where Fred was employed by 3M. He finally began playing cricket again after having been persuaded to do so by his manager, who arranged for the company to pay for his kit to be flown over. He subsequently enjoyed eight years working and playing in South Africa, having to turn down an invitation to play for Transvaal because he could not be released by his employer.

He returned to England for the sake of his children's education and found work where he could, coaching for a while at Millfield and then taking on sales positions while based in Pinner, where he and Heather were by then living.

Fred had arrived at the County Ground as a bright-eyed schoolboy, talented and full of hope for a future in the game, but he serves as an example of all those men – the vast majority of pros – who never make it to the higher echelons of the game and are forced to find ways to get by when their dreams fade.

429
Mervyn John Kitchen
29 June 1960 v. Cambridge University, Taunton

Mervyn Kitchen, known to many as Merv, was born in Nailsea on 1 August 1940. His father, Hubert John Kitchen, was a builder's carpenter and joiner and his mother, Phyllis Elizabeth (née Webber), was a housekeeper living in Long Ashton prior to her wedding. David Foot writes in *Sunshine, Sixes & Cider* that Merv 'looked like a young farmer and walked like a worldly, old sailor. He was a left-hander, vigilant and uncomplicated in defence, able to punch and pull when runs were needed.' He had first come to the attention of the Somerset hierarchy as a teenager and Somerset coach Bill Andrews recommended him to Flax Bourton CC, knowing that their excellent batting track would suit the young prodigy. Flax Bourton were rewarded with some fine innings and as a result his venture into life as a laboratory technician at the Long Ashton Research Station proved shortlived. After just six months he resigned to join the Somerset ground staff. He was soon making runs for Somerset Second XI and was in fact the leading scorer when they won the Minor Counties Championship for the first time in 1961. His progress in the First XI was slow but the county stuck with him.

Bill Andrews deserves some credit for having persuaded Somerset that Merv should be tried as an opening batsman in 1968, having drawn on his own experience of finding that a left-hander tended to disrupt his line and rhythm as a bowler. The experiment proved a success. Always at his best when he was in a more attacking frame of mind, Merv's fortunes were turned around through a combination of newfound confidence as a result of the trust placed in him and the benefits of adopting a positive approach that limited-overs cricket imbued. In Merv and Roy Virgin, Somerset had for a period a pair of batsmen often able to put opposition bowlers on the defensive. In 1966 he was the county's leading run scorer and he continued to make telling contributions.

Merv Kitchen – a left-handed opening batsman consistently in the runs and later a respected Test Match umpire. SOMERSET CRICKET MUSEUM

In the words of his opening partner, Roy Virgin, 'he never ducked a challenge'. Asked to outline his qualities, his erstwhile captain Colin Atkinson listed Merv's loyalty, genuineness and – with tongue in cheek – his pessimism. For part of the 1974 season and then throughout 1975 he was obliged to stand down as a result of injury problems but he came back in 1976 for four further seasons, playing his part with some useful cameo roles. Merv was delighted to still be part of the set-up of his beloved Somerset CCC when finally they landed the first trophies in the club's long and often tortured history. Over the course of 352 first-class games for Somerset he had averaged 26.41, with seventeen centuries to his name. He also surprised himself and his teammates by taking 2 wickets at 54.50 apiece. Another wicket in a Benson & Hedges cup match lodged long in the memory of the participants. Roy Virgin recalls that a rank long-hop was smashed straight to him at square cover and as he trudged disconsolately towards the pavilion, Gloucestershire opener Ron Nicholls was heard to mutter: 'What a death – caught Virgin, bowled Kitchen!'

After retiring as a player, Merv became a successful and widely-respected umpire for twenty-five years until his retirement in 2005 at the age of sixty-five. He remained as resolute in his decision making as he had been as a batsman. With his trademark six plastic promotional Watney's red barrels to count the overs, he stood in 393 first-class matches and 396 List A matches and also umpired in twenty Test Matches in the 1990s, together with a further thirty-two One Day Internationals or World Cup matches. His umpiring took him across the world, standing as an independent official in Test Matches in the West Indies, South Africa, Zimbabwe and the Indian sub-continent. Surely no umpiring career has ever been entirely error-free and Merv's momentary lapse came with what he himself, with his usual honesty, described as 'a shocker' in 1998 when he enraged South Africa's Allan Donald with a couple of poor decisions. Donald was later fined for stating that 'if you are not up to it, then get out of the game'. When Merv did leave the game at the age of sixty-five, he did so with his head held high, his reputation for integrity and a whole-hearted commitment to all he did intact. Ever a droll observer of life, he noted on retiring after forty-nine years in the game: 'Typical of me to end just one year short of a half-century.'

Merv Kitchen – 'looked like a young farmer and walked like a worldly, old sailor'.
SOMERSET CRICKET MUSEUM

Married in 1971 to Anne Jasper, he lives in retirement with his wife in Bristol. Anne was a spectator at many of her husband's matches as, on occasions, was their much-loved dog, Thumper, a pedigree chow, who on one occasion slipped his leash at the County Ground and followed his master loyally to the crease. Still striding toward the bowler's end, Merv was unaware of this until umpire John Langridge called out to him: 'Is that your dog?' Thumper had paused to relieve himself against the stump with Roy Virgin taking evasive action. Thumper was kept thereafter on a tight leash.

Fortunate enough and talented enough to have spent an entire career in the game he loved and having given his all for the county he loved, Merv had been a great favourite among the supporters who saw him very much as one of their own – Zummerzet to the core.

430

Abbas Ali Baig

9 July 1960 v. Warwickshire, Birmingham

Abbas Ali Baig was born in Hyderabad on the 19 March 1939 into an aristocratic Muslim family who had prospered under the benign rule of the Nizam of Hyderabad. His father was an engineer in the service of the Nizam and Abbas also had three younger brothers who played cricket professionally – Murtuza, Mazhar and Mujtaba Baig.

Known to his Indian teammates as 'Buggy', Abbas was fifteen and already regarded as a child prodigy when he made his first-class debut in the 1954-55 Ranji Trophy. By the end of that year's tournament, he had averaged 62.33 with the bat. A later description of his style talks of 'dazzling, exquisite stroke play, fleet-footed movement and incredible hand-eye coordination' and adds that 'while at the crease, he was like a composer directing his orchestra, rather than a batsman wielding his willow'. He was sent to study in England, attending University College, Oxford. Here he played regularly for the University in 1959 including in the Varsity match when, in a low scoring game, his half-century in the second innings helped Oxford to achieve their first victory in eight years. That same year, he scored 221 not out and 87 against Free Foresters, breaking Fredrick de Sarum's record of the highest run aggregate for Oxford University in a first-class match, the new record standing until 2013.

Meanwhile, the Indian Test team were having a torrid time in England, having lost the first three matches and the services of their senior batsman, Vijay Manjrekar, forced to return home with a knee injury. Abbas's exploits for Oxford made him an obvious choice as a replacement in the Test Match at Old Trafford. He hit a plucky century in the second innings, having earlier had to leave the field after being struck on the temple by a bouncer from Harold Rhodes. Still only twenty years old, he was the youngest Indian at the time to have achieved the feat and the first Indian player to have scored a Test century outside his home country. Even Fred Trueman, never one to lavish praise on a batsman, would concede that 'Abby Baig played fast bowling very well'. Abbas retained his place in the team for the final match of the series and had impressed sufficiently to be included in the Indian squad for the home series against Australia later that year.

His unbeaten half-century in the Third Test at the Brabourne Stadium, Bombay (Mumbai), sparked an unexpected chain of events. In his own words, 'I was returning to the pavilion at tea when this girl jumped the fence and kissed me.' The public display of affection between a Muslim and a Hindu sparked outrage and it would not

A. A. Baig (left) with his brother, M. A. Baig (right), going out to bat at Lord's for Oxford University against Cambridge University in 1962. SOMERSET CRICKET MUSEUM

be the last occasion on which his religious affiliation would blight his Test Match career. Despite having helped India to secure a draw, he was dropped for the final two Tests.

Abbas returned to Oxford University, gaining a further blue in 1960, the year in which he made his debut for Somerset. He was keen to continue enjoying first-class cricket during the vacation and Somerset had seized the opportunity. For his part, Abbas was no doubt relishing the opportunity to play at the County Ground, regarded as a batsman's paradise. Somerset coach Bill Andrews took him under his wing and offered him a place to stay. Abbas averaged nearly 40.00 in his eight matches for Somerset that year. Having returned to domestic cricket in India and to the Test Series of 1960-61 against Pakistan, he performed indifferently in the First Test and the selection committee were bombarded with messages asking for the 'Muslim sympathiser' to be dropped. He received an enormous quantity of hate mail and the pressure told on him in the following Test in Calcutta (Kolkata) when he was out to an ill-judged shot in the second innings. He had managed just 34 runs over the two matches. Many observers voiced the opinion – wrongly – that he had sacrificed his wicket deliberately. The selectors bowed to the pressure to drop him.

He returned to Oxford, gaining blues in 1961 and again in 1962 (on the latter occasion joined in the team by his brother Murtuza). He also played another fifteen matches for Somerset and finished his career there with an overall batting average of 30.36, also taking one wicket for 22 runs with his occasional leg-spin. Somerset would have liked to have seen more of him, but his future lay in India.

Back in his homeland, he continued to score heavily in the Ranji and Duleep Trophy tournaments and was selected for two Tests against the West Indies in 1966-67 before being dropped following failures in both innings in the Test at Calcutta. He never played for his country again but his batting performances in a strong Hyderabad team throughout the 1960s and until 1976 forced the selectors to reconsider him. Although chosen for the Indian squad, he was not asked to play and there remains a hint of injustice in his treatment by the selectors, with many suggesting that this elegant and hugely talented player had paid the price for Hindu-Muslim rivalry. A description of Abbas by Hyderabad teammate Venkateraman Ramnarayn gives a flavour of his persona. We are informed that 'appearing to look at the world around him with amused tolerance, he spoke both English and Hyderabadi with a beautiful but natural accent and was politeness personified, even when ticking you off for a poor effort'.

Abbas had been regarded as among the most eligible of bachelors in India, in company with his longstanding friend 'Tiger' Pataudi, (the Nawab of Pataudi Jnr). The pair were arguably the flag-bearers for future generations of Indian cricketing idols and were beset by female admirers. However, as Abbas later pointed out, 'there comes a time in everyone's life when you realise that you've had your flings and want to settle down'. He was married on 25 August 1968 to a Bombay girl, Vinu Mirchandani.

After his retirement as a first-class cricketer, Abbas enjoyed many seasons in club cricket playing for the Hyderabad Blues with Tiger Pataudi and then, when he moved with his family to Delhi, he played regularly for the British High Commission Cricket Club, still opening the batting with great style. As recently as 2015 he captained The Oxbridgians in the Nawab of Pataudi Challenge Cup of 2015. He also maintained his links with the Indian national cricket side and has stepped into the cauldron, managing the Indian team on a number of occasions, stating that he prefers active involvement to writing or commentary. His first taste of the role came in the Asia Cup of 1984, followed by a One Day series against Australia. Usually impeccably presented, with 'a silk handkerchief flowing from the breast pocket of his blazer' his was a softly-spoken but determined presence. He stepped into the breach again, succeeding Bishen Bedi as Manager of the Indian tour of Australia in 1991-92 and the Cricket World Cup in 1992. Abbas has said of the role that the incumbent 'must be more than just a coach: he must also be a friend, philosopher and guide, and a conduit between the players and the outside world'. He might have added that diplomacy skills of the highest order are also needed to satisfy the various warring factions.

Abbas Baig as a promising young Somerset player (top) and in latter part of his playing career (above).
SOMERSET CRICKET MUSEUM

At the time of writing, Abbas and his wife, Vinu, remain prominent figures on the Delhi social scene. Much-feted, Abbas has been the recipient of a number of awards in recognition of his outstanding contribution to Indian cricket.

1961

"Beyond all else, it was Bill Alley's year. He had been granted a benefit and, cussed and combative as ever, produced his best. He was forty-two years of age, a battered old sportsman who cursed and smote to leg and tiptoed in to bowl an impeccable line and length."

Peter Roebuck in *From Sammy to Jimmy*

Championship Position: 10 of 17

Many supporters approached the new season with low expectations. Colin McCool had called it a day and returned to Australia. Membership had slipped to a nadir of only 2,800 and a wildly ambitious plan to raise the number to 8,000 – based on blind optimism rather than a convincing strategy – fell on deaf ears. In order to inject some cash, a greyhound track was introduced around the edge of the field. Not everyone approved. In the event, the season was lit up by the batting of Bill Alley. The year was a personal triumph for the forty-two-year-old Australian with 2,761 runs for Somerset, including ten centuries and more than 3,000 runs in all first-class matches. Barring a brief run of poor form mid-season, he looked invincible, attacking the opposition bowling with fearless abandon. On two occasions he smote the first ball of the day for six. Alley was well supported by Graham Atkinson, with over 2,000 runs and Peter Wight with 1,660 to his name. Abbas Baig returned in the summer vacation and batted with great style. Ken Palmer was the most successful bowler, his 114 wickets contributing to a personal double, at the age of

Bill Alley – 1961 was his annus mirabilis *with over 3,000 first-class runs.*
SOMERSET CRICKET MUSEUM

The Somerset team in 1961.
Back row: *H. Sully, M. J. Kitchen, K. E. Palmer, G. Atkinson, K. D. Biddulph,*
B. A. Langford, B. Roe. Front row: *P. B. Wight, J. G. Lomax, H. W. Stephenson,*
C. R. M. Atkinson, W. E. Alley. SOMERSET CRICKET MUSEUM

only twenty-four. Brian Langford claimed 111 victims.

Of the ten Championship victories, two were over local rivals Gloucestershire. Given all these reasons for optimism, it is something of a surprise that Somerset managed only a lowly tenth place but the truth of the matter was that they still lacked a quick bowler to strike terror into opponents. The Second XI had fared better than their First XI counterparts. Somerset won the Minor Counties Championship for the first time in their history, helped in part by the absence of those leading counties who had left in 1959 to participate exclusively in a newly formed competition for the second tier teams of first-class counties.

None of the debutants made a lasting impression on the first-class game, although Cambridge graduate Tony Pearson had shown great promise as a penetrating quick bowler before opting for a career in the medical profession.

431
Michael Edward Latham
6 May 1961 v. Hampshire, Frome

Mike Latham was born in hospital in Birmingham on 14 January 1939, the son of Thomas (or Tom) Latham and his wife Frances (née Derry), who lived at the time in Smethwick. Tom was a toolmaker who played league cricket in the Midlands and took his family to Clevedon in 1949 where he captained the Clevedon Second XI in his fifties. Mike and his younger brother, Robert, would both become members of Clevedon CC, although Mike's interest waned and he turned to tennis for a while, before rekindling the flame at the age of seventeen. He and Robert would frequently bowl unchanged and bag all ten opposing wickets, competing together to see who would be the first to claim five victims, with Mike achieving his best bowling figures of 9 for 6 against Claverham CC. He was a versatile bowler who sent down fast-medium off-cutters or spin, depending on conditions.

Educated in Clevedon, he left school at sixteen to take up a five-year apprenticeship as a toolmaker at the Bristol Aeroplane Company (newly formed through a merger of a number of companies). After passing his Ordinary National Certificate (ONC) he attended the Muller's Orphanage College, which was affiliated to Bristol University, and while there he played regularly during the summer vacations for Gloucestershire Second XI. In 1960, he was approached on behalf of Somerset by Bill Andrews while he was enjoying a purple patch in club matches. Somerset persuaded Mike to register with them, fighting off approaches by Warwickshire and Gloucestershire. He had by then been taken on by a firm in Clevedon as a Planning Engineer and for two seasons his employer was happy for him to be released in the summer to play cricket (on a professional basis) but at the end of the summer of 1962 he was obliged to choose between a full-time career in engineering or cricket. He opted for greater long-term security. In eighteen first-class matches he had taken 29 wickets at 30.62, included best bowling figures of 5 for 20 against Nottinghamshire at Bath. He also recalls the match at Taunton in 1962 where Fred Trueman arrived late at the ground, having slept in. The rest of the Yorkshire team were despatched to the Somerset changing room while Fred was given a dressing down by his captain, Vic Wilson, and sent home. Relieved to see his nemesis off the scene, Peter Wight scored a double century and Mike, doing his bit for the fast bowling fraternity, claimed a haul of 5 for 61 in the Yorkshire first innings. Mike's career batting average was 14.77 – respectable for a supposed tail-ender.

Although he had planned to make further occasional appearances for Somerset as an amateur, his work took him to Northumberland the following spring and after a further three years, he started up a toolmaking company with his father in Hexham. He would play for Tynedale CC and for Northumberland in Minor Counties cricket between 1963 and 1972. He was married in September 1962 to Susan Lewis, with whom he had two daughters. Mike and Susan would in time go their separate ways and he would have two children with his new partner, Maureen Dick. Their son, Patrick, would have trials with Somerset and would play Minor Counties cricket for Cambridgeshire.

After having operated their business from 1963 until 1980, Mike and his father closed down their company on Tom's retirement. Mike then set up his own enterprise - Gridmaster Ltd - where he designed and manufactured a modular fixturing system for machinists in the engineering business. All his know-how and years of experience were brought to bear to offer simple solutions to clients. He was also able to bring his cricketing experience to good use, too, coaching on a part-time professional basis at Kimbolton School, close to Kettering, where the two children of his second marriage were educated.

At the time of writing, Mike continues to reside in Kettering and after a fulfilled and successful life he can say with certainty that cutting short his adventure as a first-class cricketer with Somerset proved a sound decision.

Mike Latham – a fast-medium bowler approached by Somerset after a purple patch in club cricket.
BOTH SOMERSET CRICKET MUSEUM

432
Geoffrey Harold Hall
21 June 1961 v. Cambridge University, Taunton

Geoff Hall

Geoff Hall was born on 1 June 1941 in Colne, Lancashire, the son of Harold Hall, a silk weaver, and Esther (née Carradice). By the age of fifteen, he had broken into the Colne CC First XI and soon established himself as the club's opening bowler, operating in tandem with overseas pro, the all-rounder, Stan Jayasinghe. Bespectacled and amiable, Geoff appeared an unlikely fast bowler but he became a formidable pace bowler in league cricket, according to one account 'regularly hitting the stumps'. By 1959 he had become a key figure in the Colne CC side who became the most successful in the club's history, winning the Worsley Cup and being crowned Lancashire League champions. He was drafted into the Lancashire Second XI and became a member of the ground staff at Old Trafford, appearing regularly the following season, although he never broke through into the First XI.

Word of his prowess reached Somerset, who were searching for an opening bowler

Geoff Hall surrounded by young autograph hunters. SOMERSET CRICKET MUSEUM

Geoff Hall – came down to Somerset after establishing a formidable reputation as a fast bowler in Lancashire League cricket. SOMERSET CRICKET MUSEUM

who offered genuine pace and hostility and he was offered a contract by the county. He impressed in friendly and Second XI fixtures and at the start of the 1962 season (by now qualified by residence) he took 5 for 28 and 4 for 30 against Hampshire Second XI and was immediately drafted into the First XI. His progress was halted the following season when Fred Rumsey arrived to partner Ken Palmer and opportunities became more limited. Fred's subsequent Test call-ups created openings but in five seasons between 1961 and 1965, Geoff would make only forty-eight appearances, taking a total of 111 wickets at 30.85 apiece. On one or two occasions as a batsman he demonstrated obdurate defence but he was never a run-maker and averaged only 3.60 with the bat. His former teammate, Peter Robinson, notes that Geoff was a pleasant companion and capable of devasting spells of fast bowling but adds with a smile that his feet could be deadly, too. 'Geoff had the smelliest feet on the planet,' he asserts.

Geoff was married for the first time in 1962 to Alison Sharpe and during the winter months the couple lived in Taunton where he worked as a draughtsman in the County Architect's Department. After parting company with Somerset he returned to the Lancashire Leagues as a player and coach before crossing the Pennines and continuing in a similar role until he retired from the game in 1981. He continued to work on the design of heating systems for local government, in the particular for the West Riding County Council. While based in Dewsbury, he was married again. His second wife was Mary Gaunt.

Having taken early retirement in 1994, he moved with Mary to Braunton in Devon, where he died of prostate cancer on 1 November 2009 at the age of sixty-eight.

433
Anthony John Grayhurst Pearson
19 July 1961 v. Worcestershire, Bristol

Tony Pearson

Tony Pearson was born in Pinner on 30 December 1941 although Somerset would lay claim to him on the basis of his having been educated at Downside, the Roman Catholic school in Stratton-on-the-Fosse. Tony's father, a tall, impressive Scot named John Erskine Grayhurst Pearson, known as Jack, was a distinguished consultant whose final posting was at Frenchay Hospital in Bristol. Jack also published a number of research papers and was married to Ruth Addison, an Admiral's daughter whom he met while they were both medical students. With as fine a mind as her husband's, Ruth worked as a general practitioner and raised their son and daughter in Bristol.

The Downside schoolboy was offered a place at Cambridge to study Classics but decided instead to follow in his parents' footsteps and train for the medical profession. He therefore studied the relevant science A Levels from scratch at Millfield School and gained a place at Jesus College, Cambridge, for Autumn 1960. Tony observes that during his year at Millfield 'ironically, I was unable to bowl for the school team, owing to a back injury'.

A right-arm fast-medium bowler, he was awarded blues in each season from 1961 until 1963. He played in thirty-six first-class fixtures for Cambridge University but his stand-out performance was his 10 for 78 against Leicestershire at Loughborough in 1961. He was the first Cambridge undergraduate to have accomplished the feat since Sam Woods (also of Somerset) in 1890 and the youngest, at nineteen, to have done so in any first-class game. The latter record would be

Tony Pearson – took 10 for 78 against Leicestershire in 1961. COURTESY OF JOHN LEE

taken away by Middlesex's Richard Johnson who was approximately a month younger when he performed the feat in 1994 and would later go on to play for Somerset.

Tony remained self-effacing about his performance, claiming in conversation with Barry Phillips that 'it was pure luck and actually a spinners' wicket', insisting that everything went his way, 'even down to the last wicket, where the batsman was dropped in the previous over'. Having already played on occasions for Somerset Second XI since 1959, he was given his Championship debut when regular bowler Ken Biddulph was injured and there was no obvious replacement, with Roy Palmer considered 'too young', though Tony would observe that he was only one year older. The impact was immediate with a return of 7 for 63 on debut, in Worcestershire's second innings. It is a record that, at the time of writing, has never been bettered by a Somerset debutant in a County Championship game. He would make six appearances for Somerset between 1961 and 1963 and would later recall that he loved his time playing for the county, who were enjoying a purple patch in which Bill Alley, Graham Atkinson and Peter Wight were regularly among the runs and the team were always looking to win matches rather than adopting negative tactics. 'They were confident', he would

Tony Pearson – a fast bowler who made a record-breaking County Championship debut for Somerset. COURTESY OF BRISTOL RECORD OFFICE

note, 'so different to Cambridge. Alley was a brilliant gully fielder and took some wonderful catches off my bowling. Other difficult chances that might have been dropped at Cambridge were swallowed up by the close fielders.' In total he took 26 first-class wickets for Somerset at a creditable 19.50 apiece. Asked whether he had any regrets about not pursuing a career in cricket he says he has none. 'I wasn't good enough', says the man who took ten wickets in an innings at nineteen. Tony Pearson has always set himself the high standards that one hopes for in a medic.

He was married to Elizabeth Angus in 1962 in Loughborough – the town in which he had claimed his ten-wicket haul. He was still an undergraduate at the time and the first of their four children was born the following year in Cambridge. His medical career took Tony and his burgeoning family initially to Bristol and on to Oxford for two years and then to Sheffield, before he became a consultant at Royal Free Hospital in Barnet where he remained for many years until his retirement in 2006. He had continued to play occasional games of club cricket but had turned increasingly to golf, becoming a member of the Burnham & Berrow Club whose facilities he had used when visiting his parents, who had retired to Burnham-on-Sea.

At the time of writing, Tony and his wife, Elizabeth, reside in New Barnet, where they have lived for nearly forty years. He combines brilliance with modesty in happy harmony. His bowling feat at Loughborough in 1961 and his heroics on his Somerset debut stand as lasting testimonies to his skills, however much he might protest.

1962

"It has been my pleasant, hair-raising duty since the
summer of 1962 to record Somerset affairs. In that time
they have toppled the best and been thrashed by the worst ...
How can I, the humble reporter of their deeds, be expected
to have a coherent line of thought, to be a calm purveyor
of fact, not to despair and not to be elated in
consecutive breaths, yet alone sentences?"

John Mason (Journalist for *Bristol Evening Post*)

Championship Position: 6 of 17

At the end of the preceding season, there had been the vague whiff of a mutiny
when Graham Atkinson (who had exceeded 2,000 runs), Ken Palmer (who had
achieved the double) and Brian Langford (with 111 wickets) had had the temerity to
delay signing their contracts, requesting a modest pay rise. The request was declined.
By the start of the 1962 season, the players had relented. 'I've a family to support,'
Brian Langford stated. 'If I'd not signed they wouldn't have released me and I'd have
been out of work for a year.' Perhaps some of the players' minds were elsewhere when
they failed to glean a single point from their first five fixtures, but thereafter the team
rallied and rose to a creditable sixth place, with twelve wins under their belt. Momen-
tum was building. The club was regaining a measure of self-respect.

Hot on the heels of Ken Palmer's becoming the youngest post-war cricketer to
complete the double, Bill Alley became the oldest, with 112 wickets and 1,915 runs.
Some felt that Chris Greetham might have been the man claiming the double had
Alley not demanded the ball whenever a seam-friendly track was in evidence and been
strangely reticent about shouldering the burden on bone-dry tracks. Greetham claimed
69 wickets but bowled fewer overs: of the two, his strike rate of wickets per balls
bowled was superior. Ken Palmer and Brian Langford both fell just short of 100
wickets.

Graham Atkinson and Peter Wight both exceeded 2,000 runs. They were ably supported by Brian Roe – never sparkling, forever dour, but a useful accumulator of runs and an establisher of platforms on which the more adventurous hitters could build. Peter Wight's 215 against Yorkshire was a highlight that very nearly wasn't. It is asserted by some that he had been complaining of sickness but after his nemesis, Fred Trueman, was dropped for disciplinary reasons, Wight staged a hasty recovery to rival the raising of Lazarus.

Roy Kerslake would make his debut. He would prove a thoughtful leader in due course and he would later become a pivotal member of a more forward-looking regime who embraced modernity and ushered in success at last.

The Somerset team who played Middlesex at Lord's in May 1962.
Back row: M. E. Latham, B. Roe, G. Atkinson, T. Tout (Scorer), K. E. Palmer,
M. J. Kitchen, I. R. Lomax. Front row: B. A. Langford, C. R. M. Atkinson,
H. W. Stephenson, J. G. Lomax, W. E. Alley. SOMERSET CRICKET MUSEUM

434

Ian Raymond Lomax
2 May 1962 v. Essex, Taunton

Ian Lomax.

Ian Lomax was born in Fulham on 30 July 1931. His father, Raymond Frederick Lomax, was a medical practitioner, married to Evelyn Mary (née Wolland), who was the daughter of a wealthy silk dealer who owned properties in London and Wiltshire. Their marriage was shortlived as Ian was only four when his mother petitioned for divorce. Raymond left for Tasmania and died in 1940 at the age of only thirty-six, leaving the pitiful remnants of his estate to his widow, Mavis Eva, whom he had married in Australia.

Ian was sent to Eton where he played in the First XI in 1948 and 1949. In the latter season, he enjoyed some useful partnerships with Colin Ingleby-Mackenzie, later the captain of Hampshire. They formed a striking pair, Ian large to the point of being ursine and Colin contrastingly short. One partnership descended into farce when, according to Ian's own account, they both found themselves stranded at the same end. With neither prepared to sacrifice their wicket they promptly raced to the other end and were both run out again, whereupon they turned and were both run out for a third time, leaving the umpire to adjudicate. His decision is not recorded but Ian's intimidating presence would perhaps have influenced the outcome. Certainly he was a man to give no quarter. As a batsman, his approach was to smite every delivery he could and when he succeeded, his innings were all-too-brief but wondrous spectacles of pyrotechnics.

Whilst still a schoolboy he appeared for Buckinghamshire but is more readily associated with the Wiltshire team he played for between 1950 and 1970, captaining them on a number of occasions although teammates recall that he was more successful as a hard-hitting batsman than he was as a skipper, tending to be distracted by goings-on on the racetrack and frequently having telephone messages conveyed to him from the pavilion. Mick Hanna recalls one match during which Ian was called away to the phone because his wife was in the throes of purchasing a race horse and was in need of a second opinion.

Although Ian was nominally a racehorse trainer, it was in fact his wife who undertook the role but was debarred from registering under the misogynistic Jockey Club rules of the time. Ian had been married to Rosemary Ransom in 1953 and they would have three children together, the youngest of them, Sarah, later becoming the second wife of Formula One World Champion James Hunt.

Ian Lomax – his approach was to smite every delivery he could.

Ian's six matches for Somerset all took place in 1962 when, as David Foot relates, he approached the county and fulfilled 'a long-cherished wish to sample County [Championship] cricket'. He came away with an average of 22.25 and with his curiosity sated, returning to his large farm near Baydon in Wiltshire, with his continued interest in the world of racehorse breeding and training. He was also for a while the Master of the Craven Farmers' Hunt (later part of the Vine & Craven Hunt). Thereafter, he worked for a while in London in the insurance industry and later enjoyed a spell as a pub landlord.

Sadly, Ian and Rosemary were divorced and he was married for a second time in 1975 to Joanna Rosemary (née Hebeler) who had already changed her name by deed poll to Lomax but was the former wife of Test Match Special commentator and Ian's fellow Old Etonian, Henry Blofeld.

A larger-than-life character, he divided opinion. His drinking buddies considered him the life and soul of the party. They ranged from the wealthy to the famous, including the great Australian all-rounder Keith Miller, but rarely if ever included the hoi polloi. A majority of disinterested observers regarded him as an over-bearing Old Etonian thug. He was certainly not a man to cross. It is documented that on one occasion he narrowly escaped a jail sentence for having horse-whipped a stable boy for not having packed his cricket bag correctly. There were mutterings that friends in high places had spoken up for him. Perhaps the description in *Wisden* of his having had 'an Edwardian sense of style and 18th century zest' is intentionally ambiguous. In cricketing terms, his brief spell in the Somerset side offered a fleeting but entertaining reminder of the age of the well-connected, hard-hitting amateur.

Ian died on 31 July 1996 in Deane, Hampshire, the day after his sixty-fifth birthday, denying him any claims to a long and happy retirement.

435
Roy Cosmo Kerslake
11 August 1962 v. Kent, Weston-super-Mare

Roy Kerslake

Roy Kerslake was born on 26 December 1942 in Paignton, where his father, Leo Eric Kerslake, ran a fruit, vegetable and florist shop after having left the family market gardening business. Leo was married to Patricia Louise (née Bellamy).

Educated at Kingswood School in Bath, Roy appeared both for Gloucestershire Second XI and Somerset Second XI while still a schoolboy. He went on to study Classics at St Catharine's College, Cambridge, where he observes that he was taught 'among others by a gentleman called Augustus Caesar, who apparently had a brother named Julius'. *Quod fingi non posset,* as they used to say in Ancient Rome: *you couldn't make it up*. In the event, with an eye to enhancing his career prospects, Roy switched after one year to a degree in Law. While at Cambridge he won blues in 1963 and 1964, on both occasions under the captaincy of Mike Brearley. His main contributions to the Varsity or county teams were as an off-spin bowler but he was also considered a capable middle-order batsman. During the summer vacations he played for Somerset, choosing to leave the first-class game at the end of the 1964 season in order to focus on his career in the legal profession, taking articles in London.

Prior to settling down to the planned career in law, he toured South America with MCC and he would later take part in an MCC tour of Canada. In 1968, having completed his articles, he joined the Taunton office of Clarke, Willmott & Clarke (a leading law firm with operations spread around the country) with whom he stayed, including a spell as a managing partner, until his retirement in 2007. Roy focussed on private client work and specialised in Trust and Probate Law. He jokes that he 'never appeared in court except for speeding'.

In 1968, with Colin Atkinson standing down, Roy was invited to return to Somerset and lead the side. It would prove a memorable year, to say the least. Sidelined because of a hamstring injury, Somerset's new captain missed five of the six opening fixtures, during which time they were beaten in the Gillette Cup – an anti-climax after the grand day out at the final in the preceding year – but ultimately he led Somerset to twelfth place in the County Championship. He was also married in 1968 to Lynda Lackie, known as Lynn, whom he had met while touring Canada and with whom he later had a son and daughter. Roy observes that he was at the County Ground and ready for the toss in the match against Gloucestershire a mere half an hour after his marriage, at which one of the witnesses was a youthful Greg Chappell. If Lynn had ever had any doubts about Roy's passionate commitment to Somerset cricket, they

Roy Kerslake – a useful all-rounder and a brilliant fielder.
SOMERSET CRICKET MUSEUM

would by then have been eradicated.

Wisden would note that 'his innate modesty prevented him from developing his skills to the full. His brilliant fielding never wavered, but his batting and bowling, both of value on occasions, were not given full rein.' It is certainly in keeping with Roy's self-effacing nature that he turned to others, rather than advancing his own cause as a bowler or batsman. David Foot would note in his *Who's Who* of Somerset cricketers that 'in truth he could stroke the ball powerfully for a small man, could spin it notably from the off and could field as well as anyone in the side'. His fielding indeed earned him the moniker 'Cobra'. In fifty-two first-class matches for Somerset he would take 45 wickets at 24.04 apiece and he would average 12.28 with the bat. Having stepped down from the captain's role, he would go on to appear when he could for Somerset Second XI (whom he often led) and on two occasions for the Minor Counties representative side.

Latterly, Roy has worked as a consultant on tax and probate issues. He has also continued to play an active role in the administration of his beloved Somerset CCC. In 1970, aged twenty-seven but already with vast experience under his belt, he became Chairman of Cricket and was able to offer support to the extraordinary group of young players who came together to produce a team of one-day 'Invincibles' in the late 1970s and early 1980s. In 1981 he was appointed Club Chairman and would continue to be regarded by the players as a confidant to whom they could come with concerns. Having stepped down from the chairmanship he was invited in 2004 to become President and remained in post for a twelve year period during which the facilities and running of the club were transformed for the better. Latterly, he has acted as a patron of the Somerset Cricket Museum. During the winters, Roy and Lynn spend time in Perth, Australia, with their daughter. In the summer, their son is close at hand. Jon has made appearances for Somerset Second XI and plays for Taunton CC.

Roy Kerslake stood up to the plate as a captain and later as a father-figure who has steered the club he has always loved to greater glory with gentle persuasion and a vision that marries intellect and understated passion for the cause. His deeds on the field of play were useful rather than stellar, but his overall contribution to the progress of the club has been immense.

Roy Kerslake – after retiring as a player he became an important confidant for a crop of world-class players. COURTESY OF ROY KERSLAKE

1963

"I particularly remember the match we played in June of 1963 against Somerset at Taunton ... I batted for a while with Fred Trueman ... Rumsey, it seemed, had gone completely off his head: he bowled a series of bouncers at Fred! Not just one or two but four an over, grinning all the time and clearly enjoying himself."

Geoff Boycott in *Boycott: The Autobiography*

Championship Position: 3 of 17

For the first time since the Second World War, Somerset were blessed with the presence of a bowler of genuine pace – one who could put the wind up opposing batsman and who was fearless or mad enough to exact revenge on the likes of Fred Trueman for their treatment of the Somerset batsmen. Fred Rumsey was worth his not inconsiderable weight in gold. On wickets that were greener than the norm, Rumsey took 102 wickets and his opening partner Ken Palmer an impressive 126. Although runs were harder to come by in 1963, Graham Atkinson amassed 1,454 and Brian Roe was not far behind. Chris Greetham had a sparkling season and scored 1,186 runs and Bill Alley contributed 1,076, two more than the elegant Peter Wight, for whom this was a relatively lean year.

Led once again by Harold Stephenson – a knowledgeable skipper and as nimble behind the stumps as ever, with 79 victims to his credit – the side threatened for much of the season to win the Championship, only to fall away at the death. Well practised in the art of winning the main prize, Yorkshire pressed home their advantage in the final stages.

This season also marked the introduction of the Gillette Cup which injected new life into the cricket scene at a time when attendances had been falling remorselessly. Although Somerset were knocked out in the first round in the inaugural year of the competition, the county and its supporters would take to limited overs cricket with great gusto.

Ken Palmer's efforts were rewarded with Test selection but he was twelfth man.

He did, however, win an international single-wicket competition, the first of its kind. Among the debutants, Fred Rumsey stood out, although Vince Lindo, a quick bowler and uninhibited batsman with figures of 8 for 88 and 23 unbeaten runs in his only appearance, might have been a useful addition, had his letter responding to Dicky Robinson's initial contract proposal not been lost in the depths of the Secretary's in-tray.

There were moments of reflection kindled first by the death of long-term servant (or possibly master) of the club, John Daniell, and by the installation of the main gates to the County Ground in memory of arguably the greatest of all Somerset-born bowlers, Jack White, who had died in 1961.

Roy Kerslake and Chris Greetham (front, l and r) together with Harold Stephenson and Brian Langford (back, l and r) wait for the rain to clear during the away fixture with Gloucestershire at Bristol in August 1963. SOMERSET CRICKET MUSEUM

436
Frederick Edward Rumsey
1 May 1963 v. Kent, Taunton

Once in a while, a player is released by another county and observers are surprised to find that a cricketing duckling has fledged into a swan of international class. Fred took to the County Ground and the County Ground and all its inhabitants took to him. Here was a bowler of genuine pace, capable of hurrying or intimidating the finest and, to add to his armoury, he was a left-armer. Fred was the missing piece in the Somerset jigsaw.

Born on 4 December 1935 in Stepney, London, he was the son of Frederick Rumsey and his wife Katherine Anne (née Finch). Fred Snr was a stevedore who worked in the London docks loading ships, a skilled job later rendered obsolete by the introduction of shipping containers. Fred Jnr began establishing a reputation for himself as a genuinely fast bowler in club cricket in London, also appearing for the Club Cricket Conference side, who included the pick of the local players. In 1957 he was invited to play for Essex Second XI as a twenty-one-year-old, but it was Worcestershire who offered him a professional contract. Between 1959 and 1962 he struggled to break through and only made thirteen first-class appearances, taking 31 wickets at 21.32 apiece. Ironically, he was unable to bowl in his final match for the Second XI against Somerset Second XI, owing to injury.

When Fred threw in his lot with Somerset, there was a sudden flowering of his talent. Here was a man of genuinely hostile pace, although being by nature an amiable sort, he sometimes had to be fired up to his fearsome best. Bill Alley would later observe that not only was Fred valuable as a strike bowler who would exceed 100 wickets on three occasions, but he also freed up the Somerset batsmen because opponents were suddenly 'less inclined to pepper the Somerset batsmen with bouncers', given that revenge could now be extracted. In short, Fred's arrival transformed the side. The England selectors took note and he made five Test appearances, taking 5 wickets at 27.11 apiece. Between 1963 and 1968 he would play in 153 first-class matches for Somerset and take 520 wickets at 19.78 each. His batting average was 7.66 and included a number of lusty blows that offered fleeting excitement as the Somerset tail sometimes twitched rather than wagged with Fred at the crease.

There can be no doubt that Fred has added considerably to the pockets of his fellow professionals over the years because in 1967 he set up the Professional Cricketers' Association, so that for the first time players were able to put on a united front and

Fred Rumsey – a bowler of genuine pace capable of hurrying or intimidating the finest.

Fred Rumsey – a man of courage who effected change for the better both on and off the field.
SOMERSET CRICKET MUSEUM

have a say on issues. He had sent a letter to each club secretary and senior player, pointing out that salaries were below the national average and that contracts only applied for six months of the year with no guarantees for many of winter employment. At a meeting at the Press Club in Fleet Street, he was appointed Secretary, with Roger Prideaux of Northants made Chairman and Jack Bannister of Warwickshire the Treasurer. John Arlott would later accept Fred's invitation to become the President. Fred was subsequently made an Honorary Life Founder Member and a Vice President of the PCA.

Somerset teammate, David Doughty, confirms that he knew from the outset that Fred was a leader of men and recounts the tale of Fred's unpreparedness to put up with the appalling food laid on for the players during the lunch interval. Fred broke ranks and sent out for eleven portions of fish and chips. Asked why the team had not joined their Yorkshire counterparts, he informed the club that the Somerset players had no intention of eating what was on offer. If the Yorkshire lads wished to eat it, that was their prerogative. Thereafter there was an improvement in the quality of the catering. Here was a man of courage who effected change for the better.

He was married in Bristol in 1966 to Coleen Crowther, with whom he would have three children. An inveterate organiser and a serial entrepreneur, he had opened up a new carpet cleaning business – Carpet Care Ltd – in Kidderminster in 1963 and this gave him a taste for managing his own businesses. In the winter of 1967-8 he was taken on as Somerset's Public Relations and Fundraising Co-ordinator, the first such appointment by a Championship side. Derbyshire quickly cottoned on to the value of such a role and, more importantly, of including Fred among their ranks, and offered him a similar position ahead of the 1968 season, with the business contracted out to his own stand-alone company. He was offered the added inducement of playing in List A matches. Fred had and still has a magnificent pair of broad shoulders, but at the age of thirty-two, he was beginning to feel the effects of years of pace bowling on his heavily-built frame and employed former Somerset cricketer Mike Barnwell not only as his administrative assistant but as a batsman in the nets, required to help his boss sharpen up each Friday ahead of the forthcoming fixture. On one occasion Fred appeared in a first-class game for Derbyshire but this reaffirmed the view that his days of three-day encounters were behind him.

In 1970, he became Managing Director of a property development company which merged with his Public Relations firm in the same year. In 1978, travel was added to the portfolio – initially in partnership with Caribbean Connection, a Chester-based travel company, but later independently for a total of thirty-three years. Fred applied his boundless energy and his networking skills to coordinate overseas cricket tours. He employed a number of well-known former players as his ambassadors on the trips. They included a roll-call of the great and good of international cricket, with Godfrey Evans playing a leading role, supported by the likes of Denis Compton and Sir Colin Cowdrey or Sir Garry Sobers and Wes Hall. Fred remained generous in helping others and giving of his time and was very active in raising funds through the Lord's Taverners. The wider debt that cricket professionals still owe the man who instigated the Professional Cricketers' Association continues to be recognised. Nor has he been forgotten by the supporters and the committee of the county he served so well and who honoured him as a Legend of the club in 2008.

437
David George Doughty
11 May 1963 v. Essex, Brentford

David Doughty has lived a varied and interesting life. There is an element of the Bohemian about a man who pursued twin dreams of a life in the theatre and a career as a first-class cricketer – two professions united (in the era in which he played) by the likelihood that they would leave him short of cash and vulnerable to life's vicissitudes but with a rich fund of memories.

Born in Chiswick on 9 November 1937, David was the second son of Ernest George Doughty and Violet Hilda (née Smart). During the Second World War, Ernest served as an ambulance driver with the RAF while his wife and young sons decamped to Hove. Here they remained when Ernest returned to civilian life as a skilled decorator, restoring regency properties. Educated in the state system, David blossomed as a cricketer, captaining his school First XI. Although his initial job choice was journalism, he soon set his sights on a career as a professional cricketer. His first approach was to Sussex where he was given trials in the nets. Although he failed to make the desired breakthrough, Jim Parks persuaded David that he would enjoy more success if he bowled left-arm orthodox (turning the ball away from right-handed batsmen), forsaking the chinaman that he had previously deployed. Having completed his National Service, during which time he played club cricket at the weekends at Beddington CC, sleeping overnight in the club pavilion, he was offered a trial with Essex, overseen by Trevor Bailey. He was informed by Bailey that he was 'a good player but we can't afford you'. David had by then joined Alf Gover's cricket school, initially as a client, coached by Arthur Wellard, but subsequently invited to undertake coaching sessions during the winter months. Here he befriended Arthur's acolyte Harold Pinter, at the time regarded more as an actor than the world-renowned playwright he would become. Harold helped to cement David's passion for the theatre. Indeed, David would later direct two Pinter plays – *The Lover* and *The Dumb Waiter* – in Edinburgh.

There followed a further trial for Surrey, facilitated by Jim Laker. There were also appearances for Middlesex Second XI and Leicestershire Second XI as David continued to put his case and demonstrate a dogged determination to succeed. The breakthrough into first-class cricket finally came when Arthur Wellard recommended him to Harold Stephenson at Somerset and, having bagged a five-wicket haul in a friendly against Glamorgan, David was instantly offered a three year contract. During his time at Somerset he would only make seventeen first-class appearances, with a batting average of 6.93 and 35 wickets at a respectable 20.28 apiece, including two five-wicket hauls. David confesses that his confidence took a battering when he fell victim to the deft footwork and exquisite timing of Australia's captain Bobby Simpson. During his second season, he fell out of favour and, languishing in the Second XI, lost his passion for the game. Good came out of his stay at Somerset, though. He met and was married to a Manchester girl, Linda McGawley, with whom he had a son. During the winters, David had worked as a garage attendant and – more to his taste – had then decamped with wife and son to Spain for an extended stay in a Ford Thames van he had customised as a mobile home. At the end of his three-year contract, he and his family moved to Manchester where he was offered employment as the pro at Werneth CC. Act One of the life of David George Doughty had come to an end. It was time for fresh beginnings.

While in Manchester, David worked as a salesman for the Co-op Bakery but was dogged by ill-health with hepatitis and tonsillitis. Laid low, he reassessed the trajectory of his life and applied successfully for the role of cricket coach at the Royal High School in Edinburgh, a job he held for five years. His passion for the theatre had remained undimmed and he joined the Traverse Theatre, an organisation committed to new

David Doughty – cricketer, playwright and theatre director. COURTESY OF JOHN LEE

plays. Initially, he offered his services as a director but he also became a member of the committee. Hoping to secure a full-time career in the theatre, David left his cricket coaching position and embarked on a three-year degree course in Theatre Studies at Manchester Metropolitan University.

Returning to The Traverse, he continued to help as a volunteer while resuming duties as a school cricket coach, this time at Loretto School. Some of his plays, including *Swansong* and *After Yesterday*, were performed at the Edinburgh Fringe over this period, a brochure announcing them under the banner of 'The Theatre of Ironic Absurdity'.

He had managed to generate much-needed funds with a shrewd or fortunate investment in a cottage in Lancashire which he had sold on completing his degree course. In a case of ironic absurdity spilling out beyond the confines of the theatre, this would prove the first of a number of fortuitous property investments while his first loves of cricket and the theatre proved less than lucrative. His wife Linda was by then a Social Worker when David suffered what he describes candidly as 'a bit of a breakdown'. He left Edinburgh. The curtain fell on Part Two of his life.

He and Linda led separate lives and for twelve years, David cared full-time for his parents in Hove (and later in Portsmouth) while gleaning occasional work in London as a freelance theatre director. Once again, it was shrewd property deals that saw him able to see off the threat of penury that bedevils many who opt for the life of a freelancer in the world of theatre. His son, Lawrence, now runs a successful guest house in Edinburgh.

At the time of writing David is based in the Yorkshire Dales, and in conversation reveals that he is considering living once more in the city of Edinburgh to be close to his family. This engaging character – a cricketer, coach, playwright and theatre director – deserves a happy finale.

438
Cleveland Vincent Lindo
19 June 1963 v. Pakistan Eaglets, Taunton

Vince Lindo enjoyed a brief but spectacularly successful first-class career with Somerset. 'What more do you have to do to win a contract?' wrote David Foot in his *Who's Who* of Somerset's post-war players. Blessed with a disposition as warm and sunny as the island on which he was raised, Vince bears no ill will for his shoddy treatment by the county. Indeed, he breaks into a broad smile as he tells you the tale.

He was born in Bigwoods, St Elizabeth, on the island of Jamaica on 6 June 1936, the last of ten children, only five of whom survived into adulthood. Vince was not yet six months old when his father, Lawrence Lindo, a farmer, died. His mother, Leah (née Nembhard), worked tirelessly to keep things afloat.

For many in the community, brought up in poverty and with little to entertain them, cricket was their abiding passion. On leaving school, Vince began to make a name for himself as a budding cricketer and was spotted by George Headley, who recommended him to the War Department of the British Army, where he was offered work as a clerk and drafted into the Garrison CC team, based in Kingston. By the age of twenty-three, he had decided – encouraged by some of his colleagues in the War Department – to visit England and he made his way to London with a group of friends. Vince chuckles as he remem-

Vince Lindo – played for Nottinghamshire and Somerset: 'I just ran in and bowled as fast as I could'. COURTESY OF VINCE LINDO

bers how he and his companions arrived utterly ill-prepared for their adventure. All they wanted to do was to party and play cricket. It had not occurred to them that they might need money for rent or food. Obliged to seek a refund for his return ticket from the travel agency in order to raise some cash, Vince then found work in the shunting sheds at St Pancras. While there he read a newspaper advert placed by Notting-hamshire, offering trials to fast bowlers. As a pace-man also capable of lusty blows with the bat in the best, free-spirited West Indian tradition, Vince applied. He was an instant success. On the basis of a stunning performance for Notts Second XI against Pakistan Eaglets, when he took 7 for 50 followed by 6 for 115, he was employed as a pro for eighteen months.

Although he played frequently for the Second XI and would win an award as the best bowler in the Bassetlaw League, he never broke through, enjoying only one first-class outing. Vince explains that he had never been coached – 'I just ran in and bowled as fast as I could', he says – and Notts coach Frank Shipstone attempted to change his bowling action, reducing his effectiveness in the process. He felt ready to move on, putting his faith in his natural ability. He was next offered a job as a pro with Gains-borough Britannia CC, supplementing his wages with work for Rose Brothers in Gainsborough, making packaging materials. It was while making a guest appearance

Vince Lindo – after a brilliant first-class debut in which he took 8 for 88, he never played for Somerset again. COURTESY OF VINCE LINDO

for Rose Brothers CC that he impressed a touring Somerset XI (who included Ray Robinson, the brother of Somerset Secretary, Dicky Robinson). Vince was promptly offered a trial and fast-tracked into the team that played the Pakistan Eaglets, tearing through them with 8 for 88 in their only innings and scoring 23 not out. The Eaglets must have been glad to see the back of their nemesis. Not so the Somerset supporters. Vince was offered a derisory amount of £14 10s a week and asked to fund his own travelling from Lincolnshire. Torn between his desire to play first-class cricket and the fact that this would make him sizeably worse off, he asked Dicky Robinson if he would consider a slightly more generous offer. The request appears to have languished in the Secretary's in-tray. Vince never heard from Somerset again until approached over thirty years later by the Former Players' Association. Incapable of bearing grudges, he is able to laugh about the debacle.

Vince then enjoyed success as a pro in the North Staffordshire League where he is described by cricket historian Peter Wynne-Thomas as having been 'a dominant force for thirteen seasons' with bat and ball. Over the 1965 and 1966 seasons he would also take 50 wickets in Minor Counties cricket for Staffordshire at less than 20.00 runs apiece. By 1966 he had felt ready for home but then he met and was married to Phyllis Barbara Linda Hutchinson, who worked as a nurse. A little more than a year later they had a daughter, Sonja, and Vince opted to put down roots in his adoptive country. He

Vince Lindo (left) and Sir Garry Sobers (right) enjoy a drink or two at Trent Bridge in 2017.

spent time in manual engineering jobs before fracturing two vertebrae which led to a change of direction when he joined the National Health Service in 1981, working in Occupational Therapy, assessing patients' needs.

He continued to enjoy his cricket, playing into his sixties before turning to umpiring. In the meantime he had played for and against some wonderful cricketers, foremost among them his friend Sir Garry Sobers, whom Vince describes as the most naturally gifted sportsman he has encountered. 'While the rest of us got our heads down and practised, everything came so easily to Garry,' he says.

In his eighties at the time of writing, Vince remains a hugely popular figure in the Stoke-on-Trent area, umpiring matches during which he happily gives advice to young and old, batsmen or bowlers, and always with a smile. In his free time he helps to raise money for research into the sickle cell trait, of which he is a carrier, as well as persuading clubs and players in the locality to part with unwanted kit which is sent to his native Jamaica in order to encourage participation. He is determined that young boys in the grip of poverty should be given every chance to break free.

This lovely man, with a heart of gold, descended briefly onto the Somerset cricketing scene. He could have brought sunshine, smiles and his brand of fearless cricket to the county. But alas we can only wonder what might have been.

439
Richard Kenyon Paull
3 July 1963 v. Cambridge University, Taunton

Richard Paull was born on 20 March 1944 in Bridgwater. His father, Joseph William Paull, was a motor mechanic and garage proprietor, married to Phyllis Christine Elma (née Parker).

In *The Hand that bowled Bradman* Bill Andrews cites Richard as a perfect example of someone who rose through the junior ranks as a result of sheer hard work and intelligent application of the lessons learned in coaching sessions, rather than an innate 'ball sense'. He was the archetypal late developer who 'had the brains to absorb the basic principles of batting'. His intellectual flowering came late, too. After performing poorly in his eleven-plus he would go on to gain a first-class honours degree.

Sent to Millfield, he became in time captain of the school First XI and also skippered the county youth side before going up to Hull Universty to take a degree in Maths. He appeared on a number of occasions for the university side before going on to Selwyn College, Cambridge, to study as a postgraduate. While at Selwyn he was awarded a blue.

A regular in the Somerset Second XI during the summer vacations, his six first-class appearances for the county came during the 1963 and 1964 seasons while he was an undergraduate at Hull. According to Bill Andrews 'there was the same academic application to his batting' that he had demonstrated in his studies. There was consistency in his performances but he averaged only 13.00.

While at Cambridge he met his future wife, Jacqueline Joan Hughes, to whom he was married in 1968. At the time of their wedding, Richard was working as a research engineer and Jacqueline as a teacher. They made a joint decision to 'visit Canada for a couple of years' but found the country sufficiently to their taste that they made it their permanent home, starting a family twelve years into their marriage and having three children. Working in the aerospace industry, Richard rose to become a senior manager before opting for a career change in his mid-forties and becoming a Maths teacher at Vanier College in Montreal. The new career allowed him to spend time with his family during the vacations and to travel extensively. Later he taught at Kuper Academy High School in Kirkland, Quebec. Views from his students varied from one assessment that 'Mr Paull is the funniest teacher ever' to another who found him 'impatient'. Perhaps Maths is not to everyone's taste and the pupil who noted that 'his sarcasm is top notch' has encapsulated both perspectives. Demonstrating the benefits of life in Canada, Richard described his home as 'a lovely place on a lake an hour East of Montreal'.

Richard Paull – captained the Millfield School XI and was awarded a blue while at Cambridge.

He remained an active sportsman for many years but also began buying and selling antiques as a pastime, noting with droll humour that 'I'm older and in worse condition than many of the antiques I deal in'.

The days spent in Somerset on the playing fields of Millfield School or at the County Ground in Taunton now appear a dim and distant memory. Canada has proved very much to his liking.

1964

"Beyond doubt the Gillette Cup was a triumph of innovation and in time Somerset would learn to love it, to yearn for it and, eventually, to win it."

Peter Roebuck in *From Sammy to Jimmy*

Championship Position: 8 of 17

Sparked by the success of the team in the 1963 County Championship campaign and by the first taste of Gillette Cup cricket at the County Ground, membership rose to the highest level at the time in the club's history. 4,742 paid their subscription and countless schoolboys sneaked into the ground unrecorded in the tried and tested manner of presenting a membership card before handing it over the wall for a fellow conspirator to repeat the exercise. If the Championship proved painful after the heroics of the previous season, then the second round Gillette Cup match against Nottinghamshire at Taunton offered a short-term palliative. A packed crowd, enticed by the novelty of this new-fangled format, were enthralled by a match that could not have been closer. With the scores tied, Somerset won on account of having lost one wicket fewer than Notts.

As for the County Championship, the frequent unavailability of captain Harold Stephenson, owing to injury problems, meant that Bill Alley was asked regularly to lead the side. Alley was perhaps instrumental in dropping the dour Brian Roe and replacing him with Roy Virgin as an opening partner for Graham Atkinson. Although this would act as a springboard to a successful career for Virgin, Atkinson's form would suffer as he bore more responsibility in the absence of an anchor at the other end. Such is the nature of cricket. Each and every decision has the capacity to generate a host of consequences, not all of them predictable. Graham Atkinson had nevertheless garnered 1,207 runs, a total bettered only by Bill Alley, who topped the county's averages. Peter Wight suffered a broken finger which meant that he missed ten matches, seriously weakening the side. Ken Palmer and Brian Langford both claimed more than 100 wickets, the latter enjoying success on spin-friendly wickets at Bath and Weston-super-Mare. Fred Rumsey – bowling far fewer overs and used in short, effective bursts – was not far behind with 78 victims.

The squad now included seventeen pros, but the debutants all failed to make any lasting impression.

440

Raymond Thomas Robinson

13 June 1964 v. Nottinghamshire, Taunton

Ray Robinson

Multiple Sclerosis is a debilitating condition and no respecter of persons, capable of destroying the nervous system, often in slow and incremental steps. Ray Robinson would become a victim of MS, which, although it robbed him of his athletic prowess and his sight, could not diminish his courage or his will to overcome adversity.

He was born in Charmouth on 15 September 1940. His father, Francis Thomas Robinson, married to Elizabeth May (née Murphy), had emigrated from Ireland, along with their son, Richard, who would later become Secretary of Somerset CCC. Francis worked as a farmer and during the Second World War served as a private in the National Defence Corps. After the war the family moved to Taunton with Ray being educated at The Priory School in the town and regarded as an outstanding rugby player, representing England Schoolboys against Wales in 1956 and also playing for Taunton RFC and Somerset (and also for the Royal Navy and British Police), primarily as a scrum-half although he was astonishingly versatile. Writing in the *Somerset County Gazette* in May 1960, Eric Hill reports that, on leave from his spell in the Royal Navy, Ray played successive games for Taunton at lock, scrum-half, centre, wing and full back. Eric adds that 'Ray, who is a bit sparing on words when reporters are about, told me "I was a bit tired" at the end of all that. It seems that the next few weeks will decide whether he stays in the Navy or gets another job. Taunton rugby followers will hope that his future lies in a job near Taunton.'

Ray had joined the Royal Navy straight from school and while he was training at Rosyth had met his future wife, Patricia Mary Beckett, known as Pat, whose father was an instructor at the college. Ray left the Royal Navy and married Pat in Edinburgh in 1962. They opted for a family life in Taunton where Ray worked initially as a turner at Easton & Johnson in Arbermarle Road. They had three sons, all gifted sportsmen – Sean, Richard Andrew (known as Andy) and Peter. Sean would play rugby for Saracens and Andy would play for Bath, England and the British Lions and would subsequently coach England and Scotland. Peter would in all likelihood have followed in their footsteps had it not been for a major injury. In later years, Ray, responding to being asked if he was proud of Andy, would reply: 'I'm proud of all my sons'.

He played club cricket extensively in the Taunton area and established a reputation for himself as an all-rounder. In 1964, at the age of twenty-four, he became a member of the professional ground staff at the County Ground and would be employed there for two seasons. Although a regular in the Second XI, he played in just one first-class

Ray Robinson – a fine rugby player whose son, Andy, played the game for England and the British Lions. COURTESY OF PAT ROBINSON

match where he was deployed as a middle-order batsman but was not asked to bowl. Sadly, he came away with a dreaded pair, perhaps musing as he made the walk of shame back to the pavilion that he should have stuck to rugby. Having left the Somerset ground staff, he joined the police force in 1966 and would become the archetypal village 'beat bobby' with spells in Yeovil, Curry Rivel and Somerton before returning to Taunton, by then with the rank of sergeant. His career with the police ended when, while working as an instructor at the Canonsgrove Cadet Training College, he was forced to retire through ill health. He had also taken up the post of coach to the Somerset rugby team when the onset of Multiple Sclerosis was diag-

Ray Robinson – his career as a policeman was foreshortened by multiple sclerosis, but he refused to be downcast about his condition. COURTESY OF PAT ROBINSON

nosed at the age of thirty-eight. As the condition took hold, his health declined until he became wheelchair-bound and blind. His son, Andy, reveals: 'I was thirteen when it started and I was immediately struck by the way my father took on the challenge of disability. He was so strong that I never saw him as disabled. He was just my father. And you have to be a great person to retain that same character.' Andy adds that 'even though he went blind early on in the illness, he didn't turn it into a big hardship. He was completely blind when I made my England debut in 1989. So you could say that he never saw me play for England but he was still there. He came to the ground and the game was relayed to him [by his friend and ex-colleague Bob Bruford]. It was as if he was seeing me with his own eyes.'

Ray was possessed of astonishing resilience and positivity and his efforts on behalf of the handicapped in the county of Somerset were acknowledged when he was awarded an MBE in the 1964 New Year's Honours List. He died in Taunton on 13 November 2001 at the age of sixty-one. Pat says of her late husband that 'he retained his love of life and good humour to the end, never dwelling on his problems and always interested in others. He was a joy to care for!'

Sport is what makes life worth living for many. And then life can occasionally come along and remind us – sometimes cruelly – that sport is a mere diversion.

* * *

Ray Robinson's older brother, Richard, known as Dicky, was also associated for many years with Somerset cricket. Born in 1929 in Shillelagh in County Wicklow, Ireland, he was a

left-handed batsman and wicketkeeper who appeared on a number of occasions for Somerset Stragglers and captained Taunton RFC at rugby. He is more readily associated with the role of Secretary of Somerset CCC, a post he held from 1955 until 1969. Perhaps because of his roots, Dickie arranged a tour of Ireland by Somerset at the end of the 1959 season, even donning his whites and playing for the Somerset XI. After leaving the County Ground, he ran a general store at Chilton Polden before becoming the steward at Morlands Club in Glastonbury and finally managing the Sports Centre at Wells Cathedral School until his retirement. He died at the age of eighty in 2009.

441

Frank Terence Willetts
1 July 1964 v. Yorkshire, Bath

Terry Willetts

Bill Andrews describes Terry Willetts as 'one of the most brilliant close-to-the-wicket fielders I've ever seen'. Terry was in fact also a useful attacking left-handed batman and a talented all-round sportsman who might have enjoyed a career as a professional footballer, had he not been advised against it by his father on the basis that it would have left him impoverished. Born in Birmingham on 20 November 1939, Terry was the son of Frank Willetts and Winifred Mabel Jones. Frank owned a number of successful retail outlets in Birmingham, ranging from a public house to a tobacconist's shop. For her part, Winifred was a talented seamstress and dressmaker whose services were much in demand.

On leaving school, Terry was offered an apprenticeship as a service manager with W. & T. Avery, a globally renowned manufacturer of weighing scales. He soon began making a name for himself as a cricketer and footballer. Having appeared for the Bristol Rovers Reserves, he was offered a contract but turned it down, favouring a career in business. He would however subsequently appear as a part-time professional for Bath City FC and Minehead FC.

By then he had begun to play for Weston-super-Mare CC under the watchful eye of Bill Andrews, who recommended him to Somerset, who offered him a professional contract. This time Terry opted for a career in sport and joined the ground staff, establishing himself in the Second XI as a superb fielder at forward short-leg and an opening batsman. Although capable of staying at the crease when the situation demanded it, he generally tried to force the pace, believing that matches could only be won if batsmen played with attacking intent. He was consequently regarded as a team player rather than an individualist concerned with averages. Over the 1964 to 1967 seasons he would make only sixteen first-class appearances for Somerset and would average 11.10 with the bat, including a highest score of 38. In truth, Terry was never entirely happy under the captaincy of Colin Atkinson, whom he had once accused of cowardice during a partnership in a non-first-class fixture at Beckenham where the ball was rearing up dangerously off a length at one end and Terry was black and blue after taking hits to the body for half an hour while, in his words 'Atkinson hid at the other end, refusing singles'.

During the winters he had worked variously at the County Hall in Taunton and in the Somerset indoor nets, gaining his coaching qualification. After his departure he was approached by Glamorgan, against whom he had scored 160 in a Second XI fixture in 1966, but declined them. He left instead to teach and coach at the Royal School in

Terry Willetts as a member of the Somerset team (top) and seen bowling the opening delivery for Bedminster CC after a record run-up that raised £30,000 for charity (above).

Wolverhampton and while there played for Wolverhampton CC and Shropshire, the county of his mother's birth.

Two years later he moved to Bristol to work for the South Western Electricity Board (SWEB) as a sales executive. Here he returned to the fold with Somerset Seconds and captained Bedminster CC, who won the inaugural Bristol & District League under his leadership. While at Bedminster he was able to claim the longest recorded run up when, in order to raise £30,000 for charity, he ran from Bedminster to Barnstaple before bowling the opening delivery of Bedminster's fixture.

Terry was also in discussions with Bristol City FC but this came to nothing when he was offered a job in the sales department of the construction company Taylor Woodrow. In 1975 he made Cornwall his home and would enjoy a long a fruitful career in Minor Counties cricket for Cornwall, representing them between 1977 and 1990, including a period as captain. In his forties he had been struck a sickening blow when a bouncer robbed him of his sight in his left eye. With help in the nets from former Yorkshire and England bowler Chris Old, he learned to adopt a new approach, now playing off the back foot, and his recovery was sufficient to register a further seven centuries. He subsequently opted for a less demanding life with the Cornwall Over-50s. During his career he had notched up an impressive 149 centuries in all levels of cricket and was also able to claim a record of seven outfield catches in one Minor Counties innings.

Terry worked for twenty-five years for Brewer & Bunney, a firm based in Redruth supplying commercial and industrial laundry equipment. He had risen to the level of Sales Director before his retirement. His first marriage in 1962 had ended in divorce, but he was married again in1975 to Frances Kay Martyn, known as Kay, with whom he had a son. At the time of writing, Terry and Kay remain happily ensconced in Cornwall.

442
John Douglas Martin
22 July 1964 v. Hampshire, Taunton

John Martin was born in Oxford on 23 December 1941, the son of Arthur George Martin and Frances (née Diment). At the time of John's birth, Arthur was serving in the Second World War as a lance bombardier in the Royal Artillery, but in civilian life he was an outfitter's salesman.

Educated at Magdalen College School in Oxford, John was offered a place at St Edmund Hall, Oxford University, where he was awarded blues at cricket and hockey. He won the first of his cricketing blues in 1962 and had to withdraw from the 1963 Varsity match after collapsing, having bowled five overs. It would later transpire that he was suffering from glandular fever, which put him out of action for the remainder of the season. After missing the 1964 fixture, he captained the side in 1965. He was then invited to tour South America in 1965-66 as part of an MCC team led by A. C. Smith. Bowling right-arm fast-medium, he had first come to Somerset's attention with a four-wicket haul while playing in a Minor Counties play-off fixture for Oxfordshire against Somerset Second XI. He was invited to appear for Somerset Seconds and would play for the First Team on just two occasions. Although he took 93 first-class wickets in total, the vast majority of these were for Oxford University, including a career-best 7 for 26 against Derbyshire in 1964. He took only 3 wickets for Somerset at 43.00 and with one innings of 0 not out, he never troubled the scorers as a batsman.

John was a regular in the Second XI during the summer vacations, often opening the bowling with his good friend, Cambridge undergraduate Tony Pearson. He retains fond memories of his time at the County Ground and his friendships with the likes of Merv Kitchen and Fred Rumsey, with whom he shared a flat, situated a five-minute walk from the ground. He would later relate that on rainy days, marooned in the dressing room, he perhaps learned more about the game of bridge than he did about cricket during his time at Somerset. He had also continued his career as a hockey player and would appear for Oxfordshire, Middlesex and on thirty occasions – qualifying via his maternal side – for Wales, before retiring from the international game in 1970.

John remains a gregarious man, with an easy-going and humorous approach to life but a quiet determination. Although he might have considered prolonging his career as a professional cricketer, the matter was resolved when he suffered a shoulder dislocation on three occasions and opted for a career as a schoolmaster, joining the staff at Wellington College in Berkshire in September 1966. Here he taught Geography, also

John Martin – for many years a teacher, coach and housemaster at Wellington College.

coaching the school rugby XV and the hockey XI for a number of years and playing his part in the running of the Combined Cadet Force, where one report describes him as 'unfailingly a fair bastard'. If his manner was of necessity authoritarian on the parade ground, the same was never said on the playing fields. A tribute in the Wellington College magazine informs us that 'his coaching style was invariably quiet and understated – yes, there was steel there, but good humour, too'.

Married in 1970 to June Heather Gasgoigne, known as Heather, John became a housemaster and was then seconded to Melbourne Grammar School for two years in the early 1980s, returning in 1983 to the role of Head of Geography. He continued to travel widely during school vacations, leading school tours to a number of far-flung countries. Latterly, he was instrumental in strengthening the game of golf at Wellington College. He was also appointed Second Master (or deputy head) in his final years at the school. In total he had served the institution for thirty-six years by the time of his retirement in 2002. In summarising his colleague's career, Chris Potter writes that 'in every area, John was able to bring a calming, commonsense, dry, pungent wit, good humour, a wealth of experience and a balanced professionalism'.

Revitalised after the replacement of both hips, John has been able to enjoy an active retirement along with his wife, Heather, continuing to pursue their interests with their usual unflagging energy and an unbounded sense of *joie de vivre*.

1965

"A view persisted among some of the more reactionary committee members at Taunton that players were paid to express themselves on the field and nowhere else."

David Foot in *Sunshine, Sixes and Cider*

Championship Position: 7 of 17

The core of successful professionals was beginning to flex its collective muscles again. Their first successful demand was that Bill Alley should not be appointed club captain. His ability was not questioned but his tendency towards selfishness and his stubborn partiality were resented. The captain of choice was Colin Atkinson, which satisfied all sides while not necessarily enthusing any. For some, the reinstatement of amateur captains was seen as retrograde. There was also agreement to the levelling of pay for capped players.

No individuals performed outstandingly but Colin Atkinson brought a sense of order to proceedings. Openers Graham Atkinson and Roy Virgin were the only batsmen to top 1,000 runs although Chris Greetham came close with some sparkling displays of mighty hitting, albeit too few of them. No bowler would reach the milestone of 100 wickets, although Fred Rumsey came closest with 96.

The Bath Festival might have caused a flurry of excitement but it was not to the taste of the purists with a square not fit for purpose. Somerset won their first two matches inside two days and were defeated by Nottinghamshire at a canter in the third. Demonstrating that there was something approaching strength in depth, Somerset Second XI won the Minor Counties Championship.

Among the debutants, Roy Palmer, younger brother of Ken, made occasional telling contributions as a pace bowler. Geoff Clayton proved an outstanding but truculent wicket-keeper and his roommate at the Princess Royal pub, Peter Robinson, would contribute much to his adoptive county as a player, coach and raconteur.

Geoffrey Clayton
5 May 1965 v. Lancashire, Taunton

Geoff Clayton was born in Mossley, Lancashire, on 3 February 1938. His mother, Elsie Clayton, worked at the time as a typist with Robert Radcliffe & Sons, a woollen manufacturer in the town and, she and her mother brought Geoff up. Later, Elsie became a district nurse.

Geoff's tough upbringing moulded him into a strong personality. Unprepared to accept anything he regarded as an injustice, he was seen as difficult by those who attempted to make him tow the party line but fellow pros valued his wicket-keeping skills and admired the way he was at his most resolute as a batsman when he needed to dig his side out of a hole. Discovered by the Lancashire Schools Federation, he cut his teeth with Mossley CC before being invited to join the Old Trafford ground staff straight from school. From 1956, Geoff began appearing for the Lancashire Second XI, also playing for Ashton CC and Werneth CC. His progress was delayed while he undertook his National Service, appearing for the Army and Combined Services in 1957 and 1958. From 1959 be became the first choice keeper at the county, a combination of his athleticism and simian gait earning him the nickname 'Chimp', an affectionate moniker that his friends still use. As striking as his brilliance behind the stumps were his loud and prolonged appeals, which added further theatre to proceedings.

His arrival at Somerset seemed like the proverbial manna from heaven: a leading first-class keeper able to replace Harold Stephenson. If there were any doubts about the move, they were eradicated by the eighty-five victims Geoff claimed in his first season with Somerset. He also played his part in keeping the team on their toes, enquiring of Fred Rumsey whether he should stand up to the wicket in order to fire the Somerset paceman up or, in the words of his erstwhile roommate, Peter Robinson, 'hurling the ball at you like a bullet and telling you that you weren't spinning it enough'. The termination of his contract with Lancashire had had nothing to do with his performances but everything to do with his attitude to authority. With twenty overs of the Lancashire innings remaining in their Gillette Cup semi-final against Warwickshire, and only five wickets intact, M. J. K. Smith had adopted defensive tactics, instructing his fielders to scatter to the boundary ropes. Geoff and Ken Grieves had taken umbrage and staged a go-slow. With the crowd slow hand clapping, one spectator running on to remonstrate, and team manager Cyril Washbrook furious, Geoff and Ken had continued to plough their own furrow. He was dropped for the

Geoff Clayton – a brilliant and independently-minded wicket-keeper.
SOMERSET CRICKET MUSEUM

Geoff Clayton – has always been a man to build a near-impenetrable shell around himself.

SOMERSET CRICKET MUSEUM

Roses match that followed and was released at the end of the season, along with three others regarded as trouble-makers. He remained a popular figure in Lancashire. Brian Statham had looked out for Geoff from the outset and they were friends for the remainder of Brian's life. In later years, when Brian was President of Lancashire, he arrived at the ground on one occasion to find his personal parking space taken by a battered three-wheeler. There was no mistaking the owner. Brian later joked that 'it cost Geoff a couple of fags'. Geoff has eschewed any outward show throughout his life and his taste in clothing matched his battered old car.

Lancashire cricket historian Rev. Malcolm Lorimer observes that 'I've taken a few funerals of former Lancashire players and Geoff always turns up in his tatty old raincoat looking like Columbo, walking down the middle of the chapel with a copy of the *Racing Post* stuffed in his pocket.'

Having arrived at Somerset with his wicket-keeping credentials already beyond doubt, his skills as a batsman were regarded as a bonus. Coming in as night watchman in the home fixture against Middlesex, he scored his only century. Over three seasons, he averaged 14.77 with the bat but, more importantly, claimed 209 catches and 33 stumpings, contributing to an overall first-class tally of more than 650 victims.

In a game against his old foes, Warwickshire, he staged a go-slow behind the stumps in order to reduce the over rate in the hope of securing a draw. Such behaviour was anathema to his captain, Colin Atkinson, who threatened to send him off unless he desisted. Relations between the skipper and his keeper never recovered with Geoff making little effort to disguise his irritation, resorting on some occasions, for example, to trapping with his foot balls thrown inaccurately from the boundary. His departure at the end of the 1967 season appeared sudden and unexpected to outside observers, although not to those who knew the strength of personality of the two protagonists.

Geoff might have been cussed to the point at times of being unmanageable, but he had been an invaluable member of the team. 'He was all right, was Chimp,' David Doughty reminisces. 'He was fond of his fish and chips. He used to drive three of us to away matches and we'd always have to stop off for fish and chips. Geoff would be sat there with them on his lap, eating them with one hand while he drove with the other.' 'The scruffiest roommate who ever lived,' Peter Robinson adds, 'and he was keen on Mackeson Stout and Park Drive cigarettes, too. He used to leave his cigarettes balanced on the side of the bench when he went out to bat. It's a wonder he never burned the old pavilion down.'

During the winters Geoff had supplemented his wages, working for a period as a coal delivery man. After leaving Somerset at the age of only twenty-nine, he walked away from the game he had graced. He turned his attention instead to greyhounds and horses and became a well-regarded greyhound trainer and owner.

He continued to find work where he could, never likely to take to an office job. 'I'm not a letter writer,' he confesses. 'Fred Rumsey would write my letters and do my paperwork for me at Somerset and Jack Bond before him at Lancashire.' For a while he rented a small number of grocery shops and Peter Robinson recalls encountering him at a later stage 'selling cladding to adapt street lighting for local authorities: his friend had registered the patent'. For recreation, Geoff turned in time to crown bowls, while his interest in horse and greyhound racing continued unabated.

Never married, he has changed little over the years and was saddened by the death of his beloved mother in 2004. 'She always looked after me, right till the last,' he confesses. 'I suppose it should have been the other way around.' He lives modestly and has always been a man to build a near-impenetrable shell around himself. The combination of dogged determination on certain issues and a tight-lipped wall of silence when he could have aided his own cause has won him admirers and critics in equal measure. His friends remain unwaveringly loyal to him, valuing the directness that strangers sometimes see as cussedness or defensiveness. He remains his own man, unmoved by what anyone else might think.

444
Peter James Robinson
5 May 1965 v. Lancashire, Taunton

Peter Robinson [signature]

Peter Robinson was born in Worcester on 9 February 1943, the son of Robert James Robinson, an engineer's labourer, and his wife Gertrude Ursula (née Jenkins). He had cricketing pedigree, given that Roland ('Roly') Jenkins of Worcestershire and England was an uncle. Almost from the moment he could walk, he was encouraged by his paternal uncles (of whom there were six) to play cricket. Educated at Christopher Whitehead High School in Worcester, he left at fifteen to work for Kay & Co Ltd, the large catalogue company which had been founded in Worcester in the latter part of the nineteenth century. Very shortly thereafter he was invited to join the ground staff at Worcestershire, although he would continue to work for Kay's each winter. During the seasons that followed, he was loaned out to club sides such as Kidderminster CC and then Stourbridge CC, where he honed his craft in a competitive environment.

He made his debut for Worcestershire Second XI in 1960 at the age of seventeen and put in some sterling performances, primarily as a left-arm orthodox spinner, but he struggled to break through into the First XI and made only five first-class appearances in total over the 1963 and 1964 seasons. With the blessing of his home county he moved to Somerset, where he was immediately given the opportunity to showcase his abilities as a spin bowler and superb close fielder but also as a redoubtable batsman. He knew his limitations as a stroke-maker but grafted for his runs with real application and was flexible enough to bat wherever he was asked to – from opener to tail-ender – and talented enough to notch up three centuries and twenty-one half-centuries. Between 1965 and 1977 he played in 180 first-class matches for his adoptive county, averaging 21.52 with the bat and taking 291 wickets at 27.38. He also held 168 catches.

The highlight of his playing career was the Gillette Cup Final of 1967 when Somerset supporters descended in their droves on Lord's and many of them were too drunk by the end of the day to be overly despondent about the loss to Kent. Opening the batting with Roy Virgin, Peter had top-scored for his side with 48 but the trophy had slipped from Somerset's grasp.

Married in 1966 to Elizabeth Powick, known as Liz, a secretary whom he had met during his days at Worcestershire, he would have three children. Peter retains fond memories of his time at Somerset. 'I was told I'd be staying at the Crown & Sceptre,' he recalls, 'but after two nights I was summoned by the Secretary, Dicky Robinson,

Peter Robinson – Somerset cricket's raconteur-in-chief.
SOMERSET CRICKET MUSEUM

Peter Robinson offered sterling service to his adoptive county as an all-rounder and later as a coach. He is seen here (left) in action and (below) receiving a clock in 1990 in recognition of his first twenty-five years at Somerset. Making the presentation is the club's chief executive at that time, Peter Anderson, a former police officer, known to many of the players as Panda.

BOTH COURTESY OF SOMERSET CRICKET MUSEUM

and told my room was too much for the club to afford. Being new to the town, I asked where I should stay and was told to use my initiative and find somewhere. Fortunately, there was a spare bed available in Geoff Clayton's room at the Princess Royal. Geoff looked after me but nobody warned me he was the untidiest, scruffiest man who ever lived.' The facilities at the ground were woeful, matched only by the catering. 'We used to be given these pies, supposedly steak and kidney,' Peter says, 'and Bill Andrews would take a bite and observe that another horse must have died at Blagdon, the local racecourse. They pushed the boat out one year and gave the cooks, Ethel and Betty, an increased budget to look after the Pakistani tourists. They served up a lovely pork dish and the tour manager had to inform them that they weren't allowed to eat meat from a pig on account of their religious beliefs, whereupon Ethel and Betty said not to worry as they had a spare leg of ham they could carve up and serve with salad, instead!'

Like all his fellow pros, Peter scraped a living on his meagre salary, in his case working during the winters at the Taunton goods shed, unloading railway wagons. He recalls the resistance to any bonus when Somerset reached the final of the Gillette cup. In the end, the committee agreed reluctantly to a £15 bonanza. Through the efforts of Fred Rumsey, the players contributed to a brochure – *Up from Somerset for the Cup* – which netted them a further princely £20 each.

After his playing days ceased, Peter's know-how was called on as he became First XI coach during the so-called 'Glory Years' when Somerset finally landed their first trophies. Along with other experienced pros, in particular Tom Cartwright, he was on hand to help a hugely talented crop of young players to fulfil their potential. He would later offer years of sterling service as coach to the Second XI and in 2002 was appointed coach of the Somerset Ladies Team. More recently, still based in Taunton, he has nurtured fruit and vegetables on his beloved allotment as carefully and patiently as he brought on young cricketing talent over the years. It is surely no exaggeration to claim that no one knows more of the intimate detail of the goings on at the club for the last fifty years and Peter recalls events with a whimsical sense of humour.

He has been around at the club long enough to have seen the transformation of the County Ground from a ramshackle set of facilities – characterised by leaking roofs, a communal bath so unwholesome that even the germs were possibly reluctant to enter it and with skirting peppered with poison to keep the rats in order – to a sparkling arena fit for King Viv and his successors.

445
Roy Palmer
19 June 1965 v. Cambridge University, Taunton

The brother of Somerset and England all-rounder Ken, Roy was born in Tidworth, Wiltshire, on 12 July 1942, the son of Henry Ernest Palmer and his wife, Cecilia (née Rhapps). In civilian life his parents had both been hospital workers near Devizes but by the time of Roy's birth, Henry was serving in the Second World War as a sergeant with the Wiltshire regiment, with the couple living in married quarters at the barracks in Devizes. Roy was born in the military hospital at Tidworth although brought up in Devizes.

He was nurtured through the junior ranks at Somerset before breaking into the Second XI at the age of sixteen in 1959. It was announced at the end of the 1963 season that he had left the ground staff and was working in the car repair business with Arthur Martin of Taunton, having previously worked alongside his brother, Ken, at Marshalsea's Garage. Reports of the death of his first-class career had in fact been exaggerated. Although he made only a handful of appearances in 1964, he came back taller, stronger and quicker in 1965. His progress as a cricketer proved slower than his nippy deliveries, with just two first-class appearances in 1965 and three the following season. He did however enjoy a purple patch in 1966 with two Gillette Cup Man of the Match awards, the second for a devastating spell of bowling when he took 5 for 18 against Lancashire. Between 1967 and 1970 he became a regular in the First XI capable of penetrative bursts but not of sustained excellence and with a tendency to be expensive. In seventy-four first-class matches he took 172 wickets at 31.62 apiece and he averaged 13.29 with the bat. He also chipped in with 67 wickets in limited overs matches.

After departing from the County Ground, Roy worked for a while as a groundsman employed by the local council. He explained his motivation for subsequently opting for the life of an umpire, stating: 'My brother [Ken] was always nagging me to have a go but I was happy as a groundsman until the council made me a 'group grounds-man', which meant I lost my own pitch and had to go off trimming verges here, there and everywhere.' The poacher, who had once been upbraided for picking the seam as a player, turned umpiring gamekeeper in 1980 when, after a trial period the preceding season, he was added to the umpires list. He stood in 445 first-class matches, 469 List A matches and in two Test Matches, both of which were not without incident. In the first, in 1992, he warned Aaqib Javed for intimidatory bowling against avowed tail-ender Devon Malcolm and at the end of the over, handed back the bowler's sweater with what *Wisden* described as 'more emphasis than usual, probably because it was caught in his belt'. Pakistan seemed intent on making an issue, claiming Roy had insulted them, but they were deemed to be in the wrong by match referee, Conrad Hunt. Roy was involved in a further fracas in 1993 when he reported the Australians for their excessive appealing. Once again he was supported in his actions. Roy's swan-

Roy Palmer – a fast bowler capable of devastating bursts who later became a Test Match umpire. SOMERSET CRICKET MUSEUM

song was an emotional one at the County Ground when, led by Justin Langar, Somerset secured the Division Two Championship in 2007 with a record 266 points. Roy was given a standing ovation before the celebrations began. Former England player and commentator David Lloyd has ranked Roy, along with brother Ken, in his Top Ten umpires, observing that 'Roy used to shoot you out' with the 'slowest raised trigger finger in the west'. All of which goes to prove that the amiable 'Bumble' is not a man to bear grudges, given that in his first taste of limited overs cricket he had faced three deliveries and that on the third of these Roy had uprooted his stumps, sending him back to the pavilion for a duck.

Roy was married in Barnstaple in 1966 to Ella Wescott, styling himself 'Royston' for the records. They would have a son, Nicholas (Nick), who was a good enough cricketer to represent Combined Services. Roy was married for a second time in 1983 to Alyne Goulding. In later years he has turned to golf at the Ilfracombe & The Vale Club in North Devon. His brother, Ken, states that Roy continues to be a fine golfer. 'Unlike the majority of cricketers, I could never manage to hit it straight and so I've resisted Roy's efforts to get me to play the game,' Ken reveals self-deprecatingly. At the time of writing, Roy continues to enjoy his retirement in North Devon with regular rounds of golf.

Roy Palmer (left) and older brother, Ken (right), in 2008. COURTESY OF RICHARD ISBELL

446
Michael Godfrey Melvin Groves
4 August 1965 v. Sussex, Weston-super-Mare

Michael Groves

Michael Groves was born on 14 January 1943 in Taihape, a small town on New Zealand's North Island. His father, Henry Basil Melvin Groves, known as Basil, had been a Lieutenant Colonel in the Army and had played in one first-class match for the Europeans in India. Awarded the military cross and bar, Basil had served with the Desert Rats before being invited to command the New Zealand Army Fighting School at Waiouru near Taihape. He was married to Sheila Flora (née MacKinnon) and in addition to Michael, the couple would have a daughter. Already in his late-forties when Michael was born, Basil retired from the Army in 1947 and the family moved to Cape Town the following year. The decision to relocate to the South African city was sparked by Sheila, who had been struck by the beauty of the place when the ship carrying her to join her husband in New Zealand had stopped there to take on supplies.

Educated at the Diocesan College in Cape Town, Michael made an initial first-class appearance for Western Province as an eighteen-year-old, having just completed a second year of playing for the South African Schools XI. He arrived in England in 1962 and – clearly well-connected – appeared for the prestigious Free Foresters side captained by Devonian C. H. R. Featherstonhaugh. His association with Somerset was via his godmother, whose house he lodged at in East Coker. With special registration allowed for Oxbridge cricketers, appearances for Somerset would follow.

In September 1962 Michael began his studies at St Edmund Hall, Oxford, and he would play for the Varsity side on forty-three occasions. In his first year, he narrowly missed out on his blue when he was selected as twelfth man for the Varsity match and replaced his good friend and fellow Somerset cricketer, John Martin, who succumbed on the first morning to what turned out to be glandular fever and took no further part in the match. Michael was awarded his blue in each of the following three seasons. In his last year he helped Oxford to an innings victory with what G.H.Chesterton described as a 'militant' 80 not out. His batting style indeed tended toward the forceful and expansive and this is perhaps reflected in the statistics. On twenty occasions he notched up a first-class half-century but never progressed to a hundred. His seven matches for Somerset – all in 1965 after having established his credentials in the Second XI – yielded a batting average of 23.46 (compared to an overall first-class average of 29.20). Michael made his final appearances for Somerset during the summer vacation in 1966, scoring freely for the Second XI in the Minor Counties Championship. He was asked by Bunty Longrigg to take on the captaincy of the First XI after

Michael Groves – an Oxford blue who went on to enjoy a successful business career.

COURTESY OF BARRY PHILLIPS

Colin Atkinson's departure in 1967 but had the good sense to rebuff any advances, having taken up an appointment in the City of London.

Michael was married in 1967 to Catherine Elizabeth Heathcoat Amory, a member of the illustrious family who owned Knightshayes House, near Tiverton, before it later passed into the hands of the National Trust. After leaving the City of London for the North West, he embarked on a hugely successful business career. Over more than four decades, he developed and grew a multi-million pound operation which started out as Millford Grain Limited, shipping high protein hard milling wheat to Liverpool and Tilbury. Subsequently, he set up Yeoman Backhouse, selling aggregates, Mersey Asphalt, manufacturing tarmac, and Backhouse Bloore, a shipping agency company. He has also been a leading light and director of the Grain and Feed Association. In the meantime, this man of unbounded energy was married for a second time in 1971 to Susan Irwin and then in 1991 to Julia Costa-Sanseverino (née Cockayne), the daughter of Lord Cullen. He was then married in Richmond in 2000 to Sarah Amos.

Michael still retains an active interest in the businesses he built up, along with his son and fellow director, Alistair, who has taken over the day-to-day running. He also regards his involvement in the wider community as an important element of his time in Liverpool and is Chairman and President of the inner-city youth charity Fairbridge in Merseyside, set up after the Toxteth riots. His main source of recreation is now golf rather than cricket and he is a member and past captain of the Royal Liverpool Golf Club at Hoylake. He resides in a characterful listed home in Puddington, Cheshire.

1966

"Had not injury prevented Alley bowling against Yorkshire, the eventual champions, who won by 49 runs, had not last-wicket stands twice denied them victory, the title might have been brought to Taunton for the first time."

Peter Roebuck in *From Sammy to Jimmy*

Championship Position: 3 of 17

Somerset were not alone in struggling financially, racking up a substantial loss each year. With the County Championship in a moribund state, new ideas were being explored. On 15 May at Valentine's Park, Ilford, the Essex and Somerset players gave the public their first taste of County Cricket on a Sunday. That match was drawn but Somerset won thirteen of their twenty-eight matches in a successful campaign in which they ended up in third place.

Peter Wight had been released but the five leading batsmen all exceeded 1,000 runs with Merv Kitchen in particular blossoming. The three main bowlers – Langford, Palmer and Rumsey – all reached 100 wickets and the close fielding was sharp, too. Geoff Clayton claimed 84 victims behind the stumps and Roy Virgin held 42 catches, many of them in the slips, while Peter Robinson held 32 catches, most of them at forward short leg. This was a balanced side and a settled one, with ten of the eleven appearing either in all or the vast majority of fixtures. If their captain, Colin Atkinson, was fortunate to be in the right place at the right time, he also deserves credit for bringing about a burgeoning sense of optimism and self-belief.

The Second XI also performed strongly and were runners-up in the Minor Counties Competition and eligible to challenge the other regional leaders, Lincolnshire, for the Championship. As the *Somerset County Gazette* noted, 'for the team to have taken part would have cost more than £250 and it was felt that in the present situation this would not be justified. The rights to challenge were therefore waived and Lincolnshire became champions for the first time in their history'.

1966 marked the debut of local boy Graham Burgess who, though he was never able to lay claims to greatness, became an important all-rounder for the county over the years. The other debutant, Yorkshire-born Tony Clarkson, would prove a sound opening batsman.

Taking part in fielding practice in 1966 are (left to right): W. E. Alley,
R. Palmer, R. T. Virgin, P. J. Robinson, N. K. Parker, G. Atkinson,
M. J. Kitchen, K. E. Palmer, C. H. M. Greetham and B. A. Langford.

Nigel Parker, a right-arm fast-medium bowler who hailed from Weston-super-Mare, never graduated from the Somerset Second XI and later appeared for Cormwall. SOMERSET CRICKET MUSEUM

Anthony Clarkson
25 May 1966 v. Nottinghamshire, Nottingham

[signature]

Tony Clarkson was born on 5 September 1939 in Killinghall, a village two miles from Harrogate. His father, Joseph Clarkson, was a cricket pro who, prior to the Second World War, had played for Rothwell in the Leeds League. Badly wounded during the conflict, Joe was obliged to give up cricket and became a turf accountant. He was married to Clarrie (née Avery), whose father was a joiner. Their son, Tony, attended Harrogate Grammar School and by the age of fifteen was appearing for Harrogate CC. Within a year he was opening both the batting and bowling for the club. At the age of nineteen he would change from seam bowling to delivering off-breaks after an operation to remove his appendix had caused a rethink and he began to exploit his ability to turn the ball. It would be as an opening batsman, though, that he would establish himself in first-class cricket.

Having broken through into the Yorkshire Second XI in 1958 at the age of eighteen, he finally graduated to the First XI and played six times for his native county in 1963 as a replacement for Ray Illingworth, who was on Test duty. Yorkshire were at the time paying fees on a match-by-match basis for non-capped players and Tony's main source of income was as an engineering assistant with the Harrogate Borough Council. He was married in 1962 to Yolande Nelly Anselme, who was French and with whom he would have two sons and a daughter. With no assurances about his future and stiff competition for places in a strong Yorkshire side, Tony moved to Torquay in Devon, to work as a civil engineering assistant with the town's Borough Council. His performances in club cricket soon attracted the attention of Somerset and Gloucestershire, both of whom discussed a contract. With the lure of a job as an engineering assistant at the Guildhall in Bath and the promise (which was never fulfilled) that he would be deployed as a genuine all-rounder, Tony gave Somerset the nod. After a year batting at number five, he was asked to open the innings following the departure of Graham Atkinson to Lancashire at the end of the 1966 season. Curbing his attacking instincts, Tony would play 104 first-class matches for Somerset over the course of six seasons, averaging 25.75, with two centuries and twenty-three half-centuries. In addition, his off-spin yielded 8 wickets at 34.37 apiece. Referring to Tony by his nickname, Australian Test cricketer Kerry O'Keeffe would write that 'Bunner resolutely supported the choice to walk if [he] had edged the ball.' Kerry, who spent two seasons at Somerset, would note that 'we may not have had the best team in the Championship but we were definitely the most honest.'

Tony's most successful year was 1970 when he amassed 1,246 first-class runs, but he made history in 1969 by becoming the first Englishman to score a century in the newly-formed John Player League, following hot on the heels of fellow Somerset cricketer, Greg Chappell of Australia. Inevitably, the achievement generated fewer headlines than Tony might have expected, given that his sterling effort coincided with Neil Armstrong's becoming the first man to set foot on the moon.

His release by Somerset after the 1971 season was regarded by many as premature, given that his batting average was rising remorselessly. The county had second thoughts after prospective captain Brian Close became involved and insisted that Tony be offered a contract, but in the intervening two-month period he had returned to Harrogate after securing more lucrative options, having agreed professional

Tony Clarkson – deployed by Somerset as an opening batsman, he was often obliged to curb his attacking instincts.
SOMERSET CRICKET MUSEUM

terms with Middlesbrough CC whilst also being offered a job as a District Manager for Yorkshire Water. After five successful years with Middlesbrough CC, he joined Windhill CC in the Bradford League. He would continue playing as a pro until the age of fifty-one. In 1991 he retired from the game and also accepted a severance package from Yorkshire Water. Tony then promptly set about becoming an umpire whilst concurrently starting up his own consultancy business offering architectural, civil engineering and surveying services. He began officiating in Varsity matches in 1992 and from 1996 joined the umpires panel for County Championship matches. He stood in 130 first-class and 157 List A matches until his retirement in 2004. He was married for the second time in 1999 to Cheryl Lynn Wright. At the time, Cheryl was a personal development coach and trainer, but she is now active in a number of fields from amateur dramatics to church volunteer work. The couple continue to reside in Killinghall, the village of Tony's birth. He is described by his wife Cheryl as 'the best thing that ever happened to me'. Whilst not quite the best thing that ever happened to Somerset cricket, he was a useful addition. Tony has never been a man to seek the limelight but is well-respected by friends and colleagues for the quiet and industrious way he has always gone about his business. His knowledge of the game, coupled with his air of calm authority stood him in good stead both as a reliable opening batsman for Somerset and as a first-class umpire.

Tony Clarkson – the first Englishman to record a century in the John Player League.
SOMERSET CRICKET MUSEUM

448
Graham Iefvion Burgess
16 July 1966 v. West Indies, Taunton

Known to his teammates as Budgie, Graham was born in Glastonbury on 5 May 1943 although he was brought up in Street from the age of two. His father, Mervyn Thomas Burgess and his mother, Margaret (née Howe), both worked in the Clark's shoe-making factory in Street. It was clear from a very young age that Graham was an outstanding all-round sportsman. By the time he left Hindhayes Infants School and joined the County Mixed School, he had begun to make a name for himself. Those who recall the corpulent Graham of later years – noted, in the words of David Foot, for his 'economy of effort' or, as Eric Hill wrote, his 'occasional courtly canter and underarm throw from the boundary edge' – would perhaps struggle to picture the man described by a table-tennis opponent in his younger days as a 'skinny, shock-haired Burgess'. Indeed the same report suggests that Graham could perhaps have reached international level at table-tennis had he not opted to retire from the game at seventeen, having already been Somerset Junior Champion and West of England Doubles Champion. In later years, his party piece was to trounce teammates at the game while remaining seated in a chair.

His games master at County Mixed School relates that he was obliged to give his own star out LBW every time the ball struck his pads in order to allow other boys to become involved in the game, because Graham was so much better than his contemporaries. It was also noted that he had intimidated opponents in his age group with his long run-up and pacey deliveries that contrast with the more languid style of later years. Graham also excelled at football as a right winger or inside right and would later go on to play for Street FC. He is said to have been heartbroken when told at fourteen, on winning a sports scholarship to nearby Millfield, that he was going to a rugby-playing school, although this did not stop him from winning school colours at cricket, rugby and hockey. Invited on one occasion to a county hockey trial and having had to race from another engagement, he arrived shortly before bully-off – having changed in the car as he was driven – only to be told by a punctilious official that he would have to wait until the second-half as a punishment for indiscipline. He promptly told the official to forget it and was driven off. Thus ended his career as a hockey player. Budgie's philosophy was that life was something to be enjoyed not endured and sport was his life.

He first appeared for Somerset in a Second XI fixture against Cornwall when he

Graham Burgess – Budgie's philosophy was that life was something to be enjoyed rather than endured. SOMERSET CRICKET MUSEUM

was fourteen and began playing club cricket for a strong Morlands CC side, for whom he became the first player to exceed 1,000 runs in a season. He would continue his connection with Morlands – a company based in Glastonbury and involved in the tanning industry and the manufacture of sheepskin products – when offered winter employment by them after he had embarked on his career as a professional cricketer.

He was taken on by Somerset as a member of the junior ground staff in 1965 and made his first-class debut the following year. Colin Atkinson would recall being joined at the crease by a diffident Budgie who, noticing that Wes Hall – famed for his pace and for a long, rhythmic and intimidating run-up – had been brought back into the attack, ambled up to Colin and pleaded: 'Skipper, I've never faced him before. Will you take him?' Colin Atkinson cited this as an example of a lack of confidence that held Graham back in his early years. Others have talked of a lack of ambition or a shortage of aggression and certainly the last of these rings true. Graham was an affable man, able to laugh at his own misfortune. He was fair-minded, too, and always prepared to see another point of view. If he felt that an opponent had been badly treated or the victim of an erroneous dismissal, he would say so.

There was a sense among most commentators that he never fulfilled his rich potential not because of any lack of commitment to the cause but because he was just simply too rounded a man. He could be cruising along as if his mind was elsewhere or trundling up to dole out a succession of friendly medium-paced deliveries and might then burst into devastating life and turn a game around. One incident sums up his philosophy. He was batting beautifully and was into the forties when he played a shot as ghastly as the LBW decision that followed immediately afterwards. He was approached at the interval by Eric Hill who expressed doubts about the umpire's call. 'It was a shocker,' Graham agreed. 'I think he gave me out for the shot. Fair enough, too.' And yet, no one should ever doubt that he cared passionately about the fortunes of his beloved Somerset. He sank to his knees in despair in 1976 when on the last ball of the last fixture of the season in the John Player League, he failed by one run to steer his side to the first trophy in their history. No doubt those feelings were still etched in his mind three years later when in the quarter final of the Gillette Cup he rescued Somerset with a half-century at a time when they were reeling on 95 for 5. His knock set the scene for Joel Garner at his devastating best to tear out the heart of the Kent innings with a return of 5 for 11 in 9.4 overs. Perhaps it was a degree of sentiment as well as gratitude – on top of Graham's steadying influence – that led captain Brian Rose to include him in the eleven who won their first Lord's final in 1979. Joel Garner was of course unplayable again with 6 for 29 but even that was insufficient to win the Man of the Match Award which went to Viv Richards for a nerveless century of sparkling brilliance.

Having played in 252 first-class matches for Somerset, Graham averaged 18.90 with the bat and took 474 wickets at 28.57 apiece. His ambitions had only ever been in relation to the team. His dreams had been realised in 1979 with Somerset winning their first trophies, ninety-seven years after having been granted first-class status. He left with his head held high and would enjoy four seasons in Minor Counties cricket with Wiltshire and Cambridgeshire, while employed for a number of years as a cricketing coach, including a spell at Monmouth School. In 1990 he joined the umpires panel and would stand in nearly 300 first-class matches and a number of international representative fixtures until his retirement in 2008.

Graham had been married in Taunton in 1966 to Marion Stoodley, with whom he would have two daughters. His second marriage, in 1981, was to Dagny (née Smith).

He had talent as huge as his heart, ability as big as his bulky frame. And what he lacked in hard-nosed ambition he more than made up for with the passion he had for Somerset cricket. The supporters knew it and he remained a much-loved member of the team, as delighted as they were when he played his part in helping them to land their first trophies.

Graham Burgess – a Somerset-born man delighted still to be a member of the team when they finally won their first honours.

1967

"The stateliest home of English cricket had never experienced the peculiar delights of such a vocally uninhibited crowd as flocked through the Grace Gate early on September 2nd, 1967 ... For the bulk of the side, performing in front of 25,000 spectators was definitely a new experience."

Vic Marks in *Somerset County Cricket Scrapbook*

Championship Position: 8 of 17

Eric Hill observed in his summary of the 1967 season in *Playfair Cricket Monthly* that 'it is, for the partisan, somewhat sickening that Graeme Pollock might have joined [Somerset] had the immediate registration been accepted'. If only ... Two words that form an oft-repeated refrain in the Somerset cricketing lexicon. Had Somerset's request to register the stand-out batsman of his generation been granted then the county would surely not have had to wait a further twelve years to land their first trophy. As it was, they came close when, having descended upon Lord's for the Gillette Cup Final in fine voice and well-lubricated, the supporters witnessed their team being outmanoeuvred by Kent. As David Foot wrote, 'Somerset's supporters, joyfully and noisily in evidence ... came in their farming smocks and war-paint. Their incessant banter was rustic and good-humoured, though not, one imagines, entirely to the liking of headquarters'

Somerset supporters were determined to enjoy their trip to Lord's for the Gillette Cup Final of 1967.

haughtier and more traditional cricketing residents.'

In the Championship, Colin Atkinson led the same settled side and yet the results were not forthcoming and the team slipped to eighth position. Only three batsmen – Bill Alley, Roy Virgin and Merv Kitchen – reached 1,000 runs, Virgin the most prolific among them with 1,440. Not a single player averaged 30.00 with the bat. Similarly, the three most successful bowlers – Ken Palmer, Brian Langford and Fred Rumsey – all fell short of 100 wickets. One bright spot was the improved all-round performance of Peter Robinson who contributed a useful haul of runs, wickets and catches.

The Somerset team in 1967.
Back row: *G. Clayton, T. I. Barwell, R. Palmer, F. E. Rumsey, G. I. Burgess, M. J. Kitchen, P. J. Robinson.* Front row: *R. T. Virgin, B. A. Langford, C. R. M. Atkinson, W. E. Alley, K. E. Palmer.* SOMERSET CRICKET MUSEUM

Lionel Michael Lowry Barnwell
19 Aug 1967 v. Nottinghamshire, Nottingham

Mike Barnwell

Mike Barnwell was born in Crewkerne on 12 August 1943. His father, Frederick Reginald Lowry Barnwell, a civil engineer at the time of his marriage to Norah Manning Powell, was serving in the Second World War when Mike was born. Norah was living at the time in Hinton St George.

Mike was educated at Repton, captaining the cricket First XI in 1962 and winning a place at Christ's College, Cambridge, where he studied Geography and then completed a Dip Ed to qualify as a teacher. He would appear for Cambridge four times but not in the Varsity fixture. He also captained the university at football. His family already had links with Somerset CCC, given that he was the nephew of John Barnwell, who had played for the county immediately prior to and after the Second World War. Mike had gained his first taste of cricket for Somerset as a nineteen-year-old when he became a regular in the Second XI during the summer vacation after he had left Repton. An adaptable player, who bowled right-arm medium pace and batted right-handed, he reappeared on the Somerset cricketing scene after his graduation and would play in six first-class games for the county of his birth, averaging 16.00 with a highest score of 60 but never bowling for them. He brought his all-round skills to bear, though, in reaching the final of the Somerset single wicket competition, losing out to a youthful Greg Chappell.

On leaving Cambridge, Mike had taken up a temporary teaching post at St Anselm's in Bakewell but after his brief spell back playing for Somerset he was offered a coaching contract at St Andrew's College in Grahamstown, South Africa. The place already had links with Somerset. D. J. Smith, who had played for Somerset in the 1890s, had left the county to become the school's coach and groundsman for forty-five years. In gratitude, he had left a bequest which continues to fund the Douglas Smith Scholarship to Cambridge University for one pupil of the school each year.

When Mike's contract with Somerset was not renewed, he remained at the school, adding teaching duties, and while there he played in a number of first-class fixtures for Eastern Province as their opening batsman. He feels privileged to have witnessed greatness at close quarters. Graeme Pollock, whom he describes as 'an amazing player' was a teammate and Mike is in no doubt that his most nervous time in cricket was acting as Pollock's runner during one Currie Cup match. The weight of responsibility was enormous and the opprobrium showered on him by spectators would have been tremendous, had he misjudged a run. One occasion on which Mike outshone one of

Mike Barnwell – played six first-class matches but over the years he played with or worked alongside some of the greats of the game. COURTESY OF JOHN LEE

the greatest batsmen of all time was in his only List A match when he scored 124 runs to help Eastern Province to victory over Orange Free State. His spectacular average of 124.00 would remain intact, given that he was promptly dropped, in his words, 'for having scored too slowly'.

After then working for a short while as a travel agent in Grahamstown, he returned to England in 1972 to work with former Somerset and England pace bowler Fred Rumsey, whose company was involved in public relations and fund raising for Derbyshire CCC. Although Mike's job was primarily centred around persuading potential sponsors to part with their cash, he was also required to face Fred in the nets for an hour each Friday as the well-built left-armer limbered up for each forthcoming Sunday League fixture.

He was married in 1973 to Augusta Wileen Wood. Augusta had grown up on the Isle of Harris before moving to South Africa in 1963 and becoming the Catering Manager at St Andrew's College, also acting as housekeeper for the resident staff bachelors who at one time or another had included the likes of Barrie Meyer, David Steele and Tony Greig. Augusta and Mike would have one daughter.

There followed a change of career direction when he joined the RAF in 1974 and worked in the secretarial branch for seven years. He played for the RAF and Combined Services and captained both. Then in 1981, Mike returned to South Africa to work in the Grahamstown Travel Agency. Six years later he returned for the final time to England, back to his roots and undertaking the teaching work for which he had initially trained. From 1987 until 1992 he taught at Northbourne Park Preparatory School in Kent, continuing to enjoy club cricket with Tilmanstone Ravens CC, where he took up wicket-keeping, as he puts it, 'to spare me from having to chase around after the ball'. In 1992 he accepted a new teaching post at another prep school, Hawtreys, which amalgamated with Cheam Prep School four years prior to his leaving the job in 1998. Thereafter, he took up a number of temporary appointments until his retirement.

Given the trajectory of his life it is perhaps unsurprising that Mike lists travel as one of the pleasures in his life. He is also a keen bridge player and interested in photography. His experience of first-class cricket at Somerset was fleeting but in his wider career he was able to pit his wits against some of the greats of the game such as Barry Richards and Mike Proctor, both of South Africa. He was also at the non-striker's end in a friendly fixture for R. C. Kerslake's XI against a touring St Andrew's College side when a young Viv Richards was given an early taste of cricket in England. There was a certain inevitability that the first ball would whistle past Mike and the bowler for a perfectly-timed four. Viv was always destined for greatness. Mike's career, while not touched with such greatness, offered him a rich bank of fond memories.

1968

"The club Secretary, the officious Dicky Robinson, pulled me aside and said, 'In private it's all right to call him [Roy Kerslake] Roy, but normally when you are talking to him, you should address him as 'Captain' or 'Sir'. And when you're talking to me 'Dicky' is fine in my office, but in front of the members it's 'Mr Secretary' or 'Sir'."

Greg Chappell in *Fierce Focus*

Championship Position: 12 of 17

'Nothing is so predictable about Somerset as its complete unpredictability,' wrote A. A. Thomson in a summary of the county's season in *Playfair Cricket Monthly*. He is not the only cricket writer to have been struck by the yo-yo performances of the county – so often saving up their best for the strongest sides and on occasions woeful against the most mediocre of opposition. For the supporters it has bred every emotion from exasperation to despair. Thompson would add in his article in *Playfair Cricket Monthly* that 'Chappell of Australia was a useful all-rounder, as was the daddy of them all – Alley', also noting that 'the general impression was of a side with plenty of potential who didn't make enough quick runs or take enough early wickets to challenge the leaders' (which is perhaps a polite way of suggesting that they were mired for much of the season in mediocrity). From the dizzy heights of third place in 1966, the team had continued their descent of the Championship table, a slide that they would suffer for another season until they would hit rock bottom once more in 1969.

Roy Kerslake had taken the mantle of Colin Atkinson as the amateur captain. An injury at the start of the season meant that the team had already been despatched from the Gillette Cup and were floundering in the Championship before he was able to take his place. The loss of Geoff Clayton was keenly felt. In addition, a lack of penetrative bowling bedevilled the side. Fred Rumsey was the leading wicket-taker with 72 victims, followed in the averages by Brian Langford with 70. Incapacitated for much of the season and only appearing in sixteen matches, Ken Palmer was missed. Four of the batsmen exceeded 1,000 runs. Top of the averages was Merv Kitchen with 1,730 runs, closely followed by his opening partner, Roy Virgin. Bill Alley also had a successful season with the bat but it was the arrival of the young Greg Chappell, tall, exuding class and possessed of an array of elegant strokes, whose introduction, having surprised everyone, proved a fine decision.

Greg Chappell apart, the debutants – wicket-keepers Dickie Brooks and Charlie Carter – were in truth interim choices ahead of the arrival in 1970 of Derek Taylor.

The Somerset squad and support staff in 1968. Back row: *C. F. D. Buttle, E. Woodgate, P. J. Robinson, R. T. Virgin, A. Clarkson, M. J. Kitchen, K. E. Palmer, R. A. Brooks, D. Price, D. Hunt.* Middle row: *R. Holman, G. I. Burgess, L. M. L. Barnwell, F. E. Rumsey, R. Palmer, G. S. Chappell, T. I. Barwell, T. Tout.* Front row: *Mrs A. Smith, W. E. Alley, W. H. R. Andrews (Coach), R. C. Kerslake, B. A. Langford, R. Robinson, Mrs A. Lewis.* SOMERSET CRICKET MUSEUM

450
Gregory Stephen Chappell
4 May 1968 v. Oxford University, Oxford

[signature: Greg Chappell]

The grandson via the maternal line of a former Australian Test captain, Victor York Richardson, Greg Chappell had cricketing ability writ bold in his genes but circumstances, an intense focus and a restless quest for excellence transformed him from a gifted player to an Australian legend. His association with Somerset was serendipitous. The county had agreed to employ John Inverarity but he was in the end unavailable and Greg – at the time a nineteen-year-old establishing his reputation in State Cricket – sent a speculative telegram to Somerset and was taken on with alacrity. For once, Secretary Dicky Robinson's overflowing in-tray had not proved a black hole into which hopes and dreams sank without trace.

Born in Unley, Adelaide, on 7 August 1948 – in his words 'a week before Bradman was making the most famous duck in history' – and one of three brothers who would play for Australia, he was the son of Martin Chappell, a sales rep for a pharmaceutical company, married to Jeanne (née Richardson). Martin was a useful Grade cricketer and gave his sons every encouragement. Greg and his siblings were sent to Lynn Fuller's coaching school at a young age and Greg notes that this embedded his technique while their father instilled the attitude that 'batting is about scoring runs'. Greg and older brother Ian would spend every available moment enacting their own Ashes series in their back yard, all the while honing their skills. At primary school and later at Plympton High School and Prince Alfred College, Greg's studies were neglected as he set his heart on becoming a cricketer. In the school First XI by the age of fourteen, he was physically a late developer, smaller than his peers and obliged to develop his trademark flick off the hips in order to score runs. Having put on a growth spurt and broken into the South Australia side at eighteen, he sent his speculative telegram to Somerset and was welcomed into the side, a complete unknown in England. According to fellow Australian Bill Alley he arrived 'an over-extravagant batsman and leg-break bowler and left a world-class batsman in the making and a useful medium-pacer'. By then he was 6 feet 1 inch tall and, as his teammates noted, had the presence of a guardsman walking to the crease. He came to national attention in England when he scored the first ever century in the John Player League in a match that happened to be televised. It was a chanceless masterpiece and a sign of what was to follow. Two seasons were enough to complete his education on English conditions. He came away with a batting average of 30.03 over fifty-two first-class matches and took 71 wickets at 27.70 apiece.

Thereafter he would be unavailable after graduating into the Australian side in

Greg Chappell – came to Somerset as a teenager and would later develop into one of the greats of the game. SOMERSET CRICKET MUSEUM

1970. Initially playing under the captaincy of Bill Lawry and later under the leadership of his brother, Ian (who offered no favours, with their competitive instincts never letting up), he made an immediate impact but after his initial successes his form became indifferent. The jolt he needed came in the guise of a critical article by a journalist and family friend, Keith Butler, suggesting that Greg had become complacent and was frittering his talent away. Shutting himself in his hotel room, he analysed where he was going wrong and realised that as a batsman he needed to focus single-mindedly on the moment of each and every delivery and free his mind, relaxing entirely outside those moments. Overnight he was a changed man and the runs began to flow.

Married in 1971 to Judith Donaldson, a school teacher from Sydney, with whom he would have three children, Greg was obliged to find ways to supplement the paltry income derived from cricket (as indeed was Ian, too) and this would remain a bone of contention for most of the Australian side. He was employed by Coca-Cola Bottlers as a trainee manager but was then offered the opportunity to make a name for himself outside his native South Australia as Queensland's marquee signing. He would remain in the state as a player and administrator for twenty years and was also offered a job in insurance with Friends Provident, selling Payment Protection Insurance (PPI), at a time when the practice was regarded as entirely above board. Captaining the Queensland side prepared him for his future role as captain of Australia when brother Ian decided that at thirty-three he had had enough. By now established in Queensland, he set up a business in insurance and was, like his brother, becoming jaded with the poorly-remunerated world of Test cricket when Kerry Packer's World Series transformed everything. Ian and Greg were pivotal to the success of the enterprise and after the rapprochement between the Australian Cricket Board and Kerry Packer, Greg returned to lead the Australian side. His style was entirely different to Ian's. Whereas the older brother was outspoken and combative, Greg had a reputation for aloofness that derived in large part from his need to recover alone because he had been prone to debilitating sore throats and respiratory tract infections from a young age. Both brothers, however, shared a will to win and Greg would elicit widespread condemnation when in 1981 he instructed his brother, Trevor, to bowl underarm for the final delivery of a one day match against New Zealand, denying Brian McKechnie the chance to hit the required six to tie the match. He blamed the decision on his state of mind, claiming 'I was cooked, exhausted, exasperated.'

His Test career in the round was a triumph. Going into his final match in Sydney in 1984, 68 runs short of Bradman's record aggregate of 6,996 runs for Australia and one short of Colin Cowdrey's record for all Test-playing nations of 119 out-field catches, he scored 182 and took 3 catches. His batting average in eighty-seven official tests was 53.86, including twenty-four centuries, anchoring him firmly among the pantheon of the all-time greats. In addition, fellow Australian Kerry O'Keeffe has written that Greg was the finest all-round fielder he encountered, rarely ever making an error.

Greg Chappell gets a taste of an English summer at Derbyshire's County Ground (top) and welcomes the Queen to a sunny MCG in 1977 in his role as captain of Australia (above).

335

He had been awarded an MBE in 1979 for his services to cricket and since retiring as a player he has enjoyed considerable success in business. His insurance partnership was sold in 1990 and subsequently he branched into managing property portfolios and a sports marketing business and has enjoyed success with the Greg Chappell Cricket Centres whilst also engaging in some commentary and writing. He has also acted as a Test selector. In 2005 he was appointed coach of the Indian Test side. Up for the challenge of transforming the team, he continued to be dissatisfied with mediocrity or complacency and was always on the lookout for innovative approaches that underlined his view that without 'temperament, personality and intention', technique is of little worth, but he found himself bogged down in the politics of cricket on the sub-continent. In 2010 things went full circle when he was invited by Cricket Australia to take on the roles of National Talent Manager and Selector.

Greg Chappell will forever be regarded as one of the giants of Australian cricket. His two seasons at Somerset perhaps played only a negligible part on his road to greatness, but his elegant contributions are fondly recalled by former teammates and many supporters of the club.

451
Richard Alan Brooks
4 May 1968 v. Oxford University, Oxford

When Geoff Clayton parted company with Somerset, the county turned to Richard Brooks. Dickie, as he is referred to, was born in Edgware, Middlesex, on 14 June 1943, the son of Richard Brooks, a water engineer, and Irene (née Matthews). He came to Somerset's attention while completing his degree in Physics at Bristol University, where he played as a wicket-keeper for the university side and for the combined UAU team, which called on all the undergraduate talent outside Oxbridge. During the summer vacations he appeared for Somerset Second XI. On graduating he went up to St Edmund Hall, Oxford, in 1967 to study for his postgraduate teacher training qualification and was awarded a blue. He agreed to delay his entry into the teaching profession for a year while he played as Somerset's first choice wicket-keeper. Somerset had originally planned to employ the services of Charlie Carter, following the sudden departure of Geoff Clayton, but the Army had refused to release Charlie early from his three-year commission. Dickie had come to Somerset's rescue. David Foot describes him as 'small and competent' and in twenty-six first-class appearances for the county he would effect 53 dismissals. His batting average was a modest 10.11. With Somerset's wicket-keeping crisis having been averted, he took up a position as a Physics teacher at Bradfield College

Dickie Brooks – 'a good man indeed and, as I remember, the tidiest of stumpers'.
SOMERSET CRICKET MUSEUM

in Berkshire. His sojourn at the school would prove longer-lasting than his stay at the County Ground, with Dickie serving the institution for thirty-five years.

Arriving in 1968 at a place where, in the words of one report it was 'a world of "bachelor colonies", dormitories, house rooms, "cops", fagging and beating', Dickie quietly played his part in transforming attitudes, more so after he became a house-master in 1982. To quote a tribute to him in the college magazine, 'as a housemaster, Dickie quietly but insistently established a community in which cheerful relationships were the norm and adolescent aggression seemed strangely inappropriate'. The writer adds that pupils were in awe of Dickie, that he never raised his voice and that at the first sign of anger in his eyes, the boys fell quickly into line. His sense of humour was also legendary. In short, he was born to teach.

From 1990 until 2000 he was Head of Physics and brought a reforming zeal to the department to match his energies as a housemaster. At the forefront in embracing new technology, he was also dauntingly efficient, presenting precise plans of action to his staff each week and inspiring pupils to think beyond the constraints of narrowly-defined academic disciplines with ploys such as a famed white board on which he would write up a thought-provoking 'quote of the week'. Sometimes his words of wisdom failed to have the required effect. Dickie reveals that on one occasion, a pithy quote was rounded off with the attribution to Albert Einstein (1879-1955) and met with the observation: 'Gosh. Einstein. 1955. I had no idea he was as recent as that. Wasn't he the one with the bolt through his head?'

If his approach to Physics lessons could be characterised as meticulous and thought-ful, then the same might be said of his approach to cricket coaching, which he took charge of from 1971 until the mid-1980s. His credo was 'always be available: never impose yourself'. In 1984, still a bachelor and establishing himself as a housemaster, he was interviewing candidates for the role of matron when he met Alexandra, known as Alex, whom he was married to in 1987. The college magazine notes that 'she brought a new richness to Dickie's years in charge. Alex would become as important a part of the fabric of the school as her husband: the couple and their 'faithful Labrador, Tess,' were instrumental in helping many a pupil through the vicissitudes of adolescence.

They retired in 2003 and many of their former pupils have reason to be grateful to a man who served Bradfield College for all bar the first year of his working life. Among them is former Hampshire captain and now commentator and writer, Mark Nicholas, who says: 'We Bradfield folk were lucky to have him as our guide and mentor - on the cricket field that is. In the classroom, I wasn't much into the sciences I'm afraid, only the science of the great game!' Mark adds that 'Dickie knew cricket well. He was shrewd and perceptive. I learnt more about cricket detail from him than anyone else – until, that is, I reached the first-class game. Mind you, even then very few could touch him. He liked a beer too, which was a surprise, given his size. My earliest pub visits were with him, after school matches, when he made sensible observations about the day's events with positive ideas as alternatives. A good man indeed and, as I remember, the tidiest of stumpers.'

At the time of writing, Alex and Dickie enjoy life walking the East Anglian coastal paths accompanied by their newly acquired rescue terrier. With terriers notorious for often proving wilful, his coaching skills will be further put to the test.

452
Charles Edward Peers Carter
21 August 1968 v. Leicestershire, Taunton

Charlie Carter was a debonair and well-heeled addition to the ranks of the Somerset pros. A former captain of the Radley College XI whose education at a leading public school set him apart from the other professionals, he had an easy charm and comfort in his own skin that allowed him to get along with everyone. Born on 7 August 1947 in Richmond-upon-Thames, he was the son of James Douglas Carter, who ran a Human Resources Company (a headhunter, to use the common parlance), and was married to Diana Joan (née Arthur), who worked for MI5.

After leaving Radley, Charlie was offered a commission with the Army (during which time he would play for the Army and the Combined Services) but he left when offered the chance to play as a pro for Somerset. He had in any case planned in the longer term to establish his own Broking Company. Charlie had been approached by Bill Andrews, who spotted him keeping wicket for the Combined Services at Lord's. Once it became apparent that Charlie's father was a friend of Somerset Chairman, Bunty Longrigg, and that the son had been brought up in Cornwall, the die was cast. Having previously appeared for the Second XI on an occasional basis, he became a fully-fledged member of the squad in 1968, after being given a contract and taking up lodgings along with teammate Greg Chappell in Ash Priors, a sleepy village not far from Taunton. The young men were obliged to look further afield for their post-match entertainment and Charlie confesses to 'spending too long in nightclubs on away fixtures'.

He recounts the tale of his debut appearance. Prior to the match Charlie had been practicing in the nets and learning to cope with in-swing and away-swing when he asked Bill Alley: 'Excuse me, Mr Alley, could you tell me how I can read which way you'll swing it?' Bill suggested that he didn't have a clue, either. Later, with Charlie feeling on top of the world after taking a memorable catch down the leg side to dismiss

Barry Knight, Bill came on to bowl and asked his keeper to stand up to the stumps. His first delivery was aimed well wide of the off stump and as Charlie shaped to take it the ball swung viciously to leg and went for four byes. 'Now you know how I swing the ball, son,' Bill announced, lacing his words with some antipodean colour. 'I'd been stitched up like a kipper,' Charlie admits, smiling. He would make twenty-six first-class appearances over two seasons, claiming 47 catches and 6 stumpings. Less impressive was his batting average of 2.92. In his six List A matches, he was at least able to claim that he was never dismissed in five innings, albeit, with the scorers only troubled on two occasions.

It was mooted at one point that, being 'made of the right stuff', Charlie should be invited to captain the side, but he left at the end of the 1969 season to pursue his dream of working in the City and his success in his new career was unbounded. An uncle had his own insurance underwriting syndicate with Lloyd's of London and so it was with some prior knowledge that Charlie established a name for himself at Willis, Faber & Dumas Ltd, becoming a director at a young age before branching off in 1979 and setting up his own Lloyd's broking business – Carter Brito Cunha Ltd – which proved a success, handling reinsurance on a global scale. The company later diversified, with an offshoot – CBC UK – handling retail insurance business in the UK. After selling the business in 1987, Charlie was retained and would indeed remain until the company was acquired by Marsh in 1998 and he was asked to stay on for a further year to oversee the integration. He then set up a new company – Capital BC Partners Ltd – with colleague Garth Bearman. It remains a successful concern.

Charlie was married in 1973 to Margaret Cory Willson, known as Tita, whom he had met at a party in London. They would have four children together. Tita had spent some time immediately after the Second World War living with an aunt and uncle at The Priory, a part-eleventh century and part-sixteenth century listed home near Reading. Charlie and his bride were frequent visitors after the home was sold to another couple already known to Tita. Never a man to sidestep a challenge, he vowed at the time that he would one day bring it back to the family, despite the fact that his then salary with Willis, Faber & Dumas was a mere £1,000 per annum. In 1995 his chance came and Charlie purchased The Priory. With characteristic understatement, he notes that 'my wife was very pleased with me'. Their impressive gardens are now open to the public. There is no doubt that Charlie has made a success of life. Perhaps his early departure from the first-class game can be deemed a stroke of good fortune that paved the way for greater glories.

Peter Roebuck would write in his history of Somerset cricket that Charlie was 'a delightful character, who …. proved an amusing companion'. With his usual tendency to recast events in order to craft a memorable turn of phrase, he adds that Charlie was 'apt to drop as many catches as a cockney does aitches'. The joke raises a smile but is unjust. Charlie Carter was a competent wicket-keeper, good enough to have toured South Africa with a junior MCC team and to have represented both the Combined Services and Somerset. He was and is also a team player, able to rub along with anyone and a man whose talents in the wider sphere have brought him rich rewards.

Charlie Carter – a debonair and well-heeled addition to the ranks of the Somerset pros. SOMERSET CRICKET MUSEUM

1969

"It was rather the same old story with Somerset, who won only one and lost nine matches ... The gap left by the retirement of Rumsey and Alley was never adequately filled."

Rex Alston

Championship Position: 17 of 17

Can anyone doubt that this was the most inglorious campaign in the county's history since the re-granting of their first-class status in 1891? The wooden spoon in the Championship with only one match won, sixteenth place in the inaugural John Player League and knocked out in the first round of the Gillette Cup. If there was one little cameo to stir interest rather than passion, inviting tense anticipation rather than rapture, it was the eight overs bowled by Brian Langford in the John Player League fixture against Essex at Yeovil. With Brian Ward, the dourest of the dour, determined not to yield his wicket, the man who was now Somerset captain bowled eight maidens. There had been an air of pessimism before the season began after two significant departures. Bill Alley had not taken kindly to a derisory offer of playing only in limited overs fixtures with a consequent loss of pay and Fred Rumsey had tired of putting his aching body through its paces week in and week out, wishing instead to put his restless entrepreneurial zeal to the test. In the Championship, no batsmen imposed themselves. Merv Kitchen topped the Somerset batting with an average of 30.41, though Greg Chappell was the highest aggregate scorer with 1,330 runs and Tony Clarkson and Roy Virgin both topped 1,000 runs. Only Graham Burgess and Roy Palmer scraped together more than 50 wickets. Fred Rumsey was sorely missed. To add to the county's woes, Greg Chappell announced that he would not be returning. He was about to blossom into one of the legends of Australian cricket.

Things could surely only get better. Among the debutants, a couple of blonde-haired batsmen who had worked their way through the Somerset junior ranks had done enough to sow the seeds of optimism. *Wisden* would report that 'Rose and Denning, thrust into the deep end, did enough to give much hope for the future'. Brian Rose and Peter Denning were indeed destined to become an integral part of the Somerset cricketing scene for a number of years. None of the other debutants would make a lasting impression.

453
Brian Charles Rose
17 May 1969 v. Worcestershire, Worcester

It seems fitting that a home-grown player should have been the man finally to lift Somerset's first trophy in 1979 but a twist in the tale is that Brian Rose was born outside the county he loves and has always regarded as home. His birth on 4 June 1950 took place in Dartford, Kent. His father Charles, a Sergeant in the RAF, married to Jean (née Buchanan), was stationed at the time at RAF Locking near Weston-super-Mare. Brian arrived earlier than scheduled while his parents were away on a visit and the family made their way back home immediately after Jean's recovery.

Charlie Rose was posted to Singapore for two-and-a-half years in 1959, but on his return, Brian was educated at Weston-super-Mare Grammar School and showed prodigious talent as an all-round sportsman – rugby centre three-quarter, football forward, golfer and cricketer. A left-handed opening batsman, brought through the junior ranks in tandem with Peter Denning, he also kept wicket regularly and bowled at medium pace as and when required. Brian would note that he was warned by his headmaster that 'five O Levels are more important than 500 runs'. Fortunately the school's star pupil was both bright and sporty. He and his friend Peter Denning made their first-class debuts in 1969 but there was a setback in 1971 when the club officials made the decision to offer a 'match-money' contract, rather than taking Brian on as a full-time pro. That sound judge of a player, Tom Cartwright, would declare himself 'astonished' that the committee thought that Brian 'didn't have what it takes to make a county cricketer'. For his part, Brian took the slight as a spur to train as a PE teacher at Borough Road College in Isleworth. Over the duration of his course he appeared for Somerset during summer vacations and by the time he notched up his maiden first-class century at Glastonbury in 1972, the county must surely have realised that they had misjudged things. Indeed, once he had completed his teacher training he was offered a full-time contract from 1975.

In the early days, Brian was quiet and introverted, less suited to the high octane banter of a dressing room than the world of horticulture – an interest that gained him the moniker 'Harry', a nod to noted rose grower Harry Wheatcroft. His head seemed in the clouds and his forgetfulness was a source of mirth to his teammates. But he grew in confidence and his appointment as captain in 1978 after the departure of Brian

Brian Rose – 'his quietly spoken words carried immense authority'.
SOMERSET CRICKET MUSEUM

Close proved prescient. He had the respect of a group of star-studded individuals and melded them thoughtfully into a team. Vic Marks has said of him that 'his quietly spoken words carried immense authority ... he wanted us to disown our reputation for being colourful crowd-pleasers: it was important to win matches.' It was a momentous year for Brian as he was also married in 1978 to Stephanie Browne, known as Stevie, with whom he would have two sons, Stuart and Jamie, the later known to friends and family as Joey.

On the cricket field, the agonising near-misses on the final weekend of the 1978 season left the team bereft and in Brian's own words made them 'more determined and more disciplined'. A decision in 1979 to declare after one over of their final zonal match of the Benson & Hedges Cup in order to preserve the team's run rate was a communal decision driven by paranoia about having yet another prize snatched from their grasp. In hindsight it was a bad judgement call, pilloried as unsporting (which indeed it was) but the bulk of Somerset supporters – perhaps alone in the cricketing community – understood the decision and got behind their team with even greater fervour. The side's humiliating ejection from the tournament arguably focussed their minds more firmly on securing their first honours at the end of what proved a triumphant season. More trophies followed and Brian's performances as an opening batsman won him a total of nine Test caps. He had first been selected for the 1977-8 tour of Pakistan and New Zealand and later shone against the might of the West Indies in 1980. His international career then came to a sudden halt when he was forced to withdraw from the England touring party after the First Test in the 1981-2 series owing to eye problems that would require him to wear glasses.

Back on the county circuit, at the end of an injury-plagued 1983 season in which Somerset won the Nat West Trophy and were runners-up in the John Player League, he handed over the captaincy to Ian Botham. After a fuller season in 1984, his arm was broken in 1985. The following year would – barring three additional appearances in 1987 – be his last campaign, with Brian one of six batsmen to average more than 40.00 and with Somerset gaining more batting points than any other team but still propping up the Championship table, owing to a toothless bowling attack. In 251 first-class matches for Somerset he had averaged 33.26 with the bat, including twenty-three centuries. He had also taken 8 wickets at 36.12 apiece.

After ending his playing days, he remained for many years associated with the club. For a while he was Chairman of the cricket committee and he joined Roy Kerslake and Vic Marks as a member of a review panel charged with pointing the way to greater success for the club. In 2005 he became the Director of Cricket at Somerset and remained in that post until 2012. As David Foot notes, 'he had been away from the game long enough to take a detached view of what needed to be done and done rapidly. He wasted no time in changing attitudes.' Indeed, Somerset had slipped backwards and become also-rans, but with some astute signings, a commitment to developing young players and a clear strategy, Brian played a huge role in transforming them into Championship contenders. He was then taken on by Glamorgan as a consultant. Outside the cricketing world he also ran a company with his son, Joey, offering gardening services. Dogged in later years by health issues, he has spoken candidly about a crisis of confidence when he encountered problems with his loss of teeth, a condition that caused angst and laughter in equal measure.

At the time of writing Brian still resides in Weston-super-Mare. He remains the most successful captain in the club's history. His priceless contribution to the county he loves has been recognised with the gates erected in his honour, an accolade he shares with that other home-grown captain and Test Match player, Jack White.

Brian Rose – appointed captain in 1978, he led Somerset to their first trophies and remains the county's most successful skipper.
SOMERSET CRICKET MUSEUM

454
John Trevor Holmes
4 June 1969 v. West Indies, Taunton

Trevor Holmes was born on 16 November 1939 in Holmfirth, Yorkshire, the son of Roy Holmes, a textile worker and later a manager for the Yorkshire Electricity Board, married to Lena (née Tinker). After Lena's death, when Trevor was eleven, Roy was married to Joan (née Sunderland), who worked for Huddersfield Borough as a clerk's secretary. Educated at Holme Valley Grammar School, Trevor began his cricketing career in earnest as a wicketkeeper for Shepley Juniors CC in the Huddersfield Under-18s League but made the step up to the senior ranks in 1959 when the First XI wicket-keeper lost his thumb in a mining accident. He then gained further experience with Holmfirth CC, whom he joined in 1963 and captained in 1966. During a subsequent three-year spell with Slaithwaite CC he was recommended to Somerset, having spent time at Johnny Lawrence's cricket school in Rothwell.

As well as being a useful club wicket-keeper, Trevor was a right-handed batsman who by his own admission preferred to open his shoulders rather than build an innings. He was invited down to play for Somerset Second XI at Pontypridd, Glamorgan. A modest man and not one to sing his own praises, he admits to playing out of his skin. 'It was one of those games where everything goes right for you,' he recalls. He was immediately asked by Bill Andrews to play in the forthcoming fixture against the West Indies but explained that he had to return to Huddersfield for a cup fixture. Undeterred, Bill agreed that Trevor should come down on the Tuesday night train ahead of the Wednesday start. What neither of them had anticipated was that there would be a mudslide on the tracks which resulted in a detour via Crewe Station and meant that Trevor would not arrive at his lodgings at the Cross Keys pub until 7.30 in the morning. Exhausted, he kept himself awake with a regular intake of caffeine-packed Pro Plus tablets that a club member had been sent to Boots to purchase. Things went not quite as swimmingly against the West Indies as they had done at Pontypridd. Some of his teammates might have benefitted from his supply of Pro Plus to stay awake as the West Indies piled on the runs. Unbeknown to Trevor, his father had made the trip down and slipped into the stands. It would remain a treasured memory for both father and son, with Trevor taken aback by the perfect batting track at the County Ground, which compared well with 'some of the mud baths we used to play on in Huddersfield'. In the first Somerset innings, he was left stranded before he had faced a ball when Merv Kitchen called for a quick single and a young Clive Lloyd swooped

Trevor Holmes – as a goalkeeper on the books of Huddersfield Town (top), as a member of the Broad Oak CC team (centre) and in formal attire (bottom). ALL COURTESY OF TREVOR HOLMES

in and threw down the stumps at lightning speed. Trevor had never before encountered such brilliance: he was not alone in that. In the second innings, with the game already slipping from Somerset, Trevor smote a mighty six off Garry Sobers and then attempted the same against M. L. C. Foster, missed the ball and was adjudged LBW for 8. In his only first-class match he had averaged 4.00 with the bat and had taken one catch.

Returning to league cricket in his native Yorkshire, he would continue playing until 2000 and was selected as the wicket-keeper for the representative Huddersfield League side for fifteen of those years. He would also enjoy a successful run in the Samuel Whitbread National Village Competition in 1981 when his team, Broad Oak CC, were narrowly defeated in the final at Lord's by St Fagan's CC.

Married in 1965 to Margaret Hampshire, he was later divorced and subsequently married in 1979 to Hilary Whitehead. His second wife and all his children have remained involved in the game, Hilary as club secretary and caterer, his stepdaughter as a scorer and his two sons and stepson as players.

Trevor was for many years involved in football as a goalkeeper and coach, suffering a major setback in 1984 when three fingers were broken in a goalkeeping accident. Nor was his cricketing career entirely free of trauma. In 1980, he was trapped under a sightscreen that was overturned in a gust of wind. He proceeded to go out to bat in considerable pain, unaware at the time that he had suffered four broken ribs, a fractured sternum and a cracked skull.

Progress on the work front was more serene. A partner in an architect's practice, he turned down the offer of a professional contract with Somerset as the financial rewards would have paled in comparison. In 1974 he set up his own architect's practice – J. T. Design – and continued working until the year 2000, when he suffered a major heart attack. He and his wife reside in Holmforth, a small town in the shadow of the Peak District and familiar to many as the setting for the *Last of the Summer Wine* television programmes. The ever-modest Trevor would be the first to admit the place is more famed as the home town of Compo, Cleggy and Nora Batty than as the home town of one J. T. Holmes, former Somerset cricketer.

Trevor Holmes keeping wicket for Somerset as C. A. Davis hits a boundary on his way to a century for the West Indies. SOMERSET COUNTY GAZETTE ARCHIVE

455
William Dalton Buck
4 June 1969 v. West Indies, Taunton

Bill Buck was born in Portswood, Southampton on 30 September 1946, the son of Jack Buck and Agnes (née Baird), known as 'Nan'. Bill's paternal grandfather had been Mayor of Southampton and an entrepreneur who had built the first two cinemas in the town, selling them to an American company prior to the Second World War. Bill's father, Jack, followed in his own father's entrepreneurial footsteps, owning a motor business.

Coached at Oakmount Primary School in Southampton by Lloyd Budd – who won renown as a Test Match umpire – Bill then attended Clayesmore School in Dorset where he took more than a hundred wickets in his final two years. He went on to train for the teaching profession at St Luke's College, Exeter, where he played with Somerset's Peter Denning. It was after appearing for the college in a friendly against Somerset Second XI that he was telephoned by Bill Andrews and invited to bowl against Harold Gimblett and Colin Atkinson at Millfield School. He was promptly selected for the match against the West Indies and recalls that Roy Palmer took a dim view of being asked make way for an amateur triallist. Roy was in fact further aggrieved when asked to loan his sweater to the newcomer. In the event, bowling right-arm fast-

Bill Buck – his first-class career spanned one season, two games and two teams.

medium pace, Bill took 0 for 56 in the first innings and bagged the wickets of openers Roy Fredericks and Michael Carew in the second innings, leaving him with match figures of 2 for 110. He also averaged 5.50 with the bat. Bill had in fact had two catches dropped off his bowling on the first morning and so his figures do not flatter him.

He admits that he would have liked to have signed for Somerset, who expressed the hope that he would do so, but having already played for Hampshire Second XI – he topped the bowling averages in 1969 – the county was reluctant to release him, and he was indeed selected to play for Hampshire against New Zealand when he took no wickets in a severely rain-affected match. This would be his only other first-class game, leaving him with the rare claim of playing in a total of two first-class matches, for different counties and in the same season. Bill would look back wistfully at the summer of 1969 and wonder what might have been. Although his father had advised that a career as a first-class cricketer on the margins was too precarious, Bill would write that 'I think that if I had been allowed [by Hampshire] to go to Somerset, I would have given it a go'. He also observes that 'Barry Richards and Gordon Greenidge could have probably played me with sticks of rhubarb in the nets, so perhaps teaching was the better option'.

He was a schoolmaster and a cricket and rugby coach for forty-five years, with future first-class cricketers and noted rugby players coming under his care. As a trainee teacher at Buckler's Mead School, he had failed, however, to persuade a young Ian Botham to try rugby. He taught and coached at Duke of York's Royal Military School in Dover for seventeen years and during that time was married in 1974 to Alison Guy, a psychotherapist with whom he had four children. He played for a while alongside his brother for the Sussex Martlets, a wandering side of some prestige. Bill recalls with a smile the occasion he and his late brother got lost trying the find their way to the Arundel Castle ground and ended up at a Sussex village named 'The Wannocks'. On the assumption that there was a likelihood of their being black-balled, they set up their own wandering cricket club named 'The Wannocks' in memory of their misadventure.

After his time teaching in Dover, there followed two preparatory school headmas-terships, first at Glebe House in Hunstanton, Norfolk, and then at Pembroke House School in Kenya. For the final fourteen years of his teaching career he ran the cricket coaching at Sutton Valence School near Maidstone.

Since retiring from teaching he has taken up painting in a serious way and is suffi-ciently talented to have had work commissioned. He has also continued to coach. Until 2014 he helped bring on the Sutton Valence School's cricket, hockey and rugby players and at the time of writing he runs an Educational Consultancy – Dalton Buck Educa-tion. The entrepreneurial zeal his forebears demonstrated is still in evidence. Bill derives great pleasure from the progress of his former charges on the sporting stage. He is no doubt delighted that they are able to live the dream that narrowly escaped his grasp back in 1969.

456
John Kelvin Roberts
4 June 1969 v. West Indies, Taunton

Although he was born in Liverpool on 9 October 1949, John Roberts is quick to point out that he is most certainly not a 'Scouser', classing himself as 'a true Yorkie' who happened to have first seen the light of day across the Pennines when his father was working for the Government as an architect in the rebuilding of parts of Liverpool destroyed by bombing. By the time he was four, the family were back in Leeds, where his father, Jack, married to Betty (née Sutcliffe), was similarly involved in the rebuild-ing of the city. Educated at Aireborough Grammar School in Guiseley, John left school at sixteen to work as a trainee salesman.

While touring with Harrogate Cardinals CC he took 6 wickets in a match against Taunton CC at the County Ground and was invited to appear in a friendly fixture against Gloucestershire Second XI when he again impressed with his left-arm medium pace bowling and was offered a three-year contract (the length required to allow his registration, without the need for a residential qualification period). His time with Somerset would prove short and sweet. During the 1969 and 1970 seasons he played

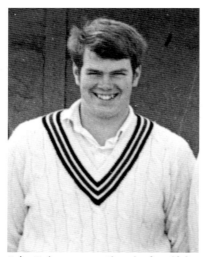

John Roberts – contributed a handful of wickets, very few runs and much laughter during his brief sojourn in the county. SOMERSET CRICKET MUSEUM

in only eight first-class matches, taking 15 wickets at 32.33. John jokes that when he was batting, he was the 'ferret', coming in after the rabbits. He notes self-deprecatingly that his first-class batting average of 1.00 was flattered by a highest score of 2 not out and also by the fact that he was not out in six of his nine innings. Styling himself jokingly as 'King of the Swingers' on account of his bowling skills, he also appeared in eleven limited overs games before his departure at the end of the 1970 season. He had been a popular member of the dressing room and had brought much laughter to proceedings with his ready wit. John says that his 'short time at Somerset was both memorable and enjoyable' and led to a number of lasting friendships. He remains a regular attendee at the annual dinner for ex-players and has on occasions been asked to deliver the after-dinner speech, drawing on his experience as a regular speaker, where his humorous observations on life and cricket are in demand. When his erstwhile captain Brian Langford was asked to sum up the contribution of the man who was once described by *Wisden* as having 'displayed a cool head and improved steadily', Brian remarked - speaking from personal experience and taking his cue from the team joker – that 'he makes a very good baby-sitter'.

John left the county in 1970 and returned to club cricket as a pro. Having started his career with Horsforth CC in the Airedale & Wharfedale League, he went on to play for Halifax CC and then for thirteen seasons for Keighley CC in the Bradford League. He finished his career at Silsden CC, finally hanging up his boots at the age of fifty-four.

Contrary to rumours repeated in more than one history of Somerset cricket, he was never a member of the police force (although his brother was). He has in fact worked for Northwest Tools, a company based in Wigan selling power tools, since the age of fifty. At the time of writing, he is still Sales Manager and showing no inclination to slow down and retire, despite being in his late-sixties. His old joints might have stiffened and his reflexes might have slowed, but his wit remains as a sharp as ever and his zest for life undiminished.

John had previously been married twice before finally settling in Keighley with his third wife Sharon (née Hooper), with whom he had two children. This amusing man had contributed a handful of wickets, very few runs and much laughter during his brief sojourn in the county.

John Roberts photographed with the Somerset team of 1970.
Back Row: *D. J. S. Taylor, J. K. Roberts, T. W. Cartwright, R. Palmer, A. A. Jones, M. Hill, G. I. Burgess, A. Clarkson.* Front Row: *M. J. Kitchen, B. A. Langford, R. T. Virgin, P. J. Robinson.* SOMERSET CRICKET MUSEUM

457
David William Cox
25 June 1969 v. Hampshire, Portsmouth

David Cox observes with a wry smile that his Championship career might not have been the longest or the most glorious but he came away from the fixture with Hampshire with one wicket for a combined 77 runs, an average of 4.00 with the bat and a future wife, whom he had met in a pub in Portsmouth during his one and only first-class appearance.

Born in a nursing home in Wells on 19 May 1946, he was brought up in Oakhill, the son of Ronald William Cox, who worked as a drayman for Courage Brewery, and

David Cox – came away from his only first-class game with one wicket and a wife-to-be.
BOTH COURTESY OF DAVID COX

was married to Gladys Marian (née Knight), who was working as a cook when the couple met. Educated at Oakhill Primary School and Sexey's Grammar School in Bruton, David was introduced to cricket at a young age by his father who played for the Oakhill village team, the son making his first appearance for them at the age of eleven. From the age of sixteen he played for Mendip Hospital CC and developed into a fast bowler, capable of swinging the ball. Between 1967 and 1970 he opened the bowling for Somerset Seconds (and in the 1968 season for the combined Gloucestershire and Somerset Second XI side). At times he put together devastating spells, such as a return of 3 for 5 in ten overs - eight of them maidens – against Sussex Second XI at Hove in 1968.

Having met Janet Rogers in Portsmouth in 1969 while playing for Somerset, his courtship would prove as pacey as his new-ball spells and they were married the following year. They would have two sons, both of whom would become successful club cricketers and both stalwarts of Midsomer Norton CC, with Andrew appearing for Somerset Second XI.

After his brief first-class adventure, David had gone on to play for Frome CC and Morlands CC in Glastonbury, before a back operation forced him to take a break from the game. He returned in due course, accompanying his sons in the Midsomer Norton side, bowling at a gentler pace. Looking back over his career in cricket, David's abiding memories are less of his bowling successes (of which there were many) and more the 'wonderful characters' he has met along the journey, among them the speed merchant whom he might perhaps wish to have emulated – Frank Tyson. Fortunately, Frank was not racing in to bowl at him at the time.

Over the years, he has enjoyed a number of jobs. They include groundsman at Mendip Hospital, followed by a period as a postman and latterly, as a coach and bus driver until his retirement.

Friends and family confirm that on the sports field he has always been hugely competitive and somewhat of a wind-up merchant, two attributes that suggest fast bowling was certainly the right calling, although these days he is often to be found on a golf course or watching the progress of his sons playing for the Midsomer Norton side in the town where he and Janet now reside.

458
Peter William Denning
28 June 1969 v. Glamorgan, Glastonbury

Known to all and sundry as 'Dasher' on account of his running between the wickets, Peter Denning was quintessentially a man of Somerset to his very bones, in the words of David Foot 'ever a village boy in spirit, with a voice, appearance and seemingly insouciant playing persona to match: he was liked because he was wholly without artifice or pretension'.

His father, Tom Denning, was the butcher in the village of Chewton Mendip and a fine club cricketer – a right-handed batsman whom many thought had deserved a shot at the first-class game. Tom was married to Maxine (née Watson). Born on 16 December 1949 in Chewton Mendip, Peter was one of two brothers, both of whom followed Tom into the Chewton Mendip CC side, Peter having starting out as the club's scorer. It was apparent from a young age that he was an outstanding prospect. Following a recommendation from his Primary School headmistress, a Mrs Smallbone, he was offered a scholarship at Millfield. Here he starred at football (although he self-deprecatingly referred to himself as 'a clogger rather than a footballer'), rugby, tennis (where he reached a junior doubles semi-final at Wimbledon) and cricket, at which he captained the First XI. In his early years he was a wicket-keeper. Colin Atkinson, his erstwhile headmaster at Millfield, notes that 'he was a handful'. Despite his education at a leading public school, Peter never shed his West Country burr and never adopted any airs or graces. Indeed, he remained unashamedly a maverick, absolutely determined never to bow before authority. It seems strangely appropriate that this rebellious character, normally to be seen in jeans and averse to modern-day accoutrements such as the tie or the comb, worked briefly for a demolition company one winter, given that whether walking into the ground or to a formal function, he gave every appearance of having been caught up in a botched demolition job.

Peter and his opening partner, Brian Rose, came up together through the ranks, first appearing together at Under-12 level and over the years developing a fine understanding when judging a single. In the early days, an additional spur for Peter beyond his competitive instincts was the promise of a ten shilling note from his paternal grandfather, Bill – also in his time a Chewton Mendip player – for every half-century he mustered. Bill was obliged to withdraw from the agreement once the young Dasher's

Peter Denning – 'wholly without artifice or pretension'. SOMERSET CRICKET MUSEUM

piggy bank began to overflow with the bounties. *Wisden* noted in 1969 that Rose and Denning offered 'much hope for the future'. Brian's range of shots was both greater and more elegant, but Dasher's selfless contributions were hugely important to the Somerset side that blossomed into greatness in the late 1970s and early 1980s. Peter was more of a risk-taker than a typical opener and a surprising percentage of his runs came in an arc from cover point to third man with the butcher's son being linked indelibly with his 'Chewton Chop', also referred to as his 'Butcher's Cut'. On one notable occasion, he slashed four fours behind point in one over by Jeff Thomson of Australia who informed him: 'Do that again and I'll nail you to the sightscreen.'

Peter's propensity for keeping the scoreboard ticking over, unsettling opponents with his cheeky singles, combined with his athletic run-saving efforts in the field, made him a valuable member of the one-day team in particular, with seven Man of the Match awards to his credit, although his contributions in the County Championship could also be telling. In six separate seasons he reached 1,000 runs, the most successful being 1979, when he totalled 1,222 runs and averaged 42.13. He was also a partner in a record Somerset fourth-wicket stand of 310 with Ian Botham in 1980. When interviewed about his involvement, he replied with his usual modesty: 'I spent the day leaning on my bat and watching Beefy, like everybody else.'

At one point he had considered a career as a schoolmaster and undertook a teacher training qualification at St Luke's College, Exeter. While there he had captained the St Luke's team and had his first encounter with a fourteen-year-old lad from Yeovil already demonstrating his precocious talents as a cricketer, although, the young Ian Botham still had a lot to learn from Dasher about the art of post-match celebrations. Ian would recall watching as the older man downed a pint mix comprising milk and beer in equal measures before turning ashen and disappearing to disgorge the contents of his stomach and then continuing proceedings. Loyal to a fault, Peter would later speak up in support of his Somerset teammate when Somerset were torn asunder in later years after Viv Richards and Joel Garner were released and Ian Botham resigned in protest. Having first played for Somerset Second XI as a seventeen-year-old, he broke into the First XI in 1969 and over the course of sixteen seasons would average 28.68 in 269 matches, with eight centuries to his name. His List A statistics were broadly similar, perhaps reflecting the fact that his approach varied little between the two formats. As for his bowling, he could at least claim one wicket and a prized one in the form of Lawrence Rowe, though the ball had allegedly bounced twice before it reached the West Indian who creamed it, only to watch in disbelief as Viv Richards took a catch of blinding brilliance. Lightning never struck twice.

Tom Cartwright coached him in his latter years and was offered a humongous joint of beef by Tom Denning if he could persuade the butcher's boy to get a haircut: a challenge he failed. Tom Cartwright felt that Peter was 'too unselfish' ever to make it to

Peter Denning – Dasher's selfless contributions were hugely important to the Somerset side that blossomed into greatness. SOMERSET CRICKET MUSEUM

the very top. After his career was ended in 1984, owing to cartilage problems, Dasher shambled off the first-class stage, as dishevelled as the day he'd arrived as a scruffy teenager.

Married in 1973 to Margaret Anne Coxall, known as Annie, he had two daughters. During his career he had found winter employment including spells for a demolition firm near Weston-super-Mare and work with Wyvern Sports. He also spent a season in 1979-80 with Waveroo District CC near Perth, playing and coaching in the Second Grade and overseeing clinics for junior teams. During his tenure he won over the locals with his wholehearted commitment to the cause and his success as a run-maker and is still as fondly remembered in those parts as he is in his beloved Chewton Mendip. Later, he worked as a regional transport manager for a farming cooperative but his life would be cut short by cancer. He died at a hospice in Taunton on 18 July 2007 at the age of fifty-seven. Shy and unaffected, he had shunned the limelight but his talent was such that he would inevitably be caught on occasions in its glare, particularly when playing his important part in Somerset's period of unprecedented one-day success. The accolades never changed him, never went to his unruly, mop-topped head.

459
James Martyn Galley
16 August 1969 v. Yorkshire, Leeds

Jim Galley was born in Bristol on 4 October 1944. His father, James Blacklaw Galley, was a laundry proprietor, married to Eileen Melita (née Burchill). Cricket was Jim's favoured sport as a boy and he was encouraged and advised by his godfather, Somerset's Horace Hazell, who would remain a close friend and confidant. Jim was also an accomplished rugby player. Educated at Bristol Cathedral School, he left to train as a teacher at St Luke's College, Exeter, before being offered a position at Monkton Combe, where he taught Geography and P.E., combining his school duties with his passion for team sports. He often had to juggle the two worlds precariously as he lurched from the boisterous environment of Bath rugby to the serenity of a service in the school chapel. He became an influential figure in the Bath sporting scene. For many years he would be a mainstay of Bath rugby, where he starred as a scrum-half and later became a selector during their heyday as the dominant force in English rugby. A larger-than-life character, he was never likely to shrink into the background.

He was married in 1968 to Fay Williams, whom he had met during his teacher training. Fay was herself an able sportswoman, noted in particular as a badminton and

The Galley family in 1981 – shown (left to right) are: Andrew, Josie, Fay and Jim.
COURTESY OF FAY GALLEY

tennis player. They would have a daughter, Josie, and a son, Andrew. For a while the couple lived near Bath but they moved to the Taunton area when Jim left teaching to work for IBM. Fay recalls the night their son was born in Wellington. 'Jim played for Taunton RFC and he was selected for the Somerset team the day before Andrew was born. I was alone and Jim came tripping in six hours after the birth after celebrating his call-up at Taunton's away match in South Wales.' The couple moved to Bristol in 1973 as part of Jim's career development with IBM, returning to Bath two years later.

He then became a leading light at Lansdown CC, whom he would captain for a period. Fay describes the club bar as 'the social centre of Bath in the 1970s, frequented both by the cricketers and the rugby side'. Jim and fellow Somerset cricketer, Len Beel, were described as the 'life and soul of the club' and Fay talks about her husband's obsession with the game with great candour and humour. 'He was their leading batsman for a while and when I was rushed to hospital with a suspected ectopic pregnancy, he finished his innings to make sure Lansdown won before he came to visit. Luckily, I'm very keen on sport, too, so probably would have done the same and I'm still here to tell the story!' Teammate Len Beel says of Jim that 'to my mind he was one of the best club cricketers I saw and even though he played a few times for Somerset, both they and Gloucestershire missed out by not picking him when he was in his prime.' Len also reveals that Jim was possessed of a competitive streak. On one occasion, Len came to the crease and, chancing his arm, found himself overtaking Jim and in his 30s. 'Jim looked up at the scoreboard and saw what was happening,' Len recalls, 'and after that he made sure I didn't face a ball until he'd reached his half-century.' A versatile player, Jim regularly kept wicket and also bowled on occasions.

His brief taste of first-class cricket had come towards the end of the 1969 season. He was in fact out on the Bath Golf Course when he received a message that he was needed the following day at Headingley. His debut would prove a memorable one. Jim later recounted the story, noting that 'Yorkshire were top of the table at the time, with Brian Close in charge. We were trying to save the match and playing out for a draw. Even though I got 0 not out, I was feeling pleased with myself but when we got back to the dressing room having saved the match, most of the players had already left and were heading back down the M1.' He and Roy Palmer had held out for fifteen overs without scoring. It had been a tense rearguard action. In the event, Jim played only three first-class matches for Somerset, averaging a modest 5.40.

Outside the world of sport, he threw himself into his work at IBM with his usual enthusiasm. Fay remembers her husband coming home in 1971 from a training conference after his appointment as a sales manager and laughing together at the outrageous claim from a speaker that 'soon every house will have a computer and televisions will be like pictures hanging on the wall with flat screens'. His work would take him

Jim Galley – for much of his adult life a towering figure in the Bath sporting scene. BOTH COURTESY OF FAY GALLEY

to most of the capitals of Europe and to the USA and finally for an eighteen-month period to Brussels where he worked at the IBM training centre, before he took early retirement. He was also the leading light in writing and performing the staff Christmas

Jim Galley (left) going out to bat with Ian Botham in a double-wicket competition in Bath. COURTESY OF FAY GALLEY

pantomime and was noted as an entertaining public speaker.

Jim retained his links with Somerset CCC, and was instrumental in organising and taking part in double-wicket competitions at Lansdown in the early 1980s, as part of the benefit activity for Viv Richards and Peter Denning. Included in a stellar cast of international players, Jim and his playing partner, Ian Botham, reached the final in 1982. Jim would also play for Wiltshire in Minor Counties cricket in 1980 and 1981.

After leaving IBM, he worked for a while as an IT Consultant but he could increasingly be found on the golf course. Both Fay and Jim were members of the Bath Golf Club and Jim served as captain in 1996 and as Managing Secretary from 2004 until 2008. Subsequently he became Manager of the Army Golf Club in Aldershot, retiring in April 2012.

He died at the Royal United Hospital in Bath on 4 October 2012 on his sixty-eighth birthday, having suffered for a while from lung cancer. The tributes flowed for an engaging and popular man and an amusing raconteur who for years had been at the epicentre of Bath's sporting life but was sadly only ever on the fringes of the first-class game.

460
Raymond Thomas Albert Windsor
23 August 1969 v. Sussex, Taunton

One of seven children, Ray Windsor was born in Wellington on 9 February 1943, the son of Thomas William Windsor, who worked as the head wool dyer for Fox Brothers, and was married to Elsie Winifred (née Vile). Thomas was a well-known local cricketer having played for Tonedale (the Fox Brothers works team) and Wellington CC. Later, he turned to umpiring at Wellington and was at the wicket when Ray made his First

X1 debut as a thirteen-year-old schoolboy. Ray also played rugby for Wellington RFC.

A slight man, Ray was a fearless and successful smiter of the ball in club cricket, reliant on superb timing rather than brute force and regularly featured in the local press for his centuries. He tended to spend precious little time getting his eye in and was as likely to be dismissed for nothing as he was to rack up a quick-fire century. In one century for Wellington he scored 114 in boundaries. He played on a number of occasions for Somerset Second XI from 1969 onwards. It was while playing for the Second X1 that he was advised by George Lambert to switch to Taunton CC in order to play a higher standard of club cricket. Although offered a one-year professional contract with Somerset, he declined on the basis that he already had a good job with Avimo (who manufactured aircraft equipment in Taunton) which offered greater long-term security. He would in fact play in a solitary first-class match for Somerset, not long after he had scored 140 against Cornwall. In his only innings in elevated company, he was bowled by Tony Greig for a duck. Peter Roebuck reports in his history of the Somerset cricket that Ray, who sported a beard, looked 'like a pirate, and he was soon all at sea'. In his one Sunday League game for the First XI against Yorkshire at Taunton, a fortnight earlier, Ray had been even less involved, watching admiringly as a twenty-one-year-old Greg Chappell took 3 for 14 in eight overs and then proceeded to knock off the runs, making 76 in double-quick time with some glorious sixes. To be so close to genius must have been both chastening and an education. By the mid-1970s, his first-class career was well in the past, although he was still playing for

Ray Windsor – a fearless smiter of the ball who enjoyed huge success in club cricket.
SOMERSET CRICKET MUSEUM

Taunton CC and in one year won separate local cricket batting awards sponsored by the *Somerset County Gazette* and by Ronson. That season he hit a double-hundred, seven centuries and six half-centuries.

Ray had been married in Taunton in 1961 to Jennifer Mitchell. He was eighteen and she was seventeen at the time and they would have two sons, Mark and Paul. The latter would prove a successful club cricketer and would captain and subsequently become President of Bridgwater CC.

Ray had moved to Bridgwater after leaving his employment with Avimo. He had spent almost twenty-five years with the firm but according to him 'the writing was on the wall for the company'. His brother was in the brewery business and suggested that he should run a pub. He became landlord of the Beauford Arms in St John's Street, Bridgwater, and it was not long before some of the pub regulars encouraged him to turn out for Bridgwater CC. In 1982, in his first full season with the club and at the age of 38, he helped them to win the Somerset Knock-Out Cup. It was a proud moment for Ray because his son Paul was also in the winning side.

Later, he refurbished the First & Last pub and renamed it The Sportsman, managing it from 1992 until 1999 and putting an enormous amount of work into building up the business at what had become a forlorn and run-down establishment. In retirement, Ray moved to within a five-minute walk of the Bridgwater CC ground at The Parks and at the time of writing he derives enormous pleasure from being able to watch his grandsons play cricket, the third generation of Windsors to have graced the ground. Many former club cricketers still recall his exploits – perhaps in the same way that Ray looks back in awe at the performances of his erstwhile teammate Greg Chappell.

*   *   *

William John Leonard Beel

Also meriting a listing in the 1969 roll of honour is William John Leonard Beel, known as Len. Although he never played first-class cricket, he appeared in the John Player League. Born in Leominster on 23 August 1945, he made a name for himself as a professional footballer, playing as a goalkeeper in league matches on three occasions for Shrewsbury Town and once, in 1965, for Birmingham City in the old First Division. On the latter occasion he was involved in a ten-goal thriller, although sadly the ball ended up in Len's net on five occasions with the match ending Birmingham City

Len Beel first to 100 wickets for Lansdown

Len Beel hits the local headlines with his exploits for Lansdown CC.

5 Blackburn Rovers 5. He then moved to Bath, where he played for Bath City. Later he played in goal for Trowbridge Town.

An all-round sportsman, Len also represented Worcester Second XI as a medium pace bowler for three seasons from 1963 until 1965. Thereafter, at Bath, he became an important member of Lansdown CC. Donald Bradfield writes in *The Lansdown Story* that 'here at last was an opening bowler capable of troubling the best of club batsmen. He combined accuracy and movement with genuine pace off the pitch.' In 1968, the year prior to his county call-up, Len had become the first Lansdown bowler to claim 100 wickets in a season. He played in only one John Player League match for Somerset – against Warwickshire at Edgbaston on 22 June 1969, a game that Warwickshire won at a canter. Having scored 1 not out, Len was not asked to bowl until the game was all but over. He took 0 for 18 in his two overs. He would also represent Wiltshire in the Minor Counties Championship.

Married in 1969 to Margaret Carpenter, Len went into sales after retiring from life as a football and cricketing pro. Following a period selling greetings cards he went on to sell pens for Watermans and then for twenty-one years worked for the Japanese company Pentel, beginning as their sales representative for the West Country and ending up as their National Sales Manager. He retired after suffering a heart attack in 2003 and observes with his usual wit that 'I now get my kicks from the odd round of golf – and some rounds are really odd.'

At the time of writing, Len and his wife, Margaret, still reside in a village near Trowbridge.

Len Beel – involved in a ten-goal thriller in his only game in the top tier of English football. COURTESY OF LEN BEEL

1970

"With perhaps fewer resources than any other county,
[Somerset] got away from the bottom of the table
thanks largely to the remarkable batting of Virgin."

Rex Alston

Championship Position: 13 of 17

The side was captained once again by Brian Langford. Roy Virgin was a man transformed. Here was an early example of a batsman who learned from limited overs cricket to adopt a fearless approach. Amassing 2,223 runs, including seven centuries, he was in scintillating form and averaged 47.29 over the course of the season. With over 1,000 runs each, Tony Clarkson and Peter Robinson offered useful support, the latter deployed increasingly as a batsman rather than as an all-rounder. Another critical element in avoiding the indignity of another wooden spoon was the arrival of Tom Cartwright from Warwickshire. A seasoned campaigner of Test Match class, he claimed 86 wickets and, perhaps almost as importantly, was parsimonious – difficult to score off in both long and short formats and thus a real asset in helping to wrest back control of games. Among the supporting cast, only Graham Burgess and Brian Langford exceeded 50 wickets, although Allan Jones and Roy Palmer injected some fire into the attack.

The introduction of four experienced debutants was a sensible way to bring stability and was a policy that would lay the groundwork to future success, with some wise heads to provide support to the next generation of players. Tom Cartwright in particular but also wicket-keeper Derek Taylor and pace-man Allan Jones made telling contributions, Maurice Hill less so, owing to injury.

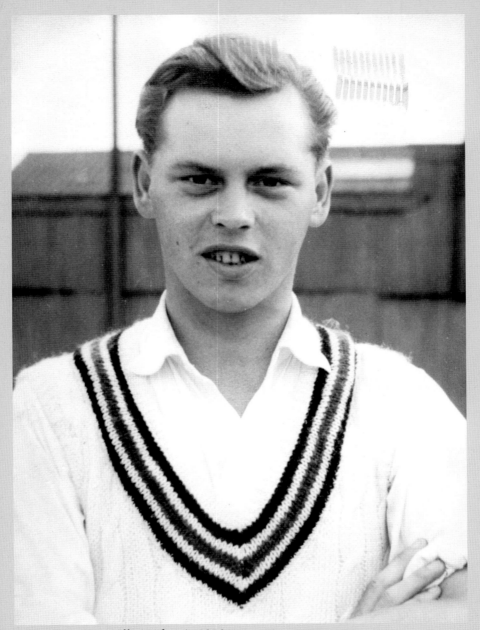

Roy Virgin – in scintillating form in 1970. SOMERSET CRICKET MUSEUM

461
Thomas William Cartwright
9 May 1970 v. Essex, Taunton

Born in Coventry on 22 July 1935 and registered at birth as William Thomas, he was always known as Tom. His father, also William Thomas and known as Tom, came from a family of greengrocers but had opted for a career in Coventry's successful car industry, assembling Rileys. Tom Snr was married to Lily (née Whitmore), a miner's daughter. The last of four children, Tom Jnr witnessed the near-obliteration of his home city by German bombing in 1940 and 1941. Educated at Foxford School, he was doubly fortunate in being blessed with talent and the guidance of a schoolmaster, Eddie Branson, who loved the game of cricket and gave his protégé every encouragement. Tom was captain of the school football and cricket teams and appeared in the cricket First XI for four years. As a young man he was on the books at Aston Villa FC but never broke through, his dreams of a career in the game ending when he injured his knee.

On leaving school, he opted initially for a career at the Rootes car factory, assembling Humber Super Snipes, but by the age of sixteen, after just one winter with his employer, he came to the attention of Warwickshire's coach Tiger Smith. Tom was offered a contract, which he accepted with alacrity, even though it meant a drop in his earnings. He appeared initially for the Second XI and whilst being loaned to Merionethshire, who were a man short, he found himself still undefeated at the end of the first innings while playing as a tail-ender. With Merionethshire needing to follow on, he was told he might as well open, given that his eye was in and he had his pads on. Thus began the first phase of his career as an opening batsman. Drafted into the Warwickshire side at Trent Bridge in 1952, while still only eighteen, he demonstrated his prowess with a dogged 82 in his debut innings, eliciting favourable reports. His burgeoning career was interrupted by National Service from 1953 to 1955, when he played for the Army and the Combined Services.

Having begun his career as a batsman, he would develop into an all-rounder and would end his playing days as a seam bowler whom Brian Close described as 'a master of accuracy, of variation and total concentration'. Tom would enjoy a hugely productive career with Warwickshire. Eager to learn and possessed of an unwavering work ethic, he would score over 10,000 runs and take over 1,000 wickets for the county, achieving the double in 1962, despite missing six matches with a broken finger. In 1960, he had been married to Joan Morwen Rees, a primary school teacher, with whom he would have a son and daughter. Tom was a devoted family man and reluctant to spend the

Tom Cartwright – a fine cricketer, an outstanding coach and a man of unshrinking honesty. SOMERSET CRICKET MUSEUM

winters away from home. Having enjoyed a spell coaching in Johannesburg in 1961-2, accompanied by Joan, he subsequently toured East Africa with an MCC side in 1963-4 before graduating to the Test team. Many of his winters were spent closer to home either employed by Courtaulds working at a capstan lathe or helping Tiger Smith with coaching duties at Edgbaston.

His Test career was limited – in part through ill-timed injuries – to five appearances. He would potentially have added to the tally had he not had to withdraw from the touring party for the 1968-9 Series in South Africa. His shoulder injury left the selectors with a dilemma. Obliged to include Basil D'Oliveira, whose claims were already strong, they sparked the dispute that led to South Africa's isolation from Test cricket until the collapse of the Apartheid regime. In 1969, at the age of thirty-four, he let it be known to the Warwickshire committee that he wished to combine a coaching appointment with playing, but his county were not forthcoming with a suitable proposal. A number of counties were keen to offer a contract, but it was Somerset who gave him the chance to play county cricket in the summer and to act as coach at Millfield School for the remainder of the year. Warwickshire refused to allow him permission to play for his new county without a year's qualification. The decision was seen by Tom himself as vindictive and unfair on a man who had served his native county well and had a wife and two children to support. An appeal was lodged with MCC, with Tom represented by Jack Bannister in his role as an official of the Professional Cricketers' Association (PCA). The case was won and he was free to play for Somerset. He proved a wonderful investment, initially as a bowler. Notably parsimonious in limited overs cricket, he was the second most economical bowler in 1972, behind John Snow and the most economical in 1973. He was also the joint leading wicket-taker in domestic first-class cricket in 1972 and headed the national averages in 1973. If his contribution as a player was valuable it would be nigh impossible to put a price on his value as a coach. When plans to build a Sports Hall at Millfield fell through, Colin Atkinson sent Harold Gimblett down to the County Ground with an invitation for Tom to buy the Millfield shop. He turned it down, and the offer to coach a promising crop of youngsters at Somerset was made instead. Tom had always believed in developing home grown talent and with some persuasive words on his part, a pool of six players was taken on and each offered £1,000 per annum. Five of them would become a pivotal part of the county's future success. Viv Richards, Ian Botham, Peter Roebuck, Phil Slocombe and Vic Marks would all recount their debt to Tom. Ian Botham, in particular, always a gifted batsman, was transformed into an all-rounder of world class, capable of imparting prodigious swing at fast-medium pace.

Tom is invariably described as a man of great integrity who was unbending in his principles and spoke the truth quietly, politely but resolutely. A Labour man to the core, he believed in standing up for his rights and those of his peers and on occasions his single-mindedness was seen to spill over into obduracy. Having left Warwickshire under a cloud, he fell out with Somerset when – ever the true professional – he refused to play in an important John Player fixture at the end of the 1976 season because an injury – sustained three months earlier during a sickening collision with John Spencer of Sussex – meant that he would not have been able to contribute as he would have hoped. In 101 first-class matches, he had taken 408 wickets for Somerset at 18.86 apiece and averaged 18.92 with the bat. Left high and dry with no contract, Tom was snapped up by Glamorgan where he played in 1977 and was appointed the Cricket Manager, a post he held until 1983. Thereafter he became Coach for the Welsh Cricket Association and the National Welsh Coach. He retired in 2000 and was awarded an MBE. From 2000 until 2007 he was responsible for the development of the Under-16s in Wales. He suffered a massive heart attack in March 2007 and died at the age of seventy-one in the Neath Port Talbot Hospital at Baglan on 30 April 2007.

Tom Cartwright – 'a master of accuracy, of variation and total concentration'.
SOMERSET CRICKET MUSEUM

Throughout his career, his appetite for hard work had remained undimmed. He was universally respected within the cricketing community: a fine cricketer, an outstanding coach and a man of unshrinking honesty. A cohort of promising young cricketers and the supporters who watched those protégés of his finally bring trophies to the County Ground have reason to be thankful for his six-season tenure at Somerset.

462
Derek John Somerset Taylor
9 May 1970 v. Essex, Taunton

An identical twin, Derek was born in Amersham on 12 November 1942, the son of Charles Norman Taylor, a provisions wholesaler, and his wife, Isabel Kathleen (née Wicks), a librarian. Derek and his brother, Mike, played for Amersham on the Hill CC as teenagers before appearing for Chesham CC and Buckinghamshire together. Thereafter they went their separate ways, Mike via Nottinghamshire to Hampshire and Derek via Surrey to Somerset. Derek had embarked on his career as a batsman and occasional off-spin bowler, making his Minor Counties debut at seventeen, but shortly thereafter he tried his hand behind the stumps and had established himself as Buckinghamshire's wicket-keeper by the age of nineteen. An all-round sportsman, he also played football in the winter months for Watford FC Juniors. While establishing himself in Minor Counties cricket, he responded to an advert placed in 1964 by Surrey, who were looking for a keeper to deputise for Arnold Long. Derek proved the outstanding applicant, and, coached by Arthur McIntyre, he developed his skills as a wicket-keeper and batsman. Over four seasons between 1966 and 1969 he would wait patiently in the wings, mustering ten first-class appearances. Uncomplaining, modest of manner and in the words of Arthur McIntyre 'a great team man', he left Surrey on an amicable basis when Somerset approached him, offering regular first team cricket.

It came as no surprise to those who knew him that Derek flourished at Somerset. There was no ostentation to his approach. He was knowledgeable about all aspects of the game, set himself high standards and applied himself with unwavering diligence. A wicket-keeper with the skill to stand up to bowlers of medium pace and one capable of effecting leg-side stumpings is an asset to any side, curtailing the attacking instincts of opposing batsmen and Derek was one such. Brian Close would state that 'he had as safe a pair of hands as anyone' and Tom Cartwright would claim that 'I wouldn't swap him if I had the pick of the whole country – I can't remember him putting down a catch off me.' Derek's eight catches in the Combined Universities innings in the Benson & Hedges Cup of 1982 – still a List A record at the time of writing – remain a lasting testament to his skill. He was also blessed with twenty years free of injury, although that came to an end when his finger was fractured while keeping to Joel Garner. He would jest that Joel's bullet-like throws from the boundary inflicted more pain than his deliveries from the bowling crease.

Derek's flowering as a batsman was a bonus. He proved hugely adaptable, reinventing himself as an opening batsman when the need arose and able either to score

Derek Taylor – set himself high standards and applied himself with unwavering diligence.
SOMERSET CRICKET MUSEUM

Derek Taylor – 'I wouldn't swap him if I had the pick of the whole country'.
SOMERSET CRICKET MUSEUM

quickly in limited overs cricket or to stay the course in the first-class game, as his 179 accumulated over five hours and twenty minutes against Glamorgan in 1974 attests. In 280 first-class appearances for Somerset between 1970 and 1982 he averaged 22.42, including four centuries. He also claimed 588 catches and 74 stumpings. 277 victims in List A matches also played their part in Somerset's success in limited overs cricket, with Derek a calming influence and a vital member of the trophy-winning team of the late-1970s and early-1980s.

For two winters at the start of the 1970s, he appeared for Griqualand West in South Africa, playing and undertaking coaching duties. Derek was married in 1971 to a school teacher and antiques dealer, Ethel Lynne Davies, known as Lynne. Having retired as a player, he emigrated with his wife and children to Sydney, Australia, where he worked in life and general insurance for ten years from 1982. For six of those years he was employed alongside former England captain Tony Greig. Derek then relocated to Queensland where he worked in real estate for fourteen years until his retirement in 2006.

He retains fond memories of his time at Somerset and, in turn, supporters and teammates remain full of praise for a modest, unassuming man who quietly went about his business as an important ingredient in what was undoubtedly the most successful spell in Somerset's cricketing history.

463
Allan Arthur Jones
9 May 1970 v. Essex, Taunton

Born on 9 December 1947, Allan Jones went by the moniker 'Jonah'. In the spirit of his Biblical namesake, he became somewhat of a cricketing nomad, although never quite resorting to travelling to any of his various destinations in the belly of an enormous fish. Indeed, he was generally seen arriving at grounds in his cherished Austin A40. His father, Leslie Harry Jones, was a painter and decorator married to Hazel Gladys (née Whitworth), an office clerk at the time of their wedding. Raised in Three Bridges and educated in St John's College in Horsham, Allan joined Sussex as a seventeen-year-old, graduating into the First XI in 1966. Throughout his stay at the county he was unable to pin down a regular place owing in large part to doubts about his fielding and batting, both of which could at times be woeful.

Recognising his talents as a devastating paceman when the mood took him, Somerset offered him a contract. As if to make a point to his former employers, Allan achieved his career-best figures of 9 for 51 against Sussex at Hove in 1973. When bowling, he would utter a grunt that echoed around the ground. He would also let fly with his verbal exchanges with spectators who barracked him for his fielding lapses. These exchanges were as fiery as the hostile missiles he sent down to opposing batsmen. When Brian Close took on the captaincy of Somerset, it was inevitable that the two strong-willed characters would clash on occasions. In *The Flame Still Burns*, Stephen Chalke recounts an incident that sums up the relationship between the unorthodox captain and his main strike bowler. In the Gillette Cup match against Leicestershire in 1973, the two of them conspired to pluck defeat from the jaws of victory. Chris Balderstone was still at the crease, having earlier been dropped on 16. With Leicester seven wickets down and reeling, Jim Parks took a blow on the thumb and, brushing aside the protestations of the team – including Brian Rose, who was familiar with the keeping role – Close announced that he would take over, on the basis that he had once similarly stepped into the breach in a Test Match. Shortly thereafter, when Allan came back on, Close – demonstrating his taste for provocation and his near-suicidal bravado – announced that Jim Parks's wicket-keeping gloves were too small and dispensed with them. Stephen Chalke takes up the story from Tom Cartwright's perspective:

> '*The only thing that would have incited Jonah more,*' *Tom says,* '*was if Closey had stood up to him. Jonah was bowling from the [Pavilion End]. Closey was trying to catch the ball as it went past him and it was going straight through him, hitting the wall and coming all the way back to the middle.*'

Allan had never bowled with more venom. His captain was deaf to all entreaties and suggestions. After a surfeit of byes, the last of them a four, Leicestershire were through, with Chris Balderstone on 119 not out.

In 1975, Jonah the wanderer would leave the county. Between 1970 and 1975 Allan had played in 118 first-class matches for Somerset, taking 291 wickets at 29.05 apiece. His batting average of 6.05 was a fair reflection of his mastery of the art of batsmanship. Given his reputation, the thirty-two catches he held are more of a surprise.

After his release by Somerset at the end of the 1975 season, he was on the verge of emigrating to New Zealand with his wife, Nina (née Harrington), whom he had been married to in 1971. At that point, Mike Brearley intervened and persuaded Allan to make Lord's his new home. Brearley's faith was rewarded. More versed in the subtle arts of captaincy than Close ever was, Brearley brought the best out of Allan and his bowling partner Mike Selvey, and led Middlesex to the County Championship title. Just as he had done against his old club Sussex, Allan made a point in a Sunday League match at Bath, after his subsequent move to Middlesex when he sprinted around the boundary to dismiss Brian Close with a blinding catch over his right shoulder. As Alan Gibson would note with droll understatement in *The Times*, 'Jones

Allan Jones – a devastating fast bowler on his day, he proved somewhat of a cricketing nomad. SOMERSET CRICKET MUSEUM

has not been hitherto distinguished by brilliant running catches on the boundary.' Perhaps Brian Close had always had his paceman's best interests at heart but had lacked the emotional acuity to achieve the desired result. He would later state of Allan that 'I told him several times in the five years we played together that if he pulled his socks up … he was good enough to play for England.'

Jonah continued his nomadic ways and spent one winter with Northern Transvaal and another with Orange Free State, but was released by Middlesex when he suffered a back injury. In 1980, he made history by appearing for a fourth Championship county, when he joined the legions of Joneses who have appeared for Glamorgan. He would remain with them for two seasons before starting up a business as a bookmaker. Allan takes up his story, confessing that 'I soon discovered that I didn't have a flair for business. What's more, I didn't like the nine to five routine and sitting in an office when the sun was shining. It surprised me how much I was missing the game – not so much the bowling as the camaraderie.'

Umpiring proved his salvation. After a year on the reserve list, he was invited to join the first-class umpires list in 1985, the year of his second marriage to Marilyn (née Jones). He surprised many of his erstwhile teammates by his calm demeanour and conscientious approach to the task. By his own confession a 'restless soul' in his playing days, he felt secure and contented. He would note with a hint of self-effacement that 'in this job if you can survive the first couple of years, you've got to do something pretty horrendous to be booted out'. Far from being ignominiously dumped, he enjoyed a long and successful umpiring career, standing in 363 first-class and 373 List A matches as well as two One Day Internationals, the second of which was abandoned without a ball being bowled, so that there was rather more sitting than standing to be done. He retired from the county circuit in 2008 before officiating for a while in the Indian Cricket League.

His days as a nomad behind him, Jonah settled down in sleepy Wiltshire where he still resides at the time of writing.

464
Maurice Hill
16 May 1970 v. Middlesex, Bath

Maurice Hill was born in Scunthorpe on 14 September 1935. His father, Edward, was a platelayer, responsible for ensuring the alignment and integrity of railway tracks, and later a locomotive cleaner, married to Gertrude Louisa (née Cross). Maurice was an elegant batsman, particularly strong on the off-side. Invited to join the ground staff at Trent Bridge, he made his first-class debut as a seventeen-year-old in 1953 but missed the 1954 and 1955 seasons while he undertook National Service. Returning to Nottinghamshire, he became a regular in the side as a middle-order batsman. He exceeded 1,000 runs in six seasons and played in 217 first-class matches for Notts, scoring seven centuries and averaging 24.79. His very occasional leg spin yielded five expensive wickets.

Having been released by Notts, he was snapped up by Derbyshire and represented them for two seasons, appearing thirty-two times and averaging 19.18. After leaving Derbyshire at the end of the 1967 season, he spent two years employed as the captain, coach and groundsman at Roth's Amateurs who played at Widmerpool in Nottinghamshire.

Maurice was offered terms by Somerset, who were looking to supplement the middle-order with an experienced and reliable pro. After a series of solid but unspectacular innings for the county during the 1970 season, his first-class career ended abruptly in June 1971. The ground and facilities had been too waterlogged for any cricket practice and so captain Brian Langford had suggested a game of two-touch football. In Maurice's words: 'I was stretching for the ball when Merv Kitchen tackled me. I tore the ligaments in my leg and was never the same again.' Given the circumstances, he agreed an early release from his three-year contract once it became apparent that further appearances were unlikely. In twenty-two matches for Somerset, Maurice had averaged 21.52, with three half-centuries.

For a while he was employed as the cricket coach and groundsman at Bradfield College in Berkshire. Dickie Brooks, the master in charge of cricket and a former Somerset player, cites Maurice as the catalyst for a turnaround in the school's cricketing fortunes. In Dickie's account, Maurice had replaced an 'indifferent groundsman' and proceeded to 'entertain and enthuse and also started to produce wickets on which good cricket could be played'. Maurice left to take up a similar role at Taunton School as replacement for Harry Parks, who had been in the post for twenty-one years. He remained there for the two seasons before in turn making way for former England cricketer and Old Tauntonian, John Jameson. Itching to continue playing competitive cricket, Maurice joined Marske CC in North Yorkshire in 1978 as their coach, groundsman and player. The following year he was debarred from appearing as an amateur on the basis that he was being employed and any amateur status would have been a circumvention of the rules. The club applied successfully for Maurice to be allowed to appear as an amateur during the 1981 and 1982 seasons, whilst continuing his paid work as coach and groundsman. He was made redundant at the end of the latter season owing to cash flow problems at the club and this would prove to be the first of two occasions where he found himself watching on powerlessly as an institution who employed him struggled

Maurice Hill – he had played for Nottinghamshire and then Derbyshire before joining Somerset to offer the benefit of his experience.

to survive. In the early 1980s he was taken on as the groundsman at Bradford Park Avenue before returning to the West Country and acting as groundsman and coach at Allhallows School in Rousdon, Devon, not far from Lyme Regis. Ultimately, his second stay in the region would prove as ill-starred as his first. When Maurice had joined in the late 1980s the school had had in excess of 500 pupils but the numbers dwindled over time to fewer than 150. As Maurice himself put it, the school had 'beautiful facilities but not enough pupils interested in playing', adding that they 'hadn't won a match in years'. Nevertheless he soldiered on and put down roots in the area, having a house constructed in Honiton, close to that of his good friend, the former Somerset player, Haydn Sully. Maurice had been married in Scunthorpe in 1956 to Josephine Harrison and their son, Greg, would play for Devon while the family resided there. Sadly, though, Allhallows continued its inexorable decline, with all staff placed on three-month contracts and Maurice was finally left high and dry when the school was forced to close its doors in 1998.

He returned to Marske-on-Sea in North Yorkshire in 1999, in order to be near his daughter and he remains there at the time of writing, a two minute walk from the Marske cricket ground he once tended and graced with his elegant batsmanship. And well out of reach, to his eternal relief, of any further crunching tackles by Merv Kitchen.

*　　*　　*

Maurice Hill had been the final debutant in 1970. Just like Johnny Lawrence, who had been the first new arrival back in 1946, here was a fine player who had not quite been able to impose himself on the first-class game. Another, too, who had welcomed the opportunity for a fresh start at Taunton. During the intervening years, Somerset had kept hoping to unearth a gem born within the county, but the truth was that

although some excellent home-grown talent emerged, the club needed to scour not just the counties of England but other continents, too, in order to compete. Despite their best efforts, the curtain had come down on the 1970 season with major trophies having proved elusive and only the Second XI having garnered any success. After a false dawn in 1946, Somerset had floundered in the doldrums and for a while had threatened to become perennial winners of the Championship wooden spoon. They appeared impotent, and after the departure of Harold Gimblett – broken by the strains of carrying the weight of expectation on his shoulders – they had lost their reputation as the entertainers of the county circuit, though some such as Bill Alley would do their best to restore lustre to Somerset's play.

Slowly but surely they had turned things around. A sprinkling of surprisingly robust Championship campaigns and one memorable but ultimately unrewarding day out at Lord's in 1967 had raised spirits. In the round, though, the twenty-five seasons immediately following the Second World War had offered much of the same for the county's longsuffering fans. Hope was draining away, but it would resurface again with the arrival in 1971 of Brian Close under whose fearless and unpredictable leadership a group of talented young players would coalesce. They would meld into a team who would not just win the county's first trophies but for a few heady years would dominate limited-overs cricket in England.

Somerset were at long last about to enjoy their time in the sun.

Tom Cartwright (foreground) orchestrates catching practice for Graham Burgess (left) and Derek Taylor (centre) in 1970. SOMERSET CRICKET MUSEUM

Index of Somerset Cricketers 1946-1970

Order of debut appearance shown in brackets.
Page reference for each player's biography is also given.